The Essential Teachings of
BUDDHISM

THE ESSENTIAL TEACHINGS OF BUDDHISM

Edited by Kerry Brown
and Joanne O'Brien

RIDER
LONDON SYDNEY AUCKLAND JOHANNESBURG

Copyright © International Consultancy on Religion,
Education and Culture 1989

All Rights Reserved

A Rider Book published in 1989 by Century Hutchinson Ltd,
Brookmount House, 62–65 Chandos Place, Covent Garden,
London WC2N 4NW

Century Hutchinson Publishing Group (Australia) Pty Ltd,
89–91 Albion Street, Surry Hills, Sydney,
New South Wales 2010

Century Hutchinson Group (NZ) Ltd,
32–34 View Road, PO Box 40–086, Glenfield, Auckland 10

Century Hutchinson Group (SA) Pty Ltd,
PO Box 337, Bergvlei 2012, South Africa

Typeset by Avocet Marketing Services, Bicester, Oxon.

Printed in Great Britain by
The Guernsey Press

British Library Cataloguing in Publication Data

The essential teachings of Buddhism.
1. Buddhist life.   Devotional works
I. Brown, Kerry   II. O'Brien, Jo
294.3′443

ISBN 0-7126-1952-6

Contents

Contributors

Ngakpa Jampa Thaye, Dharma-regent of Ven. Karma Thinley Rinpoche, Sakya Thinley Rinchen Ling

Ajahn Tiradhammo, Amaravati Buddhist Centre, United Kingdom

Dr W. G. Weeratatna, Editor of the *Buddhist Encylopaedia,* Sri Lanka

Dhanapala Samarasekara, Author and Buddhist scholar, Sri Lanka

Stephen Hodge, London Buddhist Centre, United Kingdom

James Belither, Manjushri Institute, United Kingdom

Richard Hunn, Author and Buddhist scholar, United Kingdom

Stephen Batchelor, Sharpam North Community, United Kingdom

Martine Fages, Sharpam North Community, United Kingdom

Takashi Tsuji, Bureau of Buddhist Education, San Francisco, USA

Philip Karl Eidmann, Bureau of Buddhist Education, San Francisco, USA

Venerable Myokyo-ni, Zen Centre, London, United Kingdom

Reverend Daishin Morgan, Soto Zen Throssel Hole Priory, United Kingdom

Preface

The Essential Teachings Series

This book is the third in a series of readers which is intended to offer an introductory exploration of the great religious texts of the world and the faiths for which the texts are important teachings and guides.

The series has been designed to speak to two sets of readers. The first group are those who practise these teachings for whom the series will be a source for personal reflection and a resource for teaching or study. The second group may not follow this path but may wish to open themselves to the insights which these teachings have to offer. Our intention as editors is to allow each tradition to speak with its own integrity and with the particular emphasis or approach which is its hallmark. In each book the contributors follow the logic of the teachings in the selection of texts and the purpose or intention behind the selection.

The Buddhist traditions and schools included in this text have been presented in chronological order. We have not used diacritical marks for any of the Pali, Sanskrit or Tibetan words. In the Theravada section all the textual references refer to chapter and page of the Pali texts and not to the English translations, which are usually referred to by chapter and sutta.

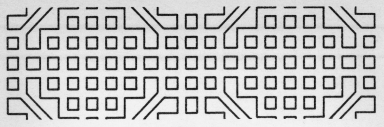

Introduction

Historically speaking, the Buddhist religion originated some 2500 years ago in northern India in the teachings of Lord Buddha, the Enlightened One, known traditionally as Sakyamuni, 'the Sage of the Sakyas'. His dates are most likely to have been in the sixth/fifth century BCE*. Following His passing, different branches of Buddhism developed in India and, after some centuries, elsewhere in Asia, each tending to focus its attention on specific aspects of the common Buddhadharma (Buddha teachings). The teaching themselves were transmitted orally for several centuries before being compiled in various recensions.

In essence these branches crystallised out of the lines of transmission of the Buddhadharma passed on from one generation to the next. These lineages of transmission from guru to disciple have from the earliest days formed the substructure of all manifestations of Buddhism. After some centuries two major traditions took shape, the so-called Hinayana or southern tradition ('lesser vehicle') and Mahayana ('great vehicle') or northern tradition. Of the eighteen sects that originally comprised the southern school that flourished in the first thousand or so years of Buddhism, only one, the Theravada school, is still prevalent today – in Sri Lanka, Thailand, Burma, Kampuchea and Laos. The Mahayana tradition developed primarily in northern India, Nepal, Tibet, China and Japan, forming a number of distinct schools in each place. Buddhism to all intents and purposes disappeared from India, the land of its origin, by the fifteenth century CE although there have been signs of its tentative re-emergence there in recent decades. The form of Buddhism most comparable to that which existed in India up to the end of the mediaeval period is that of the Newar Buddhists of Nepal.

In fourteenth century China, following a series of persecutions, the two major forms of Buddhism, Ch'an and Pure Land, amalgamated and it is this more or less unified tradition that has endured to the twentieth century. After forty years of Marxist government, the vitality of Buddhism in China today is uncertain. In Japan a number of Chinese Buddhist schools were introduced in the mediaeval period. Of these the Shingon, Pure Land, Tendai and Zen (Ch'an) schools are still extant. Korea also received its Buddhism from China in the mediaeval period and there the Ch'an school has predominated.

In Tibet Buddhism flourished from the eighth century CE, eventually

*The terms BCE and CE replace BC and AD.

creating there one of the most remarkable of Buddhist civilisations and a religious centre for much of inner Asia. Four major traditions arose there in the course of time: Nyingma, Kagyu, Sakya and Gelug. Each of these schools maintained its own distinctive presentation of Mahayana Buddhism endowed with the profound spiritual methods of the guhyamantra or tantric teachings, which were so influential in Tibetan Buddhism. Since the Chinese communist occupation of Tibet in 1950, Buddhism has been subject to ruthless persecution. Although a modicum of governmental relaxation has been apparent there in the last few years there can be little doubt that in the political conditions that presently obtain in Tibet, Tibetan Buddhism faces a sustained campaign of eradication. There can equally be little doubt of the determination of the Tibetan people to maintain their religion.

In recent decades Buddhism, in all its major Asian forms, has been establishing itself in the West, both Europe and North America. Whilst this development has so far been relatively modest, the numerous meditation and study facilities that have sprung up as Western centres for Asian lineages of Buddhism represent considerable evidence as to the power of Buddhist practice, philosophy and civilisation to survive in the modern world.

In the broadest terms, Buddhist literature can be divided into two categories: the word of the Buddha Himself and the word of saints, sages and scholars whose status as authoritative sources of Buddhist wisdom is recognised by the ongoing traditions.

Regarding the divisions of Buddha-word, superficially at least the picture is clear; it is collected in the three 'baskets' *(tripitaka):* 'discourses' *(sutra),* 'rules of discipline' *(vinaya)* and 'further knowledge' *(abhidharma).* However, a fundamental difference between the so-called Hinayana and Mahayana traditions of Buddhism emerges in this very attribution of material to the Buddha. The various Mahayana lineages defend the authenticity as Buddha-word of a number of discourses such as *The Perfection of Wisdom,* not to mention the various tantras or texts revealing the methods of secret mantra which are rejected by schools such as the modern-day Theravada.

Some idea of the extensiveness of the collections of Buddha-word can perhaps be gained from the fact that there are 108 volumes in the Tibetan canon *(bKa'. 'gyur.).* In the present collection we shall find examples of these various teachings attributed to Buddha by the differing traditions.

The works of the great saints and scholars in the continuing Buddhist traditions cover a vast range of religious and sometimes secular fields. However, it seems more appropriate here merely to give an indication of the key literary genres. Of fundamental importance are commentaries elucidating the Buddha-word such as the works of Buddhagosa in the Theravada tradition and those of Nagarjuna and Asanga in the early Indian Mahayana. Guides to the practice of meditation have also been of great importance whether in the form of systematic treatises such as those composed by many Tibetan masters or in the form of transcriptions of oral teaching given on different occasions by Zen masters. Texts of ritual practice occupy a significant place in all the major traditions though for various reasons they are perhaps of greatest importance in Tibetan Buddhism. Sacred biographies, collections of poetry and songs by revered saints comprise other noteworthy categories, all being particularly prized for their inspirational power.

In this volume of readings one is confronted by the richness and variety of Buddhism in all its varying forms. How is the reader to make sense of this dazzling and possibly bewildering array of schools and their teaching? The answer is both simple and profound. All these traditions of Buddhism represented here embody the continuing transmission of Buddhadharma. Each should therefore be regarded as a valid presentation of the Buddha's teachings.

This point is of major significance for any understanding of the phenomenon known as 'Buddhism'. Sectarian exclusiveness and claims of superiority for one's own tradition have no place here. In a similar manner the temptation, unfortunately sometimes too powerful for some westerners, to reconstruct a 'basic' Buddhism or divide it into 'mainstream Buddhism and the schools' must be resisted as an after trace of the habitual arrogance of the modernist. One glance at the history of the Buddhadharma will confirm that from the earliest period there has never been one 'Buddhism' over and above the schools. The schools or sects, as the institutionalised forms of the lineage of transmission, are 'Buddhism'.

Thus in approaching the material contained in this volume, presented by members of a number of living Buddhist traditions, one should note how each section embodies a total understanding of and guide to the Buddhist path. If one views the readings in this context much confusion and fruitless labour in attempting to discriminate between essential and inessential or 'original' and 'later' forms of Buddhism will be avoided. If this understanding is adopted one will be able to hear Lord Buddha speak out of each tradition. It is my hope that all who read this book will come to place their feet firmly on the path to liberation.

Ngakpa Jampa Thaye (Dr David Stott)
Dharma-regent of Ven. Karma Thinley Rinpoche
Sakya Thinley Rinchen Ling

I THERAVADA

1 Thailand

Compiled with commentary by Ajahn Tiradhammo

Within the Theravada tradition, as early as the Buddha's lifetime, there have existed two complementary, yet non-exclusive, lifestyles. Very simply, they are that of the study-orientated, village or town-dwelling disciple and that of the meditation-orientated, forest-dwelling disciple. The Forest Tradition emphasises the direct realisation of the Buddha's teachings through the living of a simple, morally refined life conducive to the cultivation of meditation. To assist them in this the disciples usually live in quiet, remote places adhering very strictly to the Vinaya, the detailed monastic observances.

In the early part of this century the Thai Forest Tradition experienced a major revival through the influence of the exemplary teacher Venerable Ajahn Mun Buridatto. As a tribute to his influence most of the living and recently deceased Thai Meditation Masters are his direct or indirect disciples.

One of these disciples, Venerable Ajahn Chah, has been particularly responsive and successful in teaching Westerners. At present there are nearly 100 Westerners in training as monks, nuns or novices in Ajahn Chah's branch monasteries in Thailand, Britain, Australia, New Zealand and Switzerland. Ajahn Chah's particular style of teaching, broad-minded and pragmatic, yet strict and traditional, seems especially attractive to a growing number of well-travelled and experienced people searching for some relevant, authentic and well-grounded spiritual tradition.

The following readings take us on a journey of the cultivation and unfolding of the Way of Practice in order to lead us to our own realisation of Dhamma or Truth. The majority of the readings are attributed to the Buddha himself and some to his disciples. Thus, though they may sometimes appear cryptic, they are excellent material for deep meditative reflection – the key to Buddha-wisdom.

I have tried to find a balance between including some of the more familiar texts often used to present certain aspects of the Buddha's teaching and those which are little known yet equally expressive, and perhaps even more relevant to modern, Western readers. My primary purpose in translating these passages has been merely to make them more clearly understandable to myself, as well as to others. Thus I have generally deferred to the interpretation of recognised Pali scholars when the need has arisen. Otherwise I have relied upon the experience of my own practice and the teachings of the Forest Tradition. I assume responsibility if any mistakes have occurred.

It should be noted that the Pali canon is principally 'narrative' rather than 'normative'. That is, it is the record of conversations and teachings of the Buddha given at different times and to different people, rather than being a body of prescribed doctrine. My main intent in translation has been to reduce the amount of repetition and to offer a rendering more faithful to the meaning than the letter. I have retained the conversational form by including the names of the listeners, even though they may appear unusual to a Western reader. I have also retained some basic Pali terms. Some of these are untranslatable in only a word or two, others are explained in the commentaries. For instance, I have kept the word 'bhikkhu' for what is commonly, but incorrectly, translated as 'monk'. A bhikkhu is a wandering mendicant, somewhat similar to the early friars, in contrast to the usual image of a monk as a cloistered monastic bound by lifetime vows of obedience to an abbot. It is this particular lifestyle of the bhikkhu that characterises the ideal of the Forest Tradition.

May all beings realise peace.

Homage to the Exalted, Perfected,
Fully Enlightened One

The Way

The Right Attitude

1.

*Now I say this, Nigrodha: Whatever discerning people come to me who
are honest, open and straightforward – I will instruct them, I will teach
them Dhamma. If they practise in accordance with what is taught, in
this very life within seven years they will enter on and abide in, know
and experience for themselves that unsurpassed culmination of the
religious life, for the sake of which a person of good family rightly goes
forth from the homelife into homelessness. Let alone seven years, six
years; let alone six years . . . a fortnight; let alone a fortnight, in seven
days they will know and experience this for themselves.*

Digha Nikaya, Vol. III, page 55

The Buddha has given us confidence. He has offered us the universal
possibility of nibbana – a possibility that we must recognise
individually. The Buddha offers us food for reflection not laws to be
obeyed. Anyone who approaches him with sincerity and honesty is
worthy of instruction but his instructions must be put into practice.
The Buddha does not choose his disciples according to caste, merit or
intelligence; he chooses only those who show the fundamental spiritual
qualities of honesty and integrity. These qualities alone do not merit
final release and there is no set time for achieving nibbana. The
Buddha has tremendous confidence in human beings so that if we act
according to his teachings and these teachings are put to the test, we
can realise nibbana in this life. It may take seven years, it may take
seven days. The Buddha's teachings are for all people but it is up to us
to fulfil these teachings with true wisdom.

2.

Nibbana, though very subtle and fine, is not hard to obtain for one intent upon the goal, who is skilled in mind and of gentle manner, and who practises the moral conduct of the Buddha.

Theragatha, verse 71

Nibbana, as taught by the fully enlightened one, is indeed the highest happiness: the sorrowless, stainless peace, wherein suffering is dissolved.

Theragatha, verse 227

The goal of Buddhist practice is nibbana, a state difficult to describe but within reach of every individual. Out of respect and reverence for the lofty heights of spiritual truth, we frequently push the goal into the realm of human impossibility. But the very existence of people practising the teachings should be a living reminder that nibbana is attainable. Although nibbana is above and beyond everything which is common to us, it can be realised by the honest and the persevering through the teachings of the Buddha. Nibbana is exceedingly pleasant and worthwhile and can be achieved in this life. Like human happiness, nibbana can be achieved here and now.

3.

'Any student of my teaching,' said the Buddha, 'who is eager, intelligent and aware, here and now, can find the calm of cessation for himself.'

'It is not my practice to free anyone from confusion,' said the Buddha.

'When you have understood the most valuable teachings, then you yourself will cross this ocean.'

Sutta Nipata, verses 1062, 1064

The source of suffering is our sense of self, which is out of harmony with the universe, which is selfless. We can find the calm of cessation when suffering, disharmony and unsatisfactoriness no longer exist within ourselves. The self-centred, self-affirming, self-supporting activities which are a source of suffering can cease through Dhamma (the Buddha's teachings). In our desire to escape suffering we try to manipulate the world around us but we manipulate it in relation to ourselves so we never go beyond our self and continue to create suffering. When we understand our own confusion, how it is caused and how it ceases, we can cross the ocean of sensual existence for ourselves.

Self-reliance

4.

Truly oneself is one's own refuge – what other refuge could there be?
With oneself well-tamed one acquires a refuge hard to obtain.

Dhammapada, verse 160

By oneself is wrong done, by oneself is one soiled; anti - Christ
By oneself is wrong not done, by oneself is one purified.
Purity and impurity depend upon oneself; no one can purify another.

Dhammapada, verse 165

You yourself ought to strive: the Buddhas only show the way.
Those who enter upon this way and meditate are released from the bonds
of Death.

Dhammapada, verse 276

The Buddha's teaching, in its earliest cultural context, focused on the *where is*
internal spiritual practices in contrast to the external rituals prevalent *the need*
at that time. The Buddha emphasised the need for individual effort *for God*
and self-reliance. We have little control over the external aspects of the *we do it*
world but we do have some degree of control over ourselves, so that is
where we should start our practice. 'Oneself is one's own refuge' *all*
literally means 'depend upon yourself', 'look to yourself', 'have
confidence in yourself'. It refers to the relative, conventional, *ourselves*
empirical self which can choose to do good or bad, can make decisions *?*
and initiate action. In this way we take responsibility for ourselves.
Our suffering is created by our own ignorance so we need to remedy it
by gaining confidence in our own inner wisdom.

5.

The monk must look for peace within himself and not in any other place.
For when a person is inwardly quiet, there is nowhere a self can be found;
where, then, could a non-self be found?
    There are no waves in the depths of the sea; it is still, unbroken. It is
the same with the monk. He is still, without any quiver of desire, without
a remnant on which to build pride and desire.

Sutta Nipata, verses 919–20

We realise 'inward quiet' through internalised meditation practices,
particularly through samatha (calm meditation), which develops the
quality of collectedness or concentration. When the mind concentrates on

diabolically opposed to prayer as the healer -

the meditation object of breathing all the wandering thoughts are calmed and all the mental noise is silenced. When the self-referring mental noise is silenced all reference to a sense of self and denial of a sense of self ceases, hence no pride or desire, only peaceful silence. In samatha, however, the sense of self is only temporarily quieted. It is through the practice of vipassana (insight meditation), with its emphasis upon penetrating, investigative awareness, that the sense of self is clearly seen and completely let go of.

Noble Friendship

6.

Ananda: 'Sir, fully half of this religious life is friendship with what is noble, companionship with what is noble, association with what is noble.'
Buddha: 'Not quite so, Ananda, not quite so. It is the whole, not the half of this religious life: this friendship, companionship, association with what is noble.'

Samyutta Nikaya, Vol. V, page 2

the blind leading the blind

The self has the ability to decide, choose and direct what is skilful or unskilful but we also need the guidance of a noble friend since we are still locked within ourselves. A noble friend can help us unfold the spiritual path and lead us beyond ourselves to see the aspects of our nature we are afraid of, do not want to see or do not recognise. Kalyana (the noble) can be translated as 'the beautiful' or 'the lovely' since the noble friend guides us to spiritual uplift by offering help and friendship. In Dhamma (the Buddha's teachings) companionship with the noble is formally represented by the Sangha, the community of Buddhist monks and nuns who are committed to a life of dedicated spiritual practice. Informally, the noble friend can be anyone who offers us wise reflection and skilful counsel so that we can focus more clearly upon the spiritual path.

Buddhist monks, nuns and lay people who have entered one of the paths of saintship are known as the Ariya (Noble) Sangha, the Refuge of Sangha, the most noble friends. They have attained enlightenment and cannot be identified by their appearance but by their state of mind.

7.

If you should find a wise person who, like a revealer of treasure, points out your faults and reproves you, associate with them. Association with such a one is for the better not for the worse.

Dhammapada, verse 76

If, even for a moment, an intelligent person associates with someone wise, quickly they will apprehend the Dhamma, just as the tongue apprehends the flavour of soup.

Dhammapada, verse 65

We can never underestimate the value of associating with someone wise since we can benefit from their guidance as quickly as the tongue tastes the flavour of soup. One minute with a noble friend can help us unravel the confusion in our mind and bring us closer to knowing ourselves. The noble friend guides us in the Dhamma (the Buddha's teachings) and gives us direction and dedication to the path of the Buddha. His or her words are worth far more than priceless treasures for they help us realise the faults and delusions that weigh us down and hinder our practice. They lead us to wise reflection when we begin to understand what creates the misery in our lives and through wise reflection we see that we are the creators of this misery.

Skilful Actions

8.

The Exalted One, while staying at Rajagaha on Vulture's Peak, gave abundant Dhamma-talk to the bhikkhus: such is moral conduct, such is meditation, such is wisdom.

Meditation, when augmented with moral conduct, gives great fruit and great benefit. Wisdom, when augmented with meditation, gives great fruit and great benefit. The mind, when augmented with wisdom, is completely freed from the outflows of selfhood [asavas], that is the outflow of sensuality, the outflow of becoming, the outflow of views and the outflow of ignorance.

Digha Nikaya, Vol. 11, page 81

The path can be practised and realised through our own self-motivation and with the help of noble friendship as a support. The Buddha's path is the path of morality, meditation and wisdom. Meditation when imbued with morality bears the fruit of wisdom and eventually we realise freedom from suffering, the freedom of mind.

Through meditation, that is, the cultivation of skilful spiritual practices, we learn to let go of all that is unsatisfactory and impermanent and no longer identify the sensory world as 'me' or 'mine'. We cease to demand satisfaction, security or safety and no longer expect conditions to be anything other than what they are. When the mind is peaceful we are inclining towards nibbana, to a state of mind free from selfish outflowings or pollutions.

meditation likened to prayer

(Asavas are the outflows of selfhood that pollute one's being. The word is sometimes rendered as 'cankers', 'intoxicants', 'corruptions', 'pollutions'. The four asavas are: sensuality, becoming, views and ignorance, and the ending of the asavas is equivalent to realising nibbana.)

4 vices –

9.

Ananda, skilful conduct gives freedom from remorse as its gain and advantage; freedom from remorse gives delight as its gain and advantage; delight gives joy . . . joy gives tranquillity . . . tranquillity gives happiness . . . happiness gives collectedness . . . collectedness gives knowledge and vision of things as they really are . . . disenchantment and dispassion . . . knowledge and vision of freedom as its gain and advantage. So indeed, Ananda, skilful conduct gradually leads on to the highest.

Anguttura Nikaya, Vol. 5, page 2

Skilful conduct provides the foundation for the accumulation of skilful qualities rather than merely being an end in itself. Skilful conduct gives rise to freedom from remorse, which in its turn gives rise to a series of causally related spiritual qualities. Through the practice of skilful conduct we gradually attain increasingly specialised and advantageous qualities as our spiritual progression develops more refined states. The ultimate gain and advantage of skilful conduct is freedom; freedom from attachment, disenchantment with worldly things and knowledge and vision of that freedom. We do not become wise but through skilful conduct wisdom becomes clear.

10.

Moral conduct is the beginning, the foundation, and the chief cause of all good things. Thus one should purify moral conduct.
Moral conduct is the boundary, the control and the brightening of the mind, and it is the abiding of all the Buddhas. Thus one should purify moral conduct.

Theragatha, verses 612–13

Without the stable foundation laid down through skilful living, spiritual realisation will quickly become a memory that we are unable to relate to everyday experience or to our normal level of conciousness. Moral conduct does not stand alone; it is the foundation for meditation and meditation is the foundation for wisdom. When we realise wisdom we also realise the benefit of moral conduct, and we have the confidence of virtue. The path that began with skilful practice has now travelled a full circle. We can re-establish and refine moral conduct, which again leads on to more refined meditation practice, and in its turn this produces a clearer vision of wisdom and insight.

11.

And how is a monk contented? Here, a monk is satisfied with a robe to protect his body, with alms to satisfy his stomach, and having accepted sufficient, he goes on his way. Just as a bird with wings flies hither and thither, burdened by nothing but its wings, so he is satisfied ... In this way, Sire, a monk is contented.

Digha Nikaya, Vol I, page 71

The Buddha is offering a reflection on our basic needs for survival to King Ajatasattu:

Once we have laid the foundation of moral conduct we try to simplify our life of selfish wants and dwell contented with providing the basic human needs. The Buddhist monk has four basic supports to life: almsfood, a set of three robes, shelter for one night and medicine for illness. While this is the particular reflection upon the essential material possessions for sustaining a human life, it also implies that satisfying our material needs is not the principal purpose of human life. Having few possessions to worry about keeps our life uncluttered and unencumbered so our mind can rise above the mundane concerns of the world as a bird flies aloft when it wishes. We will then have much more time and energy available for sustained spiritual practice. Just as we can train the mind to seek after material possessions for security, so we can train the mind to seek the real security of spiritual freedom.

monks live in abject poverty — denial brings spiritual freedom

Seclusion

12.

Endowed with this noble moral conduct ... with this noble mindfulness and clear awareness, and with this noble contentment, he then resorts to a secluded place to sit and sleep. He establishes himself at the foot of a remote tree, in a mountain cave or grotto, a cemetery, a jungle forest, or in the open air on a pile of straw. Then, having returned from the alms- round and taken his meal, he sits down cross-legged holding his body upright and raises up mindfulness before him.

Digha Nikaya, Vol. I, page 71

Through wisdom we recognise that the fulfilment of our basic needs is only a preliminary to cultivating more refined spiritual qualities. Once moral conduct is established our minds are free from remorse and we have the strength and confidence to live in a secluded place. When we are free from regret and fear, we no longer yearn for family, friends or comforts, and have the confidence of knowing that our lives are wholesome and our conduct skilful. We are ready to open our mind fully to Dhamma (the Buddha's teachings).

The Buddha mentioned three types of seclusion: physical seclusion leads to the development of collectedness, which brings mental seclusion; mental seclusion is conducive to the arising of wisdom, which is seclusion from attachment. When we are removed from our familiar environment we can reflect on our habits and attachments with a greater clarity since we are no longer enveloped in a world which supports our sense of self and reinforces our likes and dislikes. But seclusion is not an end in itself for we cannot run away from our own minds when we leave the environment which is the cause of our troubles. It is our own mind which creates despair and suffering. The person who goes to a secluded place does not go to escape distractions but removes himself from distractions so that he can understand the real source of the world through his or her own mind.

self idolatry

13.

> When the storm-clouds thunder in the sky and the flyways of the birds
> are awash with torrential rains, the bhikkhu who has entered a cave
> meditates – no greater pleasure than this can be found. When on the
> flower-shrouded bank of a river, bedecked with various woodland
> plants, he sits on the bank joyfully meditating – no greater pleasure than
> this can be found.
> When at night in a lonely grove, with rain pouring down, the fanged
> and tusked animals roar, the bhikkhu who has entered a cave meditates
> – no greater pleasure than this can be found.
>
> *Theragatha, verses, 522–4*

This verse refers particularly to the contentment that arises from living in harmony with nature. Once we have realised confidence and contentment through moral conduct we automatically feel at peace with nature and know the happiness of freedom. Without this peace nature can be challenging and dangerous. We become hungry and cold, we are afraid of becoming lost and are wary of the forest animals.

Through meditation in a peaceful and natural environment we can develop peace of mind, collectedness and awareness. When our senses are heightened we can see great joy and harmony in the natural world. The Buddha frequently advised people to go into the forest and meditate because its sounds are restful and its colours soothing. Our sense of self is no longer reinforced. Our sense of self is reduced to its

reliance on self

basic elements so that the sensations of hot and cold or the feelings of
fear and happiness can be seen and known in their purest state.

14.

*Abandoning worldly desires, he dwells with a mind freed from worldly
desires, and his mind is purified of them. Abandoning ill-will and
hatred . . . and by compassionate love for the welfare of all living beings,
his mind is purified of ill-will and hatred. Abandoning sloth and
torpor, . . . perceiving light, mindful and clearly aware, his mind is
purified of sloth and torpor. Abandoning restlessness and worry . . . and
with an inwardly calmed mind, his heart is purified of restfulness and
worry. Abandoning doubt, he dwells with doubt left behind, without
uncertainty as to what things are wholesome, his mind is purified of
doubt.*

Digha Nikaya, Vol. I, page 71

Through meditation in a quiet place we begin to free the mind from
hindrances. When we begin meditation practice we initially meet the
negative aspects of our nature that we have knowingly or unknowingly
been suppressing: desires, hatred, distraction, fear, dullness of mind.
These are practical expressions of our sense of self that cause suffering.
But through skilful conduct we begin to clear the fog that dulls our
clarity of mind. The so-called hindrances listed in this reading are
actually fertilisers for our practice, for as soon as we understand them
we can begin to transcend worldly desires and develop awareness and
collectedness. We become conscious of these aspects of ourself in
meditation and we should acknowledge them as challenges that help us
transcend self, not as threats to be destroyed or suppressed. Through
meditation we are given a golden opportunity to understand our
particular hindrances and relinquish our sense of self which is
identified with them.

15.

*And when he knows that these five hindrances have left him, gladness
arises in him, from gladness comes delight, from the delight in his mind
his body is tranquillised, with a tranquil body he feels joy, and with joy
his mind is concentrated. Being thus detached from sense desires,
detached from unwholesome states, he enters and remains in the first
jhana, which is with thinking and pondering, born of detachment, filled
with delight and joy. And with this delight and joy born of detachment,
he so suffuses, drenches, fills and irradiates his body that there is no spot*

*in his entire body that is untouched by this delight and joy born of
detachment.*

Digha Nikaya, Vol. I, page 73

The preliminary direction of Buddhist meditation is towards samatha
(calm meditation). From a basis of moral conduct we begin to purify the
mind of hindrances and develop stability of mind. A calm and tranquil
mind is the foundation of Buddhist meditation but there is no time limit
for realising samatha. Some people have many aversions and desires and
may take years to achieve some degree of collectedness, others may take
weeks or even days. At first we may achieve a state of collectedness only
intermittently and then it begins to become a more familiar state of mind.
Through samatha we cultivate skilful practice, but it must be reinforced
with wisdom to realise how to increase tranquillity of mind and not return
to unskilful habits. Through samatha we enter the first jhana or first stage
of meditative absorption when we think and ponder on the world around
us but are free of desires, aversions and confusion. We no longer interpret
our impressions according to our own self-interest.

Mindfulness — 4 Foundations

16.

*There is one way for the purification of beings, for passing beyond
sorrow and grief, for the disappearance of suffering and distress, for
reaching the right path, for the realisation of nibbana, and that is the
four foundations of mindfulness. What are the four? In this practice one
dwells clearly reflecting upon the body, upon feelings, upon states of
mind, upon spiritual qualities – earnestly, clearly aware and mindful,
having put away desire and disappointment concerning the world.*

Majjhima Nikaya, Vol. I, page 55

Samatha (calm meditation) is the foundation for vipassana (insight
meditation), the principal quality of which is mindfulness or awareness.
The Buddha said that the only way to realise wisdom is to practise the four
foundations of mindfulness. Without wisdom, samatha is a phenomenon
conditioned by our effort and perseverance; it is not a noble quality until it
is reinforced with the wisdom of insight into the true nature of things.
From a basis of tranquillity we can reflect upon the body, feelings, states
of mind and spiritual qualities so that our real nature is reflected in the
mind. Reflection is intuitive contemplation that arises from a tranquil
mind; it cannot be likened to analysis, discussion or speculation. If the
mind is distracted by internal dialogue which continually twists and turns
our thoughts, it is not tranquil. But when we realise samatha our internal
dialogue is quietened, we are receptive and objective. When we incline

towards vipassana we no longer want to argue or discuss, to stay or to escape, to win or to lose. We no longer form concepts of the world around us or sift our feelings into likes or dislikes. We clearly and objectively observe the true nature of things.

appeals to vanity —

I AM NOW PERFECT — so I can be passive — good teaching to hold people in subjection bound to superstition

17.

Steadfast in body and steadfast in mind —
Whether standing, sitting or lying down —
Having firmly established mindfulness,
One acquires excellence, first and foremost.
And having obtained such excellence, they go,
Unseen by the King of Death.

Udana, page 61

The four foundations of mindfulness should be cultivated as a natural way of life, as a normal way of relating to our environment. The four foundations of mindfulness should be integrated into everything we do so that we are aware of the four different expressions of self: body, feelings, states of mind, and spiritual qualities. If we do develop mindfulness to a degree of excellence we go beyond death – we enter amata (the deathless state). We are open and receptive and in complete harmony with the way things really are.

contradicts Xn belief of a resurrection

18.

I ascended the high terrace of the foundations of mindfulness and contemplated the people who were indulging in the notion of individuality that I had previously thought about so much. When I saw the Way, boarding the ship and not holding to a view of self, I saw the ultimate harbour.

The Buddha removed the ties which for a long time had been latent in me and for a long time had been established in me. He cured me of the ill effects of the poisonous defilements.

Theragatha, verses 765-6, 768

Through the foundations of mindfulness we can rise to the ultimate. Through reflection on the four foundations of mindfulness, the expressions of our individuality, we can uncover the real basis of individuality. We can identify body, feelings, states of mind and spiritual qualities and become aware of our attachments to them. As our practice develops we are carried along by it, like a ship at sea, and the way which once seemed beyond us is now part of us. When we no longer hold to a view of self we can see the ultimate harbour of nibbana. We can now remove the ties to samsara (the cycles of birth and death) which were latent within us. Our sense of self is no longer entangled with desires nor needs to be nurtured. Our sense perceptions cease to be part of our sense of self and although there is the organ of sight or hearing and the brain identifies seeing and hearing, it is no longer 'I' who hears or 'I' who sees. Through ignorance we assume that 'I' continuously exists but this assumption has no basis in reality. The Buddha said that there is the object and the process of seeing, but we create the 'I' to give the process life and so become the product of our perceptions. Through mindfulness we become aware that the physical body exists but it is no longer 'my' body; feelings arise but we no longer try to control them. They are human realities that we no longer need to manipulate.

Mindfulness of Body   *Breathing —*
bodily activity

19.

And how does one dwell clearly reflecting upon the body? To this end, one goes into the forest, to the foot of a tree or to a secluded place, sits down cross-legged with body held upright, and raises mindfulness to the forefront. Just mindful, one breathes in; mindful, one breathes out. Breathing in a long breath, one knows . . . ; breathing out a long breath, one knows . . . Breathing in a short breath, one knows . . . ; breathing out a short breath, one knows that one is breathing out a short breath.
Majjhima Nikaya, Vol. I, page 56

The first category of mindfulness is clear reflection upon the body and the first exercise is to develop awareness of breathing, the basic nutrient of life. There are forty meditation objects in Buddhism but breathing is the most fundamental and universal; it is the meditation object that the Buddha used in his own spiritual quest. Other meditation objects are more specialised; for example, the meditation on friendliness is used by people to counteract aversion or self-hatred.

This reading offers preliminary instructions for a meditation on breathing, the foundation of all meditation practice. Our attention normally wanders where it pleases but this exercise focuses our attention completely on the inhalation and exhalation of our breath. What may seem a simple exercise becomes refined through practice. We can extend and develop other meditation practices but we can always return to the meditation on breathing and continue to refine it. When we focus our attention on breathing we are developing samatha (calm meditation) but when we emphasise awareness of breathing we are inclining towards vipassana (insight meditation). We cultivate awareness when we are attentive to the subtle rhythms of breathing and sustain that attention.

20.

*He who has perfected, well developed, and practised in due order
mindfulness of breathing, as taught by the Buddha, illuminates this
world like the moon released from a cloud.*

*Truly my mind is purified, unlimited, well developed; having
penetrated and having been applied, it illuminates all the quarters.*

Theragatha, verses 548–9

What was initially a simple and obvious physical experience now becomes
a stepping stone for progressive refinement of mind through collectedness
and awareness. Through awareness of breathing the mind becomes lucid
and when attention is focused on breathing the mind becomes still and
collected. When we are instructed in meditation the emphasis is not on
willpower but on perseverance. We must work with the habits of mind
which have become rigid, which is why the support and encouragement
of a noble friend is important. If our only frame of reference is the
difficulty or pleasure we feel through awareness of breathing then we are
still entangled in the restless and confused habits of our mind. This
reading gives us confidence to persevere, for the end result is a pure,
unlimited and illuminated mind.

dependency on noble friend —

21.

*Again, in going forward or backward, one is clearly aware; in looking
ahead or around, one is clearly aware; in bending or stretching, one is
clearly aware; in wearing the robes and carrying the bowl, one is clearly
aware; in attending to the calls of nature, one is clearly aware; in
eating, drinking, chewing or tasting, one is clearly aware; in walking,
standing, sitting, falling asleep and waking up, one is clearly aware; in
speaking or being silent, one is clearly aware.*

Majjhima Nikaya, Vol. I, page 57

The second exercise for developing mindfulness is awareness of every
bodily activity. We should begin with the actions that have become so
commonplace we are no longer attentive to them, for example, washing
our hands or cleaning our teeth. Our sense of self is rooted in ritualised
habits so we can only understand our sense of self when we are aware of
these habits. We sometimes organise our daily routine very carefully, not
because we are attentive to every moment but because this is how we
express our individuality. The Buddha discovered that self-awareness of
simple activities is a source of great wisdom. There is a continuity of
awareness that leads us on from mindfulness of breathing to mindfulness
of walking, sitting, lying down, eating, and so on.

22.

*I am a disciple of the well-farer, travelling in the eightfold vehicle which
is the Way. With my dart drawn out, without asavas, having gone to an
empty house, I rejoice.*
*For well-painted puppets, or dolls, have been seen by me, fastened by
strings and sticks, made to dance in various ways.*
*This little body, being of such a kind, does not exist without these
phenomena; as it does not exist without these phenomena, on what there
would one fix one's mind.*

Theragatha, verses 389-90, 392

Once we have developed awareness of the body we realise it is like a
puppet whose actions are directed by self-affirming activities and self-
preserving habits. If our habits are unexpectedly thrown into disarray, so
is our sense of self. We attach to these habits through ignorance and begin
to relate to the world through the fixed position of ignorance. We forget
that every day is different; the weather is different, our state of mind has
altered, our body is older and our actions are slower or quicker. When we
have clarity of mind we realise that every moment is different and we are
no longer manipulated by our habits.

The body is the abiding place of our consciousness and we are
continually constructing a 'house' to accommodate our sense of self.
When the body breaks up, our craving will create a new abiding place for
consciousness. Through skilful practice the dart of craving for sense
pleasures, for becoming and for annihilation is eventually drawn out. We
are free of asavas (pollutions, outflows) and our conciousness abides in an
'empty house'.

23.

*Again, one reviews this body as it is placed or directed in regard to the
elemental qualities: there are in this body the elemental qualities of
earth, water, fire and air.*
Thus one dwells clearly reflecting upon body.

Majjhima Nikaya, Vol. I, page 57

There are a variety of meditations on the body in mindfulness practice.
The body is a coarse meditation object since it is the most substantial and
obvious.

We should learn to review the body in reference to the four elemental
qualities. Earth represents the elemental quality of hardness. The earth is
the foundation of life and in the body its quality predominates in the
bones, teeth and nails, the most obvious representations of hardness.
Water has a cohesive and fluid quality and predominates in saliva, blood,
mucus, and tears. Fire not only represents heat, warmth and radiation but

it also has a maturing and ageing quality. This quality predominates in our chemical reactions, in our metabolism or in our body heat. Air offers supportive and life-giving qualities; without it our physical being would collapse. It is air which creates movement in the body since we are given life or movement through breath.

Without water the earth would turn to dust, without fire it would become solid and without air it would be lifeless. This reading helps us reflect on our interdependence with nature so that we begin to break down the individual identification that separates us from nature. Our bodies, like the earth and everything in our environment, combine all these elements in greater or lesser proportions.

24.

Leaving the five hindrances in order to attain rest from exertion, taking the doctrine as a mirror, the seeing and knowing of the self, I considered this whole body inside and out. Both inside and outside the body seemed empty.

Theragatha, verses 171–2

Knowing the body is like foam, realising its mirage-like nature,
Cutting off the flower-tipped, sensual realm,
One goes unseen by the King of Death.

Dhammapada, verse 46

When we experience body meditation we review the body from inside and outside and realise that it is empty of self. All we see are the four elements which are combining and interacting within us. It is no longer 'I' who digests food but the elemental quality of fire which produces this digestive action. When we realise the body empty of self we also realise its fragility and impermanence. These four elements come together for a lifetime and then they disperse like foam that is thrown up on the seashore only to disappear within moments. Likewise, our body cannot last forever. We live with the delusion that we will always survive and are surprised to discover we are dying. Our preconceived ideas about the body are nothing more than a mirage for it will travel through its natural processes whatever we try to do to it.

We look at the world through our six senses but usually we try to blot out the unpleasant and hold on to the pleasant, but even these pleasant experiences bloom, wither and die like the petals of a flower.

Through wisdom we accept the transitory nature of all things so when they die there is no sorrow or regret. When we cease to be attached we no longer fear or suffer death since it is no longer 'I' who dies. We become part of a natural process that exists but has no marked beginning or end.

Mindfulness of Feelings

25.

> *And how does one dwell clearly reflecting upon feelings? To this end,*
> *experiencing a pleasant feeling, one knows one is experiencing a pleasant*
> *feeling; experiencing an unpleasant feeling, one knows one is ex-*
> *periencing an unpleasant feeling; experiencing a feeling that is neither*
> *pleasant nor unpleasant, one knows one is experiencing a feeling that is*
> *neither pleasant nor unpleasant.*
>
> Majjhima Nikaya, Vol. I, page 59

Awareness of feelings is an excellent way to understand the intricate field
of emotional reactions. Emotions are very complex mental states while
feelings are simply the affective tone of experience as either pleasant,
unpleasant or neutral. Whenever we are conscious there is one of these
three feelings present. However, it is usually a neutral feeling, or so
slightly pleasant or unpleasant that we hardly notice it. Yet feelings play a
major part in motivating our life. The central motivating force in sentient
life is seeking pleasant feeling and escaping from unpleasant feeling. This
mechanism can only be brought into the light of wisdom when we are
clearly aware of our feelings.

26.

> *One who sees that pleasant feeling is unsatisfactory,*
> *Who sees that painful feeling is like a stinging dart,*
> *Who sees that neutral feeling is impermanent –*
> *Truly that one rightly sees and understands feelings.*
> *Thus understanding feelings, one is free of pollutions in this world.*
>   *When the body breaks up, one has reached Dhamma, attained the*
> *highest knowledge and has gone beyond all ways of definition.*
>
> Samyutta Nikaya, Vol. IV, page 207

Once we recognise the range of our feelings and are familiar with all three,
we can view them with a new clarity. Pleasant feelings are unsatisfactory
because they are changeable and incomplete. It is impossible for us to
experience a pleasant feeling all our lives because other feelings naturally
arise to take their place. If we think that we can hold onto pleasure forever
we will only be disappointed. Pain can take many forms, sometimes
slight, sometimes severe, but it should never be shunned or ignored; it
should be recognised for what it is, unpleasant and impermanent.

When we recognise the truth of feeling we are no longer deluded by
pleasure or pain and become free of asavas (pollutions). When we realise
truth we enter a state that is beyond definition; we enter nibbana.

Mindfulness of States of Mind

27.

*And how does one dwell clearly reflecting upon states of mind? To this
end one knows a lustful mind as lustful, a mind free of lust as free of lust;
a hateful mind as hateful, the mind free of hate as free of hate; a deluded
mind as deluded, an undeluded mind as undeluded; a contracted mind
as contracted, a distracted mind as distracted; a developed mind as
developed, an undeveloped mind as undeveloped; an inferior mind as
inferior, a superior mind as superior; a collected mind as collected, an
uncollected mind as uncollected; a liberated mind as liberated, an
unliberated mind as unliberated.*

Majjhima Nikaya, Vol. I, page 59

Our awareness is refined when we move from meditation on feelings to
meditation on states of mind. There are infinite states of mind as opposed
to three feelings and this reading suggests sixteen states of mind that we
should use as a frame of reference. The first three states, lustful, hateful
and deluded, are the three roots of unskilfulness. The other states are
more refined but are by no means exclusive of each other. The Buddha
has mentioned these states of mind as particular areas of investigation that
can lead us to reflection upon increasingly specific states of mind.

Through reflection upon states of mind we begin to understand what
these states are, where they arise from, how they are created, how they
affect us and what our preferences are. Unless we have this understanding
of the mind's basic mechanisms we will continue to manipulate situations
and place our own preferences first. We have to be aware of and objective
to the states that exist regardless of the feelings that they arouse. We can
only achieve real mindfulness when we have cultivated objective or
'choiceless' awareness.

28.

*Mind precedes all things,
Mind is supreme, produced by mind are they.
If one should speak or act with mind defiled,
Suffering will follow,
Just as wheel follows hoof of the drawing ox.
Mind precedes all things,
Mind is supreme, produced by mind are they.
If one should speak or act with purified mind,
Well-being will follow,
Like a never-parting shadow.*

Dhammapada, verses 1–2

These are further themes for reflection and further areas that we discover through continued awareness. In Buddhist teachings the mind is dynamic; it is the continuum of mental processes, like the wind which cannot be described as air, but as air in motion. Unlike the brain, the mind has no fixed form or dimension. The mind precedes all things; it has the capacity to integrate all experiences, to define them and to qualify them. Mental and physical phenomena are inter-dependent but it is the mind which is the most dominant and important. The mind knows the physical but the physical will never know the mind. Mind recognises and acknowledges, co-ordinates and organises, integrates and separates; it is, therefore, supremely important.

29.

Bhikkhus, I don't know of any other single thing so conducive to such misery as this undeveloped, unpractised mind. The undeveloped mind is indeed conducive to much misery.

Bhikkhus, I don't know of any other single thing so conducive to such benefit as this developed, practised mind. The developed mind is indeed conducive to much benefit.

Anguttura Nikaya, Vol. I, page 6

The mind is the source of suffering and defilement but it is also the source of purity and well-being. This is why the mind must be trained and cultivated. A mind that is not trained causes suffering and arouses confusion to the point of creating physical illness. When the mind is highly developed it can attain extraordinary psychic powers which can arise quite naturally. It is only through meditation that we can develop the clarity and collectedness of the developed mind to be free from suffering and realise nibbana.

30.

Brightly shining, luminous is this mind, but it is defiled by the stains which visit it. This the unlearned common folk do not really understand; so for them there is no development of the mind. Brightly shining, luminous is this mind and it is freed of the stains which visit it. This the learned noble disciple really understands; so for them there is development of the mind.

Anguttara Nikaya, Vol. I, page 10

Through profound insight the Buddha realised that the mind in its natural state is brightly shining and luminous. This was the source of His exceptionally positive outlook on human nature. He realised that all human beings are naturally pure and their moods – their anger, aggression and so on – are merely visitors who come and go. Our defiling tendencies are not our true nature, so we can be free of them. Of course, most people identify so strongly with their visiting moods that they are unable to experience, or even recognise, their true nature. Our practice is patiently to observe the coming and going of these moods so that the insight that penetrates into their impermanent and impersonal nature enables us to let go of them.

31.

Just as a solid mass of rock is not moved by the wind, so sights, tastes, sounds, smells and all things to touch, mental objects, pleasant and unpleasant, do not cause a venerable one's mind, which is steadfast and uncluttered, to tremble and he sees their passing away.

My mind stands like a rock, and does not quiver; unattached to lustful things, it is not shaken amidst the shaking world. My mind is thus developed; whence will pain come to me?

Theragatha, verses 192, 633–44

The developed mind is not subject to the 'shaking' of the ephemeral world. If our minds are not cluttered by our subjective ideas about the world we can remain free of the turbulence that will erupt when those ideas eventually change. The well-developed mind is firm and steady in its practice. The collected mind is strong and resolutely established upon the meditation object. Sights, sounds, tastes and so on arise, but they arise to the unshakable mind, rather than the mind going out to them. The usual desires and aversions associated with most sense impressions do not arise, or if they do arise, they are clearly observed and not chased after or chased away. In this way there is no pain of disappointment or sorrow of loss.

32.

There are, Nigrodha, unwholesome things that have not been abandoned, tainted, conducive to rebirth, fearful, productive of painful results in the future, associated with birth, decay and death. It is for the abandonment of these things that I teach Dhamma. If you practise accordingly, these tainted things will be abandoned, and the things that make for purification will develop and grow, and you will all attain to and dwell, in this very life, by your own insight and realisation, in the fullness of perfected wisdom.

Digha Nikaya, Vol. III, page 57

Through the clear investigation of states of mind we discover many amazing things about ourself. In particular, what we are most likely to discover are those aspects of ourself that we have been ignoring or repressing out of consciousness, the so-called unwholesome aspects of ourself which we are either too frightened to observe or too ashamed to acknowledge. But these are precisely what we need to awaken to, to be enlightened to. It is very important, however, that we investigate thoroughly and observe very carefully and objectively. We have inherent, habitual tendencies that make us want to manipulate what we observe by either abandoning it or clinging to it. When we become conscious of unwholesome, unpleasant aspects of ourself, our main tendency is to ignore them through distraction or repress them with a cosmetic gloss of piety or niceness.

The Buddha's way is to try to understand all aspects of ourself and so we learn to transcend them with wisdom, not to annihilate them.

33.

> *When, having kept in check discursive thoughts, sheltered in a cave between the hills, fearless and without impediments, he meditates – no greater pleasure than this can be found.*
>
> *When, abiding in well-being, having destroyed corruptions, impediments and grief – free of obstruction, greed and the dart of craving – with all outflows ended, he meditates – no greater pleasure than this can be found.*
>
> *Theragatha*, verses 525–6

The greatest pleasure is the peaceful, undisturbed mind. It is not that easy to realise but it is well worth the effort, as most people who have attended a meditation retreat will attest. Many seek pleasure in the sensual world but the meditator has seen this frustration and disappointment. Through collectedness and awareness of mind a world of true pleasure and security emerges into consciousness. It is, of course, very subjective and therefore difficult to explain to others. Perhaps only the serene, enigmatic Buddha-smile is able to hint at the experience.

Mindfulness of Spiritual Qualities

34.

> *And how does one dwell clearly reflecting upon spiritual qualities? To this end one dwells clearly reflecting upon spiritual qualities in respect of the seven factors of enlightenment. How? If the enlightenment factor of*

mindfulness is present, one knows; if it is absent, one knows. One knows how the enlightenment factor of mindfulness comes to arise, and how it comes to full development. And likewise with the enlightenment factors of investigation-of-reality, energy, joy, tranquillity, collectedness and equanimity.

Majjhima Nikaya, Vol. I, page 61

This reading concentrates on factors conducive to enlightenment. Once we have observed how skilful and unskilful states of mind rise and pass away we are ready to focus on specific spiritual qualities. The skilful qualities of mindfulness, investigation-of-reality, energy, joy, tranquillity, collectedness and equanimity are conducive to enlightenment and are therefore called the factors of enlightenment.

Mindfulness is a neutral quality, investigation-of-reality, energy and joy are energising qualities, and tranquillity, collectedness and equanimity are calming qualities. Mindfulness keeps a balance between the energising and the calming.

The energising qualities give us inspiration and encouragement, but if there is too much energy it can incline to restlessness and distraction. The calming qualities give us serenity and peace, but excessive calm can lead to apathy and dullness. Energy is balanced against collectedness, joy is balanced against equanimity and investigation-of-reality is balanced against tranquillity. It is through mindfulness that the balance is maintained and the balanced mind is receptive to enlightenment.

35.

In this, Udayi, one develops the factors of enlightenment based upon seclusion, dispassion, cessation and maturity of relinquishment – which is abundant, made great, boundless and free of ill-will. As one cultivates the factors of enlightenment in this way, craving is relinquished; with the relinquishing of craving, intentional actions [kamma] are relinquished; with the relinquishing of intentional actions, suffering is relinquished.

Samyutta Nikaya, Vol. V, page 86

One whose mind is rightly established in the factors of enlightenment, who, not clinging, is intent upon the giving up of grasping, free of pollutions, a bright light – realises nibbana in this world.

Dhammapada, verse 89

When we carefully observe states of mind we notice how the factors of enlightenment arise and pass (see no. 34). Through meditation practice we can now make a concerted effort to bring these factors to full development so that they are abundant, great and boundless.

These factors do not lead directly to enlightenment but mature the mind into a state receptive to enlightenment. Through their cultivation the mind learns to free itself of many obstructions such as craving, clinging, grasping, etc. In freedom the mind shines brightly and knows nibbana.

The Four Divine Abidings

36.

Here one, with mind of friendliness, continuously pervades one direction, then the second, the third and the fourth; so above, below, across, in all directions, everywhere, throughout the whole world with mind of friendliness – abundant, made great, boundless, free of hate and ill-will.

Digha Nikaya, Vol. III, page 223

The practice of the divine abidings is a way of opening the spiritual heart and cultivating an emotionally balanced approach to life. When the heart is open, meditation practice can mature and find expression in altruistic and compassionate actions. These are not just noble ideals to live up to but meditational exercises to be developed and realised in our own heart so that we become the personification of these qualities. They are called divine abidings because anyone abiding in these mental states is 'godlike', that is, exceptionally pleasant and lovable, emotionally radiant and compassionate.

Friendliness is the first divine abiding.

We should initially internalise friendliness by befriending ourselves. In doing so we learn to be kind and welcoming to all aspects of ourselves, especially the aspects we are usually unfriendly to. When we learn to be friendly to the unkind aspects of ourselves we naturally respond with friendliness to the unkindness of others. It is this openness which is a fundamental basis of insight. If our hearts are not open our minds are closed. Friendliness is a beautiful quality but it is also a necessary one for developing the spiritual path. We don't just act with friendliness but by befriending all the negativity in our own minds we naturally respond with friendliness to all negativity everywhere and in everyone.

37.

Here one, with mind of compassion, continuously pervades one direction, then the second, the third and the fourth; so above, below,

*across, in all directions, everywhere, throughout the whole world with
mind of compassion – abundant, made great, boundless, free of hate and
ill-will.*

Digha Nikaya, Vol. III, page 223

Compassion is the second divine abiding (see no. 36).

The word 'compassion' literally means 'to suffer with'. Really to
understand compassion we need to know what it is to have compassion
for our own suffering, otherwise we merely end up feeling sorry for
other people or just pitying them from a position of superiority.
Knowing compassion for ourselves we can enter into someone else's
suffering as equals – we are all suffering together. This dissolves the
barriers that separate us from others, so instead of 'me' feeling
compassion for 'you', compassion manifests itself as a natural human
response.

38.

*Here one, with mind of empathetic joy, continuously pervades one
direction, then the second, the third and the fourth; so above, below,
across, in all directions, everywhere, thoughout the whole world with
mind of empathetic joy – abundant, made great, boundless, free of hate
and ill-will.*

Digha Nikaya, Vol. III, page 223

Empathetic joy is the third divine abiding (see no. 36).

By developing the quality of empathetic joy we can counteract
jealousy and rejoice wholeheartedly in the good fortune of others. We
must contact the jealousy or envy within ourselves and understand its
cause before these destructive states of mind cease. We must also learn
to rejoice in our own good fortune and not feel guilty about
experiencing moments of happiness and success. We cannot celebrate
with others until we can celebrate within ourselves.

39.

*Here one, with mind of equanimity, continuously pervades one
direction, then the second, the third and the fourth; so above, below,
across, in all directions, everywhere, throughout the whole world with
mind of equanimity – abundant, made great, boundless, free of hate and
ill-will.*

Digha Nikaya, Vol. III, page 223

Equanimity is the fourth divine abiding (see no. 36).

Equanimity is the most refined of the four divine abidings. We must step out of personal involvement with ourself and others. By practising this exercise we achieve serenity and even-mindedness in joyous or depressing circumstances. We must be careful not to mistake equanimity for indifference. Indifference detaches the senses from everything that is going on, but equanimity is open, calm and receptive to the world whatever difficulties or pleasures arise.

40.

When I went forth from the house to the houseless state, I was not aware of having any ignoble hate-ridden intention. But I have been aware of love, infinite, well-developed, practised in due order, as taught by the Buddha. I am friend to all, comrade to all, sympathetic to all beings, and I develop a mind of love, always delighting in non-harming.

Theragatha, verses 645, 647–8

In this reading one of the Buddha's enlightened disciples confirms his sincerity and noble intentions in living the religious life through the practice of the divine abidings. A 'non-harming intention' is one of the aspects of right intention on the noble eightfold path and therefore a necessary attribute of the spiritual way. Developing the divine abidings is not merely painting on an ingratiatingly friendly smile or being compassionately interfering, but involves an earnest attempt to manifest these as heart-felt responses to all beings. Out of good intentions we very often masquerade these qualities, as opposed to drawing out their opposites within our hearts so that positive expressions can blossom forth.

The noble eightfold path is the basic formula expression of the path of spiritual practice. It is more properly called the eight-factored way, that is, the coming together of these eight factors constitutes the way rather than compromising eight consecutive steps on the way. The eight aspects – right view, right intention, right speech, right action, right livelihood, right effort, right mindfulness, and right collectedness – are sometimes explained in terms of morality (3rd, 4th and 5th factors), meditation (6th, 7th and 8th factors), and wisdom (1st and 2nd factors).

Insight Meditation

41.

All conditioned things are impermanent;
*   All conditioned things are dukkha;*
*   All things are non-self;*
*   When one understands this with full realisation,*

One turns away from suffering –
This is the path to purity.

Dhammapada, verses 277—9

These three characteristics of all phenomena are the foundation for vipassana (insight meditation). Vipassana is penetrative insight into the truth of impermanence, dukkha (suffering, unsatisfactoriness) and non-self. These three themes are particularly fruitful areas of investigation because they help us to cut through our usual perception of reality as permanent, perpetually satisfying and self-centred. These themes must not just be believed in but must be thoroughly penetrated by reflective insight. True reflection comes from the silent mind and its quality depends upon the degree of collectedness, tranquillity and clarity of mind. The mind begins by discursively exploring a theme, then as the mind inclines towards collectedness, the reflection becomes intuitive and eventually we attain penetrating insight.

Impermanence

42.

Impermanent, alas, are all conditioned things,
  Their nature is to arise and pass.
  They come into existence, then they cease;
  Their allaying, their calming, is peace.

Samyutta Nikaya, Vol. II, page 192

The first, and perhaps most approachable, theme for insight is impermanence, changeableness, transience. A skilful reflection on impermanence can lead us to realise the way things really are beyond our normal conceptual understanding. Without practice we can still recognise to some degree the impermanence of feelings, events and life itself, yet we are still surprised or upset when they come to an end. Our anxiety is often rooted in the impermanence of life, for example, in sickness and death, but when we penetrate the nature of impermanence, sickness and death cannot be anything other than natural and peaceful.

This is one of the readings that Buddhists chant at funerals when the body is laid down and is at peace, for it is the nature of all things to arise and pass away.

43.

Just as in summer when the sky is clear and without cloud, the sun,
ascending into the heavens, expels all darkness and shines forth bright

and brilliant. Even so the awareness of impermanence, if developed and practised, exhausts all desire for sensuality, exhausts all desire for material forms, exhausts all desire for becoming, exhausts all ignorance, and removes all·'I am' conceit.

Samyutta Nikaya, Vol. III, page 156

Insight into impermanence can have a profound effect upon our lives – like the blazing forth of the summer sun. Impermanence does not just mean changeableness but also uncertainty, unreliability, undependability, instability and insecurity: that which changes is unreliable. When we insightfully realise that much of our time and energy is spent chasing after fleeting and unreliable things, we stop. We now know that sensual pleasures and material forms are ephemeral and insecure. Even the 'I am' conceit which we see arise and pass, come and go, appears as nothing dependable or worthy of holding on to. Letting go, we are free.

44.

It would be better for an untaught ordinary person to regard this body, formed of the four elemental qualities, as self, rather than the mind. Why? Because this body is seen to last for a year, two years, three years . . . a hundred years or more, but that which is called 'thought' or 'mind' or 'consciousness', by day or by night, arises as something else, ceases as something else. It is just like a monkey swinging through the forest grabbing a branch, letting it go, and grabbing another.

Samyutta Nikaya, Vol. II, page 94

Here the Buddha is challenging us to look at things in a new way. Most of us are usually willing to recognise that the body is not our permanent self but we have strong identification with our consciousness, that part of us that knows, feels or is conscious. One of the reasons for this identification is that the mind changes so fast that we rarely see it as changing, just as we see a stream as a permanent thing rather than as a continuously changing flow of water. Whenever there is identification with something, its changeableness is obscured by the stability of identity. So we might say 'I change', yet we still hold that it is the same 'I' which undergoes change, but in fact change is that very thought of 'I'.

45.

Observing the impermanence, the changing nature, the fading and the ending of body, feelings, perceptions, mental activities and consciousness, one knows that: 'Now, as well as formerly, body, feelings, perceptions, mental activities and consciousness are impermanent, unsatisfactory and subject to change.' So, seeing in this way – as it really is, by perfect realisation – one abandons sorrow, grief, suffering, distress and despair. Leaving this, one is untroubled; untroubled, one abides in well-being; abiding in well-being, one is called 'truly calmed'.

Samyutta Nikaya, Vol. III, page 43

As an aid to insightful investigation the Buddha has given us a reflection upon the human being as five distinct components: physical body, feelings, perception, mental activities and consciousness. These are known as the five khandhas. Instead of trying to investigate 'me' or 'my body and mind', we try to investigate in terms of 'this physical body, these feelings, these perceptions, these mental activities, and this consciousness'; we are then in a much better position to view them objectively and honestly. In doing this we realise some amazing things about ourself and learn to unravel the mystery of self.

46.

While seated in my hut, spiritual anxiety arose in me. 'I have followed the wrong path! I have come under the power of craving! My life is insignificant, old age and illness are crushing it. There is no time to be negligent before this body is destroyed.' Contemplating the rising and passing away of the aspects of a human being [khandhas] as they really are, with liberated mind I rose to my feet. The Buddha's teaching has been done.

Therigatha, verses 94–6

These words were spoken by a bhikkhuni (a Buddhist nun). Inspired by the Buddha's teachings, she realised that her body was the vehicle for the practice of the Dhamma (the Buddha's teachings) and that her increasing years left her little time to practise Dhamma. Deeply stirred by this perception of creeping old age, she quickly rallied her energies and investigated the rising and passing away of the aspects of a human being – the five khandhas (see no. 45). Suddenly she had insight into the emptiness of all things. Before her death the Buddha's teachings had been fulfilled – she achieved nibbana.

47.

So transient is everything, bhikkhus; so unstable is everything, bhikkhus; so uncomforting is everything, bhikkhus; so much so that it is suitable for you to be disenchanted with all and everything, to detach yourself, to free yourself.

Samyutta Nikaya, Vol. II, page 191

If we could really penetrate the truth about impermanence our life would be lived very differently. We could live with more joy and spontaneity – able to rejoice in the continuously emerging wonder of life. We could learn to flow with life's ups and downs because we know them to be changing situations. It is not that life changes but that change is the very essence of life. Change and impermanence are the fundamental characteristics of life which we need to learn to be in harmony with in order to be free and untroubled. Some people may be frightened to investigate or accept change. Yet the joy and freedom which come from realising the truth of change far surpass the mundane happiness of holding on to illusions and dreams. Change is life. Change is the wonder of life.

Dukkha

Dukkha is one of the characteristics of all conditioned things. This word has a multitude of meanings at once specific but also comprehensive. The specific expressions are simply symptomatic manifestations of its more universal meaning. Thus it is pain, suffering, dis-ease, discontent, unsatisfactoriness, incompleteness and imperfection.

48.

When the Exalted One knew that the mind of Yasa, a young man of good family, was receptive, pliable, unobstructed, exalted and clear, he explained to him the Enlightened One's succinct Dhamma teaching: dukkha, the cause of dukkha, the cessation of dukkha, and the way to the cessation of dukkha.

Vinaya, Vol. I, page 16

Now, as formerly, I just point out dukkha and its cessation.

Majjhima Nikaya, Vol. I, page 251

The insight into dukkha is the very essence of the Buddha's teachings. It was the experience of dukkha which roused the Buddha to seek for its solution. And the greatness and uniqueness of the Buddha lie in his discovery of the way to the ending of dukkha.

It is dukkha as the imperfection and incompleteness of life which is our best spiritual teacher – if we are open to learn from it. This is why the Buddha explains the four noble truths in the form of observing the symptoms of dukkha, diagnosing its cause, knowing that curing the cause will give health and well-being, and prescribing the way of treatment as remedy. The whole purpose of this is to bring us to the ultimate well-being of spiritual enlightenment.

49.

Just as, when rain pours down upon a hilltop, the water courses with the slope, filling the clefts, the gullies and the creeks; these being filled fill the streams... the rivers... the great ocean. In the same way... dukkha is a cause for trust, trust is a cause for gladness, gladness is a cause for joy, joy is a cause for serenity, serenity is a cause for happiness... for collectedness... for knowledge and vision of things as they really are ... disenchantment ... dispassion is a cause for liberation, and liberation is a cause for knowledge of the ending of the outflows of selfhood.

Samyutta Nikaya, Vol. 2, page 32

This reading explains the place of dukkha (suffering, unsatisfactoriness) in spiritual practice. We often try to escape or eradicate suffering but the Buddha said that suffering is the main focus for the spiritual practice. Once suffering is understood in its right context it is a support that will stay with us in life's crises. We need to trust in the Buddha, the Dhamma (the Buddha's teachings), the Sangha (the community of enlightened beings) and in the Way itself. Suffering can give rise to trust when we hear the Dhamma – trust in the Buddha Dhamma Sangha and trust in ourselves. Trust gives rise to gladness and joy, and joy gives rise to tranquillity since we have confidence in a solution. Tranquillity and happiness are important foundations for samatha (collectedness) and collectedness gives rise to vipassana (insight) into the nature of everything. When we gain insight into the unsatisfactoriness and impermanence of life we become disenchanted and understand how others suffer with delusion. Liberation has dawned and we know that the asavas (pollutions) have come to an end.

50.

These things should be often reflected upon by woman and man, by householder and homeless one. What are they?
I am of the nature to age, I have not gone beyond ageing;
I am of the nature to sicken, I have not gone beyond sickness;
I am of the nature to die, I have not gone beyond dying;
All that is mine, beloved and pleasing, will become otherwise, will become separated from me.

Anguttura Nikaya, Vol. III, page 71

The concept of dukkha is to be contemplated and wisely reflected upon. In this way we come to realise its multifaceted aspects. At its most basic level dukkha is physical pain and hurt. At a broader level it is mental suffering in its various forms as discontentment, depression, frustration, attachment and longing, fear and doubt, etc. In its comprehensive and most inclusive aspect dukkha is the fundamental disease, unsatisfactoriness, imperfection of life. Dukkha is a characteristic of life which we are most reluctant to acknowledge. It is not a condemnation or pessimistic criticism of life but a skilful reflection on life that enables us to see life as it really is.

These four themes – old age, sickness, death and loss of the beloved – are the most practical expressions of this concept of dukkha. We can all accept that they are true, yet how many of us still fall into despair or bewilderment when they actually occur? The Buddha suggests that we contemplate these themes so that we will gradually be able to understand them when they eventually occur.

51.

The Buddha: Passion and hatred spring from egoism. So do discontentment, attachment and terror. Speculative thoughts also spring therefrom and harass the mind as do boys a crow. They spring from desire, are in one's self like the shoots which spring from the branches of a banyan tree. They are attached to sense desires like a maluva creeper which overgrows the jungle.

Sutta Nipata, verses 271–2

Dukkha (suffering, unsatisfactoriness) is not an ultimate reality. It has a cause. If we are able to remove the cause of dukkha it will cease to be nourished, and peace and well-being will rise in its place. The cause of dukkha is diagnosed in the active expressions of selfhood such as desire or craving. This is not the simple desires for food and warmth and so on, but the self-centred wants and needs such as pleasure, comfort and self-esteem. And since the sense of self is a false illusion, this enslaved tributary craving is craving for things other than the way they are – craving for them as 'I' want them to be. Since the way 'I' want things to be and the way things really are differ, there is disease, frustration and suffering. Letting go of this foolish craving is the way to end dukkha.

52.

Incomprehensible is the beginning of this continuous wandering. The very beginning of the running on and wandering on of beings obstructed by ignorance and bound by craving is not evident. Thus for a long time have you undergone suffering, undergone acute pain, undergone misery and enlarged the cemeteries.

Samyutta Nikaya, Vol. II, page 178

The Buddha did not offer a first cause for samsara (the cycles of birth and death). He offered the way of release from the cycle. Rather than be caught in or preoccupied speculating about where we came from or where we are going, the Buddha pointed to the truth of what is. Dukkha (suffering, unsatisfactoriness) is to be understood and its cause relinquished. Unless we can free ourselves from ignorance and craving we will be caught on the treadmill of life and can expect only more of the same suffering and unsatisfactoriness. This reading is a firm warning not to waste time being complacent or apathetic. The way to the cessation of dukkha is explained. It is up to us to realise the cessation of our own disease, however great or small it may be.

53.

The whole world is ablaze, the whole world has flared up, the whole world is blazing, the whole world is shaken.

The Buddha taught me the doctrine, unshakable, incomparable, not cultivated by ordinary people. Thereto my mind was deeply attached. Having heard his utterance, I dwelt delighting in his teaching. The three knowledges have been obtained. The Buddha's teaching has been done.

Therigatha, verses 200–202

The first stage of the investigation of dukkha (suffering, unsatisfactoriness) in meditation practice is the recognition of and receptiveness to dukkha. In the second stage we realise that dukkha is a product of the self's craving and is, therefore, self-created. Continuing our practice we learn to let go of craving and no longer suffer. Dukkha as the characteristic of life's pain and incompleteness still exists, but it is no longer 'I' who suffers. Dukkha is simply the nature of life which we can fully acknowledge and live in harmony with. The body still grows old but my non-resistance to it does not cause any anguish or despair. The world is blazing with the fires of passion but I cease to be burnt by those fires.

54.

Buddha, hero, homage to you, O best of all creatures, who released me and many other people from pain.

All pain is known; craving as the cause is dried up; the noble eight-fold way has been developed; cessation has been attained by me.

Therigatha, verses 157–8

In this reading Mahaprajapati, the Buddha's stepmother and bhikkhuni (Buddhist nun), proclaims her realisation of enlightenment. Through the Buddha's direct and forthright teachings on the nature and cause of human misery many people were liberated from dukkha. The Buddha once said that just as the great oceans have but one flavour – that of salt, so his teachings have but one flavour – that of deliverance. Dukkha is but the stepping stone which needs to be thoroughly understood so the noble eightfold way of spiritual practice (see no. 40) can be developed and the cessation of dukkha finally attained.

Non-self

55.

The wandering ascetic Vacchagotta visited the Exalted One . . . and asked:
'How is it, master Gotama, does self exist?'
When this was said the Exalted One was silent.
'But then, master Gotama, does self not exist?'
For a second time the Exalted One was silent.
Then the wandering ascetic Vacchagotta got up from his seat and went away.
Now not long after he had gone, the Venerable Ananda asked the Exalted One:
'How is it, sir, that when the Exalted One was asked a question by the wandering ascetic Vacchagotta, he did not answer?'
'If, Ananda, when asked by the wandering ascetic Vacchagotta: "Does self exist?" I had replied: "Self exists", would that have been in conformity with the understanding that: All things are non-self?
'If when asked by the wandering ascetic Vacchagotta: "Does self not exist?" I had replied: "Self does not exist", then, Ananda, the bewildered Vacchagotta would be even more bewildered, thinking: 'Formerly I surely had a self, but now I have not!'
Samyutta Nikaya, Vol. IV, pages 400–401

Gotama was the Buddha's family name or clan name, i.e. Siddhatha Gotama (Pali), Siddhartha Gautama (Sanskrit).

As this reading indicates, the teaching on non-self is not very easy to comprehend. This is primarily due to the fact that our sense of self is so precious, pervasive and personal. However, we should note that the Buddha did not say that there is no self but that all things are non-self. He is not denying the existence of the empirical relative self which arises conditionally in response to situations, as this would just be nihilism. But he is denying that there is a permanent, constantly abiding self or soul-like entity.

This theme of non-self cannot be understood by the conceptual, thinking mind, because thought is entirely based upon a sense of self. That is why Vacchagotta would have become bewildered by merely thinking about this idea. Only through meditative reflection is there the possibility of insight into the truth about non-self. Through investigation of what we take self to be we are able to see through the illusion.

56.

'I am' is an imagining; 'I am this' is an imagining; 'I will be'...
'I will not be'... is an imagining. When the sage has gone beyond all
imaginings he is called at peace. The sage at peace is not born, does not
age, is unagitated, is unobstructed. He has nothing of which to be born.
Not being born, how could he age? Not ageing, how could he die? Not
dying, how could he be agitated? Not being agitated, how could he be
obstructed?

Majjhima Nikaya, Vol. III, page 246

The sense of self is expressed through the 'I am' conceit. It is maintained
and reinforced through the mechanisms of appropriation: 'I am this; I
will be, I will not be'; etc. As long as everything is harmonious and suits
our needs the sense of self flourishes. As soon as something upsets self's
reinforcing habits we have a crisis, because it doesn't slot into our usual
responses. The sense of self constantly needs to be supported and
reassured precisely because it is an imaginary illusion. If it were truly real
it would not need to assert itself, just as truth does not need to assert itself
because truth is real. Once we are able to see through all illusions we
realise the peace of truth. When we are at peace we do not need to give
birth to any more illusions. Unborn illusions do not age or die.

57.

If anyone says that the body is self... the mind is self... feeling is
self... craving is self, it is not tenable. The arising and decay of these is
evident. Now, since their arising and decay is evident, it is to be
concluded that self arises and passes away. Thus if anyone says that
body is self... mind is self... feeling is self... craving is self,... it is
not tenable. In this way body is non-self... mind is non-self... feeling
is non-self... craving is non-self.

Majjhima Nikaya, Vol. III, page 283

The sense of self as an illusion is not to be believed in; this would even be
dangerous. We wouldn't know who we were – self or non-self! The
Buddha is merely giving us a skilful reflection: look at this, reflect in this
way. One of the basic sources of the illusion of self is its apparent
permanence and persistence, for example, we have the same identity for a
lifetime. In this reading the Buddha is giving us a reflection to help us
uncover this false view. We assume that this body is 'my self' because we
have it for a lifetime. But actually this body is a dynamic biological process
continuously digesting food, breaking down, healing and repairing itself,
growing old, and so on. Which of these various processes is the real me?
When we investigate the aspects of what we assume this self to be, we
discover its true nature. The illusions of self evaporate in the light of
wisdom.

58.

Body is non-self; if body were self it would not lead to sickness, and it could be obtained of body that: my body may be like this; my body may not be like this. But because body is non-self, it leads to sickness and one cannot obtain of body: my body may be like this; my body may not be like this.

[*The same is also said of feelings, perceptions, mental activities and consciousness, which, with the body, form the five groups or categories comprising a human being and known as the five khandhas. See no. 45.*]
                                  Samyutta Nikaya, Vol. III, page 66

The second source of the illusion of self is the apparent control we have over ourselves, for example, I can move the body around, I can think, I can feel. However, if the body and mind were really self we should be able to exercise ultimate control over them. As long as we keep within our own self-imposed, familiar domain, we seem inviolate. We can easily stand, run, sit, raise our arms and perform hundreds of other movements, but if we reflect upon the limits of that control we perceive a different picture. If we try to control our thoughts or try to forbid sickness, old age and death, we come to the limits of our control over 'our' mind and body. At this level our assumptions about our self reach their limit. We have a relative self that has a relative amount of control within its own limited world, but not an ultimate self which has ultimate control over all and everything.

59.

Bhikkhus, body is impermanent; what is impermanent is dukkha; what is dukkha is non-self; what is non-self is not mine, is not what I am, is not my self. So should one look upon it as it really is by perfect realisation. Thus seeing by perfect realisation the mind is disenchanted and freed from the outflows without clinging.

[*The same is also said of feelings, perceptions, mental activities and consciousness, which, with the body, form the five khandhas. See no. 45.*]
                                  Samyutta Nikaya, Vol. III, page 45

The teachings on impermanence, dukkha (suffering, unsatisfactoriness) and non-self are all interrelated so that insight into any one of them reveals the truth of the others. While the usual logical sequence of explaining these themes is contained in the reading, each individual may have a particular preference or affinity for investigation of one or other of these themes. So if our life is particularly distraught or stressful perhaps a thorough investigation of its intrinsic dukkha can be revealing, if not enlightening. Whereas if we have suffered the tragic loss of a relative or a friend, reflection upon impermanence or the impersonal aspects of death may be a source of great peace and insight. The whole point of insight is to be able to see these characteristics within our own life. At first they may be only abstract themes until we are able to internalise them in the experience of our own mind and body.

The following readings provide material for further reflections upon various aspects of the Buddha's teachings and give guidelines for insight which rises along the way.

Views

60.

Speculative view, Vaccha, has been given up by the Buddha. Therefore I say that the Buddha, with the passing away, fading away, cessation, giving up and forsaking of all imaginings, all mental disturbances, all selfishness, egoism and tendency to conceit, is liberated without clinging.
Majjhima Nikaya, Vol. I, page 486

The most important aspect of meditation in the Forest Tradition is to go beyond attachment to views and speculation which reinforce conceit and self-centredness. Right view is one of the categories of the noble eightfold way. The Dhamma (the Buddha's teachings) are a support and a reassurance that we are travelling in the right direction, but it is hard for many people to take the step from rational criticism to trust in Dhamma and in themselves. We like to measure our progress, calculate our results, and are often blinded by our views of what we see and what we want to see. The way of practice is like embarking upon a journey. We understand the goal but in order to reach it we must step out of our familiar environment onto an unknown path. This is why we are caught up with views and opinions in this exploration. Through meditation practice we know that there is something to discover – we have to trust in the Buddha Dhamma Sangha, in wisdom, truth and virtue, for us to realise it. When our views are no longer blinkered we can accept everything as a learning experience, whether it is pleasant, unpleasant or neutral. We begin by developing insight into the truth of impermanence, suffering and non-self and what began as trust in Dhamma ripens to complete confidence in Dhamma.

61.

They do not speculate, they do not esteem any views and say 'This is the highest purity'. They release the knot of dogmatic clinging and do not long for anything in the world.

Giving up the notion of a permanent abiding self, and not grasping it again, they do not even depend upon knowledge. Not conforming with those of dissenting views, they do not fall back on any view at all.

Sutta Nipata, verses 794 and 800

This reading points out the danger of views which easily become dogmatic positions. The Buddha encourages direct meditative experience as opposed to a prescriptive theological position. Even holding on to spiritual knowledge or insight becomes the source of pride and conceit and produces dogmatic views. The experience of meditation is an ongoing experience; since we are continually learning we should never stop and hold on to what we have learned. The world frequently demands that we hold a view or choose a side. But the wise meditator knows that these are just thoughts arising and passing away. By not holding on to anything we do not lose anything and we can be at peace with all sides and all views. This is the true way to peace and tolerance.

62.

Even though one recites the scriptures only a little, but lives in accordance with the teachings – giving up greed, aversion and delusion, rightly knowing, with mind truly freed, not clinging to this realm or another realm – one thus shares in the religious life.

Dhammapada, verse 20

The Forest Tradition emphasises meditation practice in preference to scholastic learning. It emphasises direct experience of the Buddha's teachings as a priority over learning about the teachings. And the formal meditation exercises are only part of that experience. Unless we have a grounded and comprehensive expression of the teachings in our everyday lives they will remain only peripheral or superficial teachings. The religious life is the living of the teachings, that is, continuously striving to transcend greed, aversion and delusion each and every moment of our conscious life. It is in this way that we come to embody the teachings rather than merely preserve the body of the teachings.

63.

Vaccha, to resort to the views: the world is eternal, or the world is not eternal, or the world is finite, or the world is infinite . . . is to enter the thicket of views, the wilderness of views, the agitation of views, the writhing of views, the fetter of views. They are connected with suffering, with vexation, turmoil and distress. They do not lead to disenchantment, to dispassion, to ending, to calming, to higher knowledge, to awakening, or to nibbana. I, Vaccha, seeing this danger, do not adopt or resort to any of these views.

Majjhima Nikaya, Vol. I, pages 485–6

Many hours are often spent deliberating, discussing and debating these particular points or ones similar to them. But it is questionable whether these things can actually be known and, if they could be known, would it bring us any closer to liberation? The Buddha encouraged us towards the peace which comes from direct realisation of the way things are, the peace that is possible through meditational practices. If we enmesh ourselves in speculative thought we will become entangled in a mass of concepts – the wilderness of views. The practice of meditation is learning to change our perspective on reality from dependence upon questionable concepts to realisation through direct experience. Concepts are like mental bubbles which come and go with the changing moods, but direct experience knows unquestionably, otherwise it is not direct experience.

The World

64.

Friend, that in the world, by which one perceives the world, and conceives conceits about the world, is called 'world' in this noble training. And what is it in the world by which one does that? It is through the eye, ear, nose, tongue, body and mind that one perceives the world and conceives conceits about the world.

Samyutta Nikaya, Vol. IV, page 95

As our meditation practice develops we become far more aware of the subjective aspects of the world. We realise how we create the world through our sense impressions and then conceive conceits about the world. We believe that 'I' am the one who sees, 'I' am the one who knows and 'I' am the one who acts. We do this because we conceive the world through the filter of conceit or, more simply, we perceive what we allow ourselves to perceive in order to preserve and reinforce the view of the world that our self creates.

65.

I say, friend, that where one is not born, does not age or die, or pass from one state to another, or arise again – that world's end is not to be known, seen or reached by travelling.

Yet I do not say that there is an end of dukkha without reaching

world's end. Rather, it is in this fathom-long body, with perception and
thought, that I make known the world, the arising of the world, the
cessation of the world and the way to the cessation of the world.
Samyutta Nikaya, Vol. 1, page 62

The world's end is a name for nibbana. The world itself is not destroyed
but that world which we create for ourselves and perceive for ourselves
ends when we realise the way the world really is. The world's end cannot
be travelled to but it can be arrived at by practising the Buddha's
teachings within the sphere of the mind and body. Instead of searching
for the way to nibbana in the external world, we must look within
ourselves and practise within ourselves. It is in ourselves that we will find
that state where one is not born, does not age or does not die.

66.

Whoever, having attained to knowledge, being quiet, with self
restrained, destroys longing for this world or the next, he, not clinging to
all phenomena, would know the arising and passing away of the world.
Theragatha, verse 10

We create our own world through our attachment to views which
reinforce our sense of self, and through ignorance of the truth of the
world. It is the nature of the sense of self to distort and manipulate our
perception of the world to suit its own selfish needs. Someone who is very
selfish suffers a great deal since the world never satisfies them, never suits
them and never fulfils their desires. When we cease searching for a special
world to fulfil our expectations we can allow the world to be as it is –
arising and passing away as we see sights, hear sounds, taste flavours,
smell odours, sense bodily contacts and know thoughts.

67.

'Empty world, empty world' is said, sir; in what respect is it said 'empty
world'?
   It is because of being empty of a permanent abiding self, or of the
nature of a permanent abiding self, that it is said 'empty world'.
Samyutta Nikaya, Vol. IV, page 54

Look upon the world as empty, Mogharaja, always being mindful.
Remove any view of a permanent abiding self, and you may pass beyond
death. If you view the world like this, the King of Death sees you not.
Sutta Nipata, verse 119

A world of ever-changing sights, sounds, smells, tastes, touch and thoughts exists, but the world is empty of permanent existence. If we become attached to the concept of a permanent world we create the concept of a permanent self and vice versa. The Buddha understood the relative and experiential nature of the world. He recognised the act of seeing, but we, out of ignorance, assume that there is a permanent someone who sees and there is a permanent something to be seen, and so we create a permanent world which sees a permanent self. When we can let go of the sense of self and abide in the seeing, we move through the world unhindered and there is no self who dies from the world.

Conditional Causality

68.

Kaccayana, the world usually depends upon the duality of 'existence' and 'non-existence'. But for those who see, with perfect realisation, the truth of the arising of the world, there is not for them any 'non-existence' in the world. And for those who see, with perfect realisation, the truth of the passing away of the world, there is not for them any 'existence' in the world.

'It exists' is one extreme; 'it does not exist' is the second extreme. Not going to either extreme, the Buddha sets forth a teaching by the middle way . . . [of conditional causality].

Samyutta Nikaya, Vol. II, page 17

When we understand the relative nature of the world we see things arise and pass away, we realise that the world is a dynamic living process of birth and death. We are able to let go of rigid fixed views and opinions and become free from the restraints of the restless mind swinging back and forth between the extremes of 'it is' or 'it isn't'; 'yes' or 'no'; 'black' or 'white'.

The Buddha discovered that the arising and passing away of things is not due to mere chance, or accident, or divine sanction, but to the principle of conditional causality. Only nibbana is beyond the influence of this principle; it is not caused by anything since nibbana, truth, is always present.

69.

The Awakened One has told the cause
Of causally arisen things,
And what brings their cessation too.
Such is the teaching of the great sage.

Vinaya, Vol. I, page 40

This is a succinct summary of the Buddha's teachings by one of his early disciples. Through a penetrating, meditative investigation into reality the Buddha awoke to the truth of conditional causality, that is, things come to be and pass away, dependent upon a conditional cause and effect relationship. Many conditions need to be fulfilled for a cause to give a certain effect and although we are responsive to these causal laws we are not slaves to them. When we understand the factors that cause our suffering we can remove the cause and be free from suffering. This is formally represented in the phrase: 'When this is, that comes to be. When this is not, that passes away'.

70.

Neither self-made is this puppet,
Nor made by another is this misfortune.
Dependent on a cause it comes to be;
By dissolution of the cause it fades away.
Just as a seed sown in a field will sprout
Due to touch of earth and damp, these two;
Likewise the personality groups, elements and senses:
Dependent on a cause they come to be;
By dissolution of the cause they fade away.

Samyutta Nikaya, Vol. I, page 134

In this reading an enlightened bhikkhuni (a Buddhist nun) expresses her insights into the causal nature of a human being.

Through meditative reflection upon the nature of the human being we discover how we come to be and how we pass away. We are like a puppet controlled by the laws of nature and are pushed to our limits with disease and death. The creation of a human life combines a biological process with diverse psychological and spiritual factors, what some call the 'divine spark' but lucid insight reveals this to be another causal factor. Our pride says that we are a special and unique person, but the insights into the causal nature of our being uncover those impersonal aspects of our existence which we have ignored. Self is unmasked as a parasite upon the universal, spiritually infused principle of causality. Life unfolds as an awe-inspiring display of nature's wonder. As one master said, 'Life is its own magic'.

71.

Chieftain, for one who truly sees the pure and simple arising of phenomena and the pure and simple continuity of conditioned things, there is no fear.

When with wisdom one sees the world as just like grass and wood, not finding any selfishness, one does not grieve with the idea, 'It is not mine'.

Theragatha, verses 716–17

In this reading one of the Buddha's enlightened disciples speaks to a robber chief who has threatened him with death. When we realise that our mind, body and all the world are subject to the principle of conditional causality, we realise that they cannot have an owner. Without an owner nothing is lost, no one grieves and no one is frightened. Since all things are naturally selfless, they are mutually interrelated in a complex web of interdependent relationships and we are the intricate parts of that greater whole.

Kamma

The Pali word 'kamma' has been used in preference to the Sanskrit word 'karma' to avoid any allusion to the anglicised definition of karma, often interpreted as fate or destiny. This is very different from the Buddhist definition of kamma.

72.

By kamma the world goes on, by kamma people go on.
Beings are bound by kamma as a wheel is bound to the cart by a linchpin.
Sutta Nipata, verse 654

Beings are the owners of their kamma, heirs of their kamma, born of their kamma, related to their kamma, supported by their kamma. Whatever kamma they do, for good or for bad, of that they are the heirs.
Anguttara Nikaya, Vol. V, page 288

The principle of kamma is the principle of causality relating to human beings; it is ethical causality. Whether we know it or not we are all subject to this principle. Kamma is intimately related to the nature of self – as we do, so we are; as we are, so we do. We will always be heirs to our kamma as long as we act to achieve results for ourselves. Kamma literally means 'action' or 'deed'. It is the active side of our self-expression and if we persist with certain actions they become habit. In the words of a common saying: 'Sow a thought, reap a habit; sow a habit, reap a personality; sow a personality, reap a destiny.'

73.

Of these three kinds of action [body, speech and mind], divided and differentiated in this way, I say that action of mind is the most blameworthy in the doing of a bad action. Action of body is not the same, and action of speech is not the same.

Majjhima Nikaya, Vol. I, page 373

It is intention I call 'kamma'; having willed, one produces kamma through body, speech or mind.

Anguttura Nikaya, Vol. III, page 415

The Buddha explicitly pointed out the supreme importance of mind in coordinating, initiating and motivating human life. The mental quality of intention, volition or will, implying choice and initiative, is kamma. It is usually will which we most closely associate with our sense of self because 'I' can initiate action by willing a particular result. Whether or not I achieve that result depends upon my understanding of the principles of conditional causality. Our actions also create a sense of self which has a will of its own; it is a will that wants to retain and reinforce a sense of self.

74.

There are three sources for the origin of kamma. What three? Greed aversion and delusion are the sources of the origin of kamma. An action done in greed, aversion or delusion, born of, originating in or arising out of greed, aversion or delusion, is unskilful, blameworthy, and has a painful result. It leads to the arising of [further] kamma, not to the cessation of kamma.

That action done in non-greed, non-aversion or non-delusion, born of, originating in or arising out of non-greed, non-aversion or non-delusion, is skilful, it is not blameworthy, and has a pleasant result. It leads to the cessation of kamma, not to the arising of [further] kamma.

Anguttura Nikaya, Vol. I, page 263

We express ourselves through bodily actions, speech and thought, and our most basic responses are greed, aversion, delusion, or their opposites. Greed, aversion and delusion are the unskilful origins of kamma because they are self-affirming, selfish actions. Very simply, greed is 'I want', aversion is 'I don't want' and delusion is 'I don't know'.

Actions done in non-greed, non-aversion or non-delusion are completely selfless actions and, therefore, not kamma. This is the state of a realised saint.

Actions which incline towards selflessness are called 'skilful kamma'. These include generosity to counter lust or greed, loving-kindness to counter aversion, and understanding to counter delusion. These three actions are the basis for skilful, wholesome or good kamma. This principle of kamma provides the purpose and meaning for moral conduct which inclines to selflessness.

75.

*Those monks and priests who say or hold the view that whatever
pleasant or unpleasant or neutral feeling a person experiences is the
consequence of what was done in the past – they go too far. Therefore, I
say they are wrong.*

*Experiences of feelings arise from bile, from phlegm, from wind, from
the union of bodily humours, from seasonal changes, from stress of
circumstances, and from chance external happenings, as well as from the
ripening of kamma.*

Samyutta Nikaya, Vol. IV, page 230

If all our experiences in the present are the result of what we have done in
the past then we could never experience liberation and there would be no
point living the spiritual life. We need to distinguish between kamma and
its result (vipaka). These are distinct from one another but mutually
interrelated through the principle of conditional causality. If we assume
that kamma equals result then we are prisoners of our kamma. The
Buddha taught that kamma is not the same as result for between the two
there is an arena of qualifying conditions. Intentional actions merely
provide a momentum towards a particular result but before the result can
be realised various conditions need to be fulfilled. For example, if we are
angry with someone we can alleviate or cancel the effect through skilful
action such as an apology. Through our own initiative and choice of action
in the present we can change the momentum we have set going in the past
and thereby influence the results.

76.

*The results of kamma cannot be known by thought, and so should not be
speculated about. Thus thinking, one would come to distraction and
distress.*

Anguttura Nikaya, Vol. II, page 80

*Therefore, Ananda, do not be the judge of people; do not make assumptions
about others. A person is destroyed by holding judgements about others.*

Anguttura Nikaya, Vol. V, page 140

It is impossible to predict the precise results of kamma due to the
conditional causal nature of kamma. We can only speak of our intentional
actions inclining towards certain possibilities. The results of some actions
are obvious since they need very few conditions to be fulfilled: for
example, anger results in immediate emotional upset. When our
intentions are complex or unclear we can never be sure of their results.
This is why mental clarity and self-awareness are extremely important
and should be developed in meditational practice. In order to know

ourselves we must know our intentions clearly, and unless we know ourselves clearly, we can never be liberated from self.

Rebirth

Buddhists use the term 'rebirth' rather than 'reincarnation'. Reincarnation literally means that something, usually a soul, transmigrates from life to life, or is incarnate again and again. The Buddha referred most specifically to the dynamic processes constituting rebirth rather than to the static substances characteristic of reincarnation.

77.

Here someone produces an activity of body, of speech and of mind which is hurtful ... [producing these activities] they arise in a hurtful realm ... they are touched by hurtful stimulations, and experience hurtful and extremely painful feelings, just like those who are in the realm of purgatory. Thus it is that someone comes into being from what is produced, they come into being from what they do and, having thus come to be, they are touched by [related] stimulations.

Here someone produces an activity of body, of speech, of mind which is not hurtful ... they arise in a realm which is not hurtful ... they are touched by non-hurtful stimulations and experience non-hurtful and extremely pleasant feelings, just like those who are in heavenly realms.
Majjhima Nikaya, Vol. I, pages 389-90

We are heirs to the atmosphere or emotional environment that our actions create. Many of us have probably noticed the moods that some people are caught in and carry around with them. This is known as association, another aspect of the principle of kamma. Our moods expressed through body, speech or thought attract or elicit similar moods in ourselves and in other people, in the same way as we tend to attract and be attracted to people who have similar interests and attitudes.

The Buddha is pointing out the interrelation between our actions and our environment to show that we are the creators of our own heaven and hell. Rebirth is the arising of the thought of 'I' and 'mine' which is always dependent upon the object it identifies with. When we are reborn it is not the same 'I' which is reborn since birth refers to the birth of the sense of self, which is always changing.

78.

Sariputta, there are these five realms of existence: realm of purgatory, animal realm, ghost realm, human realm and heavenly realm. I understand these realms of existence, the way to these realms of existence, the means to these realms of existence; and I also understand how at death, when the body breaks up, one is born into them.

> *Majjhima Nikaya,* Vol. I, page 73

Bhikkhus, there is kamma which is to be experienced in purgatory, there is kamma which is to be experienced in the animal realm, there is kamma which is to be experienced in the ghost realm, there is kamma which is to be experienced in the human realm, and there is kamma which is to be experienced in the heavenly realm. This is called kamma's distinction.

> *Anguttura Nikaya,* Vol. III, page 415

The Buddha understood that consciousness is the principal factor in conditioning rebirth. We do not need to wait for the death of the body to experience realms of existence; some people can experience the whole variety of these realms in the course of a single day. We say that purgatory is the searing heat of hatred and aggression; the animal realm is stupidity and dullness; the ghost realm is the pain of obsessive greed; the heavenly realm is happiness and pleasure; and the human realm is a mixture of these states. If our consciousness dwells much of the time in one of these states then we are reborn into that realm of existence. At the death of the body the consciousness dwelling in one of these states creates a body as the basis for abiding in that realm more substantially. But it is perhaps comforting to know that none of these realms is permanent. When the supporting kamma-vipaka (see no. 75) is exhausted the support for consciousness is removed and consciousness goes on to seek another support.

79.

What we think about, plan and dwell upon becomes the foundation for the persistence of consciousness. With this foundation, establishment of consciousness comes to be. With consciousness thus established and growing, renewed existence takes place in the future.

> *Samyutta Nikaya,* Vol. II, page 65

Radha, that desire, that lust, that delight in, that craving, that means of attachment, that state of mind, that dogmatic adherence in regard to the aspects of a human being [khandhas] are called 'the basis for coming into existence'. Their ending is called 'the ending of the basis for coming into existence'.

> *Samyutta Nikaya,* Vol. III, page 191

The activities of thinking, planning and dwelling upon things are called the 'kammic formations'. They provide the form and content of consciousness and are traditionally symbolised by a potter forming various types of vessels. Since we all think, plan and ponder in our own ways, this becomes the form for 'my' consciousness or consciousness of 'me'. In this way the birth of 'I' takes place.

According to the kammic quality of these formations, consciousness will be formed and a sense of self is born and abides there. Skilful thinking produces an exalted type of consciousness while unskilful thinking produces a clouded, distracted or shrunken consciousness and attendant sense of self. Consciousness, in order to persist, then conditions the arising of mentality and materiality. Mentality is the group of concomitant mental factors functioning in conformity with consciousness, and materiality is the physical body providing the base for the six senses. In this way a human being comes into existence and is maintained by desire, craving, attachment, etc. Craving is the volatile fuel of the kammic formations which, bringing about the existence of a human being, is then unleashed in its own right to keep human life fuelled. Dhamma (the Buddha's teachings) directs us to a thorough investigation of this whole conditioning process so that, understanding it, we can transcend the whole process.

80.

Constant travelling from birth to birth, from this form to that form, again and again – this is what results from ignorance. It is due to this ignorance that people's [minds] become dulled and muddled, that they go on endlessly wandering from life to life. But if you walk towards knowledge, you leave these rebirths behind, you do not go on becoming.
Sutta Nipata, verses 729–30

Because we are ignorant of the process by which our sense of self is reborn we are continually being reborn as someone or something: for example, 'I am sad' or 'I am happy'. When there is a sense of self it homes in on an object, mood or feeling that it can identify with. But nothing lasts for ever and we must eventually face the pain of separation from that which eventually changes and fades. To escape this endless disappointment we need to cease this restless becoming something or other. The end of all becoming is nibbana, the state beyond rebirth in any realm, where no 'I' exists to be reborn; where there is complete peace.

Nibbana

81.

If greed, aversion and delusion are given up, one does not plan for their

*own harm, for another's harm or for the harm of both, and one does not
experience any mental anguish or distress. Thus is nibbana seen here and
now, independent of time, inviting inspection, leading onwards, and
experienced by the wise for themselves.*
Anguttura Nikaya, Vol. I, page 159

Ananda, one without attachment realises nibbana.
Majjhima Nikaya, Vol. II, page 265

Radha, the end of craving is nibbana.
Samyutta Nikaya, Vol. III, page 190

The word 'nibbana' literally means 'extinguished', that is, the fires of
passion are extinguished. It is compared to the end of craving. At this
level nibbana can be described as a positive ethical and emotional state,
the ending of all unskilful, selfish attitudes and reactions. Although it is
frequently described in the negative, it is the ending of the unpleasant,
troublesome and disturbing which is referred to. If we try to find nibbana
we still have desire and greed, and if we try to abandon our passions we
still have aversion. Some of us, however, can recognise a little nibbana
when strong emotional states have subsided and we are at peace.

82.

*There is an island, an island which you cannot go beyond. It is a place of
nothingness, a place of non-possession and of non-attachment. It is the
total end of death and decay, and this is why I call it nibbana [the
extinguished, the cool].*

*There are people who, in mindfulness, have realised this and are
completely cooled here and now.*
Sutta Nipata, verses 1094–5

When there is nothing and no attachment, there is no ground for a sense
of self; self is not able to come into being or be reborn. What is not born
does not decay and die. We do not need to experience the 'heated' agony
of death since we are cooled. This can be realised any time in this life. We
can even say that in those (usually rare) moments when there is no sense of
self disturbing us, there is the 'coolness' of nibbana.

'Island' is often used as an epithet for nibbana since it is secure from the
floods of existence, which is another name for the asavas or outflows of
selfhood (see no. 8).

83.

There is a not-born, a not-become, a not-made, a not-constructed.

Since there is a not-born, not-become, not-made, not-constructed,
Thus there is a leaving behind of the born, become, made, constructed.
Therefore there is the escape, the true,
The beyond-conceptual-thought, the stable,
The not-born, unproduced, sorrowless, stainless state:
The end of painful things, calming of conditions – bliss.

Itivuttaka, page 37

Nibbana is usually described in negative terms because all things or states that we are familiar with or can relate to are not what nibbana is. Nibbana is beyond all these; it transcends all our familiar values and frames of reference. It is not-made, not-constructed, the beyond-conceptual-thought. Words and definitions are not able to encompass it but it can be experienced through meditation practice.

We have our own sense of happiness and pleasure which we can relate to our world, but we do not really know happiness until we know nibbana. Nibbana is the supreme happiness, the greatest peace. Truth, peace, security, purity, freedom are among the positive epithets given to nibbana.

84.

As a blazing spark struck from iron
Gradually fades to an unknown course [state],
So the one who's truly won release,
Crossed the floods of sensuality's bonds,
And reached immovable peace,
Goes to a course that transcends definition.

Udana, page 93

Since nibbana is frequently described in negative terms and appears so illusory some people have assumed it is annihilation. However, it is only the annihilation of selfishness, the end of self-centredness, conceit, pride and all things which cause us so much suffering and distress.

Since nibbana is beyond all concepts it transcends definition, and so whatever we try to define it as it is not. This is perfect for the practice in which we learn to let go of those things which nibbana is not. Letting go completely of what nibbana is not, we arrive at what nibbana is – the truth behind all our concepts.

Helping

85.

It is not possible, Chunda, that someone stuck in the mud could pull out another who is also stuck in the mud. But it is possible that someone not stuck in the mud could pull out another who is stuck in the mud.

It is not possible that someone untamed, untrained, not completely calmed, could tame, train or completely calm another. But it is possible that someone tamed, trained, completely calmed, could tame, train or completely calm another.

Majjhima Nikaya, Vol. I, page 45

Explanations of the Buddha's teachings often end with nibbana, but realising nibbana does not mean we stop living. Now we are truly living selflessly and with wisdom. Someone who has achieved nibbana is in the best position to help others and this is the true help which the Buddha praised. We can only teach others when we know for ourselves. But this does not mean that we have to wait for nibbana. If we had to wait for fully enlightened beings to teach us we might never be able to learn. We teach others from what we know ourselves, however great or small that may be. If we speak from our own experience we do not need to fear conceit, and to help others we need to know ourselves very well.

86.

Protecting oneself one protects others; protecting others one protects oneself. And how does one, in protecting oneself, protect others? By the repeated and frequent practice of meditation. And how does one, in protecting others, protect oneself? By patience and forbearance, by a non-violent and harmless life, by loving kindness and compassion. 'I shall protect myself', in that way the foundations of mindfulness should be practised. 'I shall protect others', in that way the foundations of mindfulness should be practised. Protecting oneself, one protects others; protecting others, one protects oneself.

Samyutta Nikaya, Vol. V, page 168

The Buddha realised the mutual interdependence of ourselves and others but it is with ourselves that we have the greatest ability to make changes. The purification of our own minds has salutary effects on others. If it does not, or if we have to relate to difficult people, we should respond with compassion. At least this will not compound a difficult situation and will have salutary effects upon ourselves.

Many people think that helping oneself is selfish, but the Buddha understood that we cannot really help others until we have helped ourselves. Peace begins in our own minds.

87.

In this, bhikkhu, a wise person, one of great wisdom, does not intend harm to self, intend harm to others, or intend harm to both self and others. Thinking in this way, such a one intends benefit for self, benefit for others, benefit for both, benefit for the whole world. Thus is one wise and of great wisdom.

Anguttura Nikaya, Vol. II, page 179

'Great wisdom' is knowing how to live without causing harm and making one's life a benefit to the world. Even our best intentions are not enough as they still contain some degree of self-interest; for example, 'I want to help you the way I think you should be helped' or 'I'll help you my way'.

Harmlessness may sound easy but when we observe just how often our careless words cause hurt to others we begin to realise just what an art it is to live harmlessly. When we have realised this we can start to be a benefit to others.

Buddhadhamma

88.

Ananda, it may be that you will think: 'The Teacher's instruction has ceased, now we have no teacher!' It should not be seen like this, Ananda, for what I have taught and explained to you as Dhamma and discipline will, at my passing, be your teacher.

Digha Nikaya, Vol. II, page 154

The Buddha: 'Who indeed, Vakkali, sees Dhamma, sees me; who sees me, sees Dhamma.
'Surely, seeing Dhamma, one sees me; seeing me, one sees Dhamma.'

Samyutta Nikaya, Vol. III, page 120

Even though the Buddha has entered final nibbana and is following a course that transcends definition, a teacher still exists so we can practise Dhamma (the Buddha's teachings). The Buddha's clear guidance is contained in the body of scripture and the living practice of Buddhists today. In the Dhamma and discipline, which the Buddha proclaimed and which has been recorded and preserved for the last 2500 years, is the outline of the many ways of practice which anyone can follow to realise nibbana, if one is sincere and diligent. The Buddha was awakened to Dhamma, the truth, so at that time he became that Dhamma, that truth itself; his whole being entered into Dhamma rather than being someone who merely knew Dhamma. He has left us the way of practice which we can develop to realise Dhamma for ourselves.

89.

The things of which you know: These things lead to dispassion, not to passion; to detachment, not to attachment; to diminution, not to accumulation; to wanting little, not to wanting much; to being easily satisfied, not to being hard to satisfy; to seclusion, not to socialising; to putting forth energy, not to indolence; to frugality, not to luxury; of them you should surely know that they belong to the teaching, to the training, to the Teacher's instruction.

Anguttura Nikaya, Vol. IV, page 280

The Buddha's teachings are universal and cannot be found in a particular temple, ceremony or formula. The Buddha is pointing to the enlightened state of mind and offers guidelines to that state of mind. We need to develop the guidelines within ourselves to make them a living reality.

The Buddha is not teaching Buddhism but wherever and in whatever teaching or philosophy we find these guidelines we will also find the truth.

90.

And the Lord said: 'Ananda, these sal-trees have burst into an abundance of untimely blossoms... Divine music and song sound from the sky in homage to the Tathagata [Buddha]. Never before has the Tathagata been so honoured: male or female lay-follower dwells practising the Dhamma properly and perfectly fulfils the Dhamma-way, he or she honours the Tathagata, reveres and esteems him and pays him the supreme homage. Therefore, Ananda, "We will dwell practising the Dhamma properly and perfectly fulfil the Dhamma-way" – this will be your watchword.'

Digha Nikaya, Vol. II, page 138

It is often easier to worship great masters than to practise what they taught. But the Buddha emphatically reminds us that true reverence is practising Dhamma, living by truth. The Buddha did not live to be worshipped but to teach the way to liberation – the way to nibbana. If we do not practise his teaching we are being disrespectful to the Buddha and to all his efforts. To practise is to become Buddha-like so that the Buddha lives on in our own hearts. With Buddha-like people, with great wisdom and great compassion, the world will truly be a better place in which to live.

2 Sri Lanka

Compiled with commentary by
Dr W. G. Weeratatna and Dhanapala Samarasekara

These readings were chosen by Buddhists living and working in Sri Lanka. The Buddha's teachings are a guide for all people and the commentaries reflect an understanding of the Buddha's discourses from Theravada Buddhists of the lay community in Sri Lanka. This section begins with a brief outline of the daily homage that is paid to the Buddha and ends with the popular story of Kisagotami, an episode from the life of the Buddha.

Homage

> Honour to the Blessed One, the Exalted One,
> The Fully Enlightened One.

In countries following the Theravada tradition, it is customary to open any Buddhist ceremony or meeting with the recital of these words in the Pali language. It is called 'Vandana', a form of adoration and expression of respect with gratitude to the Buddha, the Supreme Teacher who taught the way to liberation. This is followed by the observation of the three refuges or three jewels (tisarana).

> I go to the Buddha as my refuge
> I go to the Dhamma as my refuge
> I go to the Sangha as my refuge.

A Buddhist seeks release from suffering by taking refuge in the Buddha, Dhamma (teachings), and the Sangha (the community of monks and nuns). The Buddha is the Teacher, the Dhamma is the unique way, and the Sangha are the ones who have chosen to follow the way as Buddha himself has done. Therefore one becomes a Buddhist out of free choice without any fear or compulsion. Buddhism does not proclaim a formal code of laws or prohibitions, in contrast to many world religions which depend mostly on faith.

After the recital of the three refuges, Buddhists undertake to observe the five precepts which are:

I undertake to refrain from harming any living things
I undertake to refrain from taking what is not given
I undertake to refrain from the misuse of the senses
I undertake to refrain from wrong speech
I undertake to refrain from taking drugs or drinks which tend to cloud the mind.

It is the practice among Buddhists to repeat the Vandana and the undertaking to observe the five precepts in the morning and before going to bed at night. There is no religious compulsion attached to this observation and it is all done freely and voluntarily.

Investigation

91.

'Sir, there are some recluses and brahmins who come to Kesaputta who explain or illustrate their doctrines only while despising, condemning or spurning that of others. This has created perplexity and doubt in us as to who among these recluses and brahmins spoke the truth and who spoke falsehood.'

'Yes, Kalamas, it is proper that you have doubt, that you have perplexity, for a doubt had arisen in a matter which is doubtful. Now, be careful, Kalamas, when you find out for yourself that certain things are bad, reprehensible, condemned by the wise, not rightly taken upon oneself, and lead to harm and suffering, then you should abandon them. But whenever you find out for yourself that things are wholesome and good, extolled by the wise, rightly taken on oneself and lead to welfare and happiness, then accept them and follow them.'

Anguttura Nikaya, Vol. I, pages 171-2

When the Kalamas townsfolk from Kesputta in the kingdom of Kosala came to the Buddha and asked him who they should or should not believe he pointed out that personal investigation was vital to all his teachings. On another occasion, the Buddha said that a disciple should examine Buddha himself so that the disciple might be fully convinced of the teacher he followed.

Buddha said, 'As a wise man tests gold on a touchstone, heating and cutting, so you, bhikkhus, should take my words only after investigating thoroughly and not because of reverence for me.'

Even on his deathbed the Buddha asked his disciples several times if they had any doubt about his teachings so that they could voice their worries before his death. When his disciples did not ask any questions the Buddha advised them, 'If it is through respect for the teacher that you do no ask anything, let even one of you inform his friend so that the friend may ask the necessary questions in his place.'

According to the Buddha, freedom of thought was essential for one to realise the truth and achieve emancipation which is independent of an outside force. Elimination of doubt builds sraddha (confidence) which is the opposite of blind faith. In the words of the Buddha, 'Confidence is the greatest wealth of man in the world.'

92.

Among highest matters of our spirit's growth
Nothing ranks above forebearing patiently.
Surely he that has the upper hand
And he that bears patiently with him that's down;
Ever to tolerate the weaker side:
This has been called the supreme forebearance.
Who thinks the strength of fools is strength
Will say of the strong man, 'He is a weakling.'
For the strong man who is guarded by righteousness,
To bandy words comes not into his thought.
Worse of the two is he who, when reviled,
Reviles again. Who does not, when reviled,
Revile again, a twofold victory wins.
Both of the other and himself he seeks
The good; for he does understand
The other's angry mood and grows calm and still.
He, who is a physician of both, since
He heals himself and the other too,
Folk deem him a fool, knowing not the norm.

Samyutta Nikaya, Vol. I, pages 285–6

Things do not always happen as we would want and it is the nature of the
average person to become excited, irritated or impatient. Our friends and
neighbours invariably anger or disturb us but retaliation only exacerbates
conflict. There are eight vicissitudes in life which we cannot escape. They
are gain and loss, fame and ill fortune, blame and praise, happiness and
sorrow. Through mindfulness we can train ourselves to face these
vicissitudes with patience, sobriety and balance of mind – the
characteristics of one who is spiritually advanced.

Citta (Mind)

93.

This mind, monks, is luminous, but it is defiled by taints that come from
without. But the uneducated folk do not understand this as it really is.
For the uneducated folk there is no cultivation of mind.

That mind, monks, is luminous, it is cleansed of taints that come from
without. The educated noble disciple understands this as it really is.

For the educated noble disciple there is cultivation of mind. Monks, if
for just the lasting of a finger snap a monk indulges a thought of good
will, such a one is to be called a monk. Not empty of thought is his

musing, he abides doing the Master's bidding. He is one who takes good advice and he eats the country's alms-food to some purpose. What then should I say of those who make much of such a thought?

Monks, whatsoever things are evil, have part in evil, are on the side of evil, all such have mind for their causing. First arises mind as the forerunner of them, and those evil things follow after. Monks, I know not of any other single thing of such power to cause the arising of evil states, if not yet arisen, or to cause the waning of good states, if already arisen, as negligence. In him who is negligent, evil states, if not already arisen, do arise, and good states, if arisen, do wane.

Monks, I know not of any other single thing of such power to cause the arising of good states, if not yet arisen, or to cause the waning of evil states, if already arisen, as earnestness. In him who is earnest, good states, if not yet arisen, do arise, and evil states, if arisen, do wane.

Anguttura Nikaya, Vol. I, pages 8–9

The normal state of the mind is as clear, clean and reflective as a dust-free mirror. But when our senses come into contact with external stimuli it is easily clouded with greed, lust, hatred, ill-will, jealousy and miserliness. These dominating elements control and confuse our mind to such an extent that we run after all types of sense objects.

We can cleanse the mind by developing mindfulness or alertness (sati) so that the strength of defiling elements already existing in the mind is diminished and entry of further defiling elements ceases. Through meditation and skilful practice the mind becomes attuned to looking at external stimuli without prejudice. Greed does not arise in a detached mind and hatred does not arise in the mind repelled by external stimuli. When the burning elements of greed and hatred are under control the mind is free of conflict and there is true peace.

The Middle Path (Majjhimapatipada)

94.

Monks, these two extremes should not be followed by one who has gone forth as a wanderer [one who is searching for truth]. What two?

Devotion to the pleasure of sense, a low practice of villagers, a practice unworthy, unprofitable, the way of the world [on the one hand]; and [on the other hand] devotion to self-mortification, which is painful, unworthy and unprofitable.

By avoiding these two extremes the Tathagata has gained knowledge of that middle path which giveth vision, which giveth knowledge, which causeth calm, special knowledge, enlightenment, nibbana.

Samyutta Nikaya, Vol. V, pages 356–7

Buddhism is called the 'religion of the middle way' since it advocates avoidance of extremes in all matters. Anyone concerned for their spiritual and social well-being should avoid self-indulgence at pleasurable or painful extremes, and adopt the middle way which can be realised through the noble eightfold path (see no. 96).

In keeping with this basic tenet, the Buddha avoided extremes in most matters. He avoided eternalism and nihilism and taught the doctrine of causal genesis to explain all phenomena. He also avoided the theory of chance occurrence, the theory of strict past kamma, and utilised instead the doctrine of causal genesis to explain condition and matter (see no. 99).

The Four Noble Truths

95.

'Suppose, monks, a man should throw into a mighty ocean a yoke with a single hole, and there were a blind turtle to pop up to the surface once in every hundred years.

'Now what do you think, monks? Would that blind turtle push his neck through that yoke with one hole whenever he popped up to the surface, once at the end of every hundred years?'

'It might be so, Lord, now and again, after the lapse of a long time.'

'Well, monks, sooner I declare would that blind turtle push his neck through that yoke with one hole, popping up to the surface once in a hundred years, than would a fool who had fallen into a lower state of existence become a man again.'

'What is the reason for that?'

'Because, monks, here prevails no practice of the holy life, no righteous living, no doing of good deeds, no working of merit, but just cannibalism and preying on weaker creatures.'

'Why so?'

'Through not seeing the four noble truths: the noble truth of suffering, the noble truth of the arising of suffering, the noble truth of the ceasing of suffering, and the noble truth that leads to the ceasing of suffering.

Samyutta Nikaya, Vol. V, pages 383–4

In the realms of animals, ghosts and hellish creatures there is no teaching regarding the four noble truths or a religious life based on that teaching. Therefore, if we are reborn, after death, in a lower state of existence as an animal, a ghost, or a creature in hell, it is unlikely that we will soon free ourselves from those states to become a human being again. Although the four noble truths exist, they would be beyond us, like a yoke adrift in a great ocean. The Buddha has pointed out the path that we, as human beings, are able to follow. If we lose sight completely of all that he has taught and are born in one of these lower states of existence, the chances of ever finding the four aryan truths again is as slight as the blind turtle searching for the yoke once in every hundred years.

The Buddha declared the four noble truths to the world in his first sermon after enlightenment. The first truth is that samsaric existence (the cycles of birth and death) is full of suffering. The second truth is that suffering has a cause, namely, the threefold craving: craving for sensual gratification, craving for future existence, and craving for annihilation. The third truth is that there is a ceasing of this samsaric suffering; and the fourth truth is that there is a way leading to the ceasing of this suffering. The way leading to the ceasing of this suffering is the noble eightfold path.

The Noble Eightfold Path

96.

Just as if, brethren, a man faring through the forest, through a great wood, should see an ancient path, an ancient road traversed by men of former days.

And he were to go along it, and going along it he would see an ancient city, an ancient prince's domain, wherein dwelt men of former days, having gardens, groves, pools, foundations of walls, a goodly spot. And that man, brethren, should bring word to the prince or to the prince's minister, 'Pardon, lord, know this. I have seen as I fared through the forest, through the great wood, an ancient path, an ancient road traversed by men of former days. I have been along it and, going along it, I have seen an ancient city... Lord, restore that city!' And, brethren, the prince or his minister should restore that city. That city should, thereafter, become prosperous and flourishing, populous, teeming with folk, grown and thriving. Even so have I, brethren, seen an ancient path, an ancient road traversed by the perfectly Enlightened Ones of former times. And what, brethren, is that ancient path...?

Just this noble eightfold path, to wit, right views, right thoughts, right speech, right action, right livelihood, right effort, right mindfulness, and right concentration of mind. This, brethren, is that ancient path, that ancient road, traversed by the rightly Enlightened Ones of former times. Along that I have gone, and going along it I have fully come to know decay and death, I have fully come to know the ceasing of decay and death. Along that have I gone, and going along it I have fully come to know birth, and becoming, and grasping, and craving, and feeling, and contact, and sense, and name, and shape, and consciousness. Along that I have gone, and going along it I have fully come to know the ceasing of activities, I have fully come to know the way going to the ceasing of activities.

Samyutta Nikaya, Vol. II, pages 72–5

The Buddha advocated the noble eightfold path for laity as well as clergy, to attain peace and happiness in our present life as well as ensuring better rebirth. But the final goal to be realised through the eightfold path is release from samsara (the cycles of birth and death).

The noble eightfold path is not an invention of the Buddha but a rediscovery by him of a goal and a path that were there in the world and were pursued by sages prior to himself. The first limb of the path is right views. Along this way we have to cleanse our minds of all irrational, dogmatic and superficial views. We should try to harbour views that are, at the same time, rational, practical and beneficial for individual and social well-being and happiness, and conducive to spiritual progress. The second limb is right thoughts. Benevolent thoughts such as charity, thoughts of loving kindness such as sympathy, and thoughts of non-violence are the thoughts that should motivate and direct all our actions.

The third limb is right speech which constitutes refraining from falsehood and speaking the truth alone, refraining from slander and speaking in a way that will bring amity and concord, refraining from all harsh and unpleasant speech, refraining from gossip and frivolous speech, and speaking with relevance at the appropriate time. The fourth limb is right action, which is refraining from killing and causing injury to life, refraining from theft, and refraining from wrongful gratification of sense pleasures. Right livelihood is the fifth limb, which rejects deceitful, fraudulent or cunning occupations in favour of pursuing innocent and harmless occupations. The sixth limb is right effort, which is nothing but initiative, will and determination to avoid what is wrong and to do what is right. The seventh limb is right mindfulness. The sixth and seventh limbs are important since they should be applied at all times to the previous five limbs. The eighth limb is right concentration, which is the pacified and peaceful state of the mind achieved through practice of the first seven limbs and through meditation.

Anicca (Impermanence)

97.

The untaught manyfolk, brethren, might well be repelled by this body, child of the four great elements, might cease to fancy it and wish to be free from it. Why so? Seen is the growth and decay of this body, child of the four great elements, the taking on and the laying down of it. Hence, well might the manyfolk be repelled by it, cease to fancy it, and wish to be free from it.

Yet this, brethren, that we call thought, that we call mind, that we call consciousness, by this the untaught manyfolk are not able to feel repelled, they are not able to cease fancying it or to be freed from it. Why so? For many a long day, brethren, has it been for the uneducated manyfolk that to which they cleave, that which they call 'mine', that which they wrongly conceive thinking: 'That is mine'; 'This I am'; 'This is my spirit.' Hence, the untaught manyfolk are not able to feel repelled by it, are not able to cease fancying it, are not able to be freed from it.

It were better, brethren, if the untaught manyfolk approached this body, child of the four great elements, as the self rather than the mind. Why so? Seen is it, brethren, how this body, child of the four great elements, persists for a year, persists for two years, persists for three, four, five, ten, twenty, thirty, persists for forty, for fifty years, persists for a hundred years, and even longer. But this, brethren, that we call thought, that we call mind, that we call consciousness, that arises as one thing, ceases as another, whether by night or by day. Just as a monkey, brethren, faring through the woods, through the great forest, catches hold of a bough, and letting go seizes another, even so that which we call thought, mind, consciousness, that arises as one thing, ceases as another, both by day and night.

Samyutta Nikaya, Vol. III, pages 65–6

Everything in this world, including our self, is in a constant state of flux. Human beings are made up of a mental or psychological aspect and the body or material aspect. The material aspect is continually growing and changing, but this occurs so slowly and subtly that we barely notice the change, although everyone can observe the difference between baby and adult, between youth and old age.

We usually expect others to have a permanent identity but if we analyse that identity we cannot say that someone aged sixty has not changed since the age of thirty.

It is much easier to recognise the fleeting changes of our thoughts or emotions and yet we sometimes try to cling to them, as we do to our identity, and so reinforce our sense of a permanent self. When we are still tied to a concept of permanent self we are also bound to greed, hatred and illusion.

Tilakkhana (The Three Signata)

98.

*Body, brethren, is impermanent. What is impermanent, that is
suffering. What is suffering, that is not the self. What is not the self,
that is not mine, that I am not, that is not the self of me. This is the way
one should regard things as they really are, by right insight.*

*So, likewise with regard to feeling, perception, the activities and
consciousness. So seeing, brethren, the well-taught noble disciple feels
disgust at body, at feeling, perception, the activities and consciousness.*

*Feeling disgust he is repelled; being repelled he is released; in him who
is released, knowledge arises that he is freed, and he knows 'Destroyed is
rebirth; lived is the righteous life; done is the task'; for life in these
conditions there is no hereafter.*

Samyutta Nikaya, Vol. III, pages 68–9

Anicca (transitoriness), dukkha (unsatisfactoriness) and anatta (without
soul) are the main characteristics of all phenomena. Through this doctrine
the Buddha refutes theories regarding creation and soul. Belief in the
eternal soul is the dogma that hinders our social and spiritual growth since
it is the belief that encourages selfishness, pride and conceit. Once we
realise the transient, unsatisfactory and essenceless nature of all things we
are freed from greed, hatred and illusion. It is only when we free ourselves
from these three basic roots of evil that we can realise true mental peace
and happiness.

Causality

99.

What, brethren, is the causal law?
Conditioned by ignorance, activities come to pass;
Conditioned by consciousness, name and shape come to pass;
Conditioned by name and shape, sense comes to pass;
Conditioned by contact, feeling comes to pass;
Conditioned by feeling, craving comes to pass;
Conditioned by craving, grasping comes to pass;
Conditioned by grasping, becoming comes to pass;
Conditioned by becoming, birth comes to pass;
*Conditioned by birth, old age and death, grief, suffering, sorrow and
despair come to pass. Such is the uprising of the entire mass of ill. This,
brethren, is called causal genesis.*

But from the utter fading away and ceasing of ignorance comes ceasing of activities; from the ceasing of activities, ceasing of consciousness; . . . ceasing of name and shape; . . . ceasing of sense; . . . ceasing of contact; . . . ceasing of feeling; ceasing of craving; . . . ceasing of grasping; . . . ceasing of becoming; . . . ceasing of birth; from ceasing of birth, old age and death, grief, lamenting, suffering, sorrow and despair cease. Such is the ceasing of this entire mass of ill.

Samyutta Nikaya, Vol. II, pages 1–2

In the Buddha's lifetime there were many with dogmatic views regarding the origin of things. Some maintained that the world and everything in it were created by an almighty creator and that things happened the way that he liked them to happen. Some maintained a materialistic view, saying that there is no hereafter and that everything ended with death. Some maintained that things happened without cause or condition, by chance.

The Buddha examined all the prevalent ideas and theories that he heard and rejected them as unsatisfactory since none could fully explain the world and its various phenomena. Instead the Buddha analysed things rationally, objectively and scientifically to find their nature, to understand how things come to be and how things cease to be. The causal law or the doctrine of dependent arising is the alternative explanation that the Buddha presented. The Buddha did not postulate about the first beginning of things; instead he took all things and analysed them into their composite parts. Through analysis he was able to show that each part was impermanent, unsatisfactory, essenceless and dependently originated. Things come to be when certain causes and conditions are present and with the change or ceasing of the causes and conditions that bring about a certain thing, that thing also changes and ceases to be. The Buddha also applied this general law of causality to the nature of human beings. We have psychological and physical aspects. The psychological aspect is divided into feelings, perceptions, energies and consciousness. The material aspect is divided into four elemental physical qualities: solidity, cohesion, heat and motion.

The law of causation can be further analysed and applied through the twelve links in this reading. We come to be due to a chain of causal factors and we are not annihilated at death as long as these causal factors contain that psychological energy called kamma (activities). Activities in turn give rise to consciousness and the chain continues as in the reading.

100.

It is just as if, because of oil and because of wick, an oil lamp were to be burning, and in it no man should from time to time pour oil or adjust the wick. Truly, such an oil lamp, when its first fuel were to come to an end, and no other fuel were brought to it, would without fuel become extinct.

Even so in him who contemplates the misery that there is in all that makes for enfettering, craving ceases, and so grasping ceases, becoming, birth, decay and death, and sorrow cease. Such is the ceasing of this entire mass of ill.

Samyutta Nikaya, Vol. II, page 61

We are not created by ourselves or by another. We are the result of a conglomeration of causes and conditions. Every bit of our self is impermanent and subject to change and cessation. Just like a lamp that burns because oil and wick are present, our life continues in samsara (the cycles of birth and death) because of conditions such as ignorance and greed. The causes change and disintegrate when greed and ignorance are dispelled through knowledge. Like the lamp that no longer burns without oil, we cease to be.

Samsara

101.

Incalculable, brethren, is the beginning of this round of rebirth. No beginning is made known of beings wrapt in ignorance, fettered by craving, who run on, who fare on the round of rebirth.

There comes a time, brethren, when the mighty ocean dries up, is utterly drained, comes no more to be. But of beings hindered in ignorance, fettered by craving, who run on, who fare on the round of rebirth, I declare no end-making.

Just as, brethren, a dog tied up by a leash to a strong stake or pillar keeps running round and revolving round and round that stake or pillar, even so, brethren, the untaught manyfolk, who do not discern those who are nobles . . . , who are untrained in the worthy doctrine, regard body as the self, regard feeling, perception, the activities, regard consciousness as having a self, regard consciousness as being in the self or the self as being in consciousness . . . , run and revolve round and round from body to body, from feeling to feeling, from perception to perception, from activities to activities, from consciousness to consciousness . . . they are not released from there, they are not released from rebirth, from old age and decay, from sorrow and grief, from woe, lamentation, despair . . . they are not released from suffering, I declare. But the well-taught noble disciple, brethren, who discerns those who are nobles . . . who is well trained in the worthy doctrine, regards no body as the self, regards not the self as being in consciousness. He runs not, revolves not round from body to body . . . from consciousness to consciousness, but is released from there. He is released from birth, old age and decay, from sorrow and grief, woe, lamentation and despair. I declare he is released from suffering.

Samyutta Nikaya, Vol. III, pages 126–7

Samsara is the technical term used to describe the continuous rebecoming of beings. Each being is a samsaric process that is not annihilated at death. The beginning of samsara cannot be reckoned and its end cannot be imagined. The Buddha taught that this recurring rebecoming of beings is due to psychological force within each being; this force is known as kamma. The kammic force cannot be compared to a soul that passes from one birth to another. Due to ignorance of the true nature of things we harbour a threefold thirst: thirst for sensual gratification, thirst for existence and thirst for annihilation. Because of this threefold thirst we are led to all types of volitional activities by thought, word and body; these activities generate the kammic force.

Gati (Destinies of Beings)

102.

'Now what do you think, monks? Which is the greater: this little dust I have taken up on the tip of my fingernail, or this mighty earth?'

'Why, Lord, this mighty earth is the greater. Exceedingly small is the little dust taken up on the Exalted One's fingernail. It cannot be reckoned, cannot be compared therewith. It does not amount to the merest fraction of a part when laid beside this mighty earth.'

'Just so, monks, few indeed are those beings that deceasing as human beings are reborn as human beings.'

Samyutta Nikaya, Vol. V, pages 396–7

There are five destinies or spheres that we can be born into as we fare along in samsara (the cycles of birth and death). There is the sphere of the divine beings, the sphere of the humans, the sphere of animals, the sphere of ghosts and the sphere of hellish creatures. The first two spheres are called good destinies and the remaining three are known as bad destinies. The kamma which is generated by our volitional activities has the potency to direct our rebirth into one of these spheres. If we engage in volitional activities harmful to ourselves and to others, the psychological force that we generate can result in a rebirth in one of the bad destinies. If we engage in volitional activities that are wholesome and beneficial to ourselves and others, the psychological force that we generate can result in a rebirth in one of the good destinies. In this reading the Buddha points out that only a few humans who die are reborn as humans since the great majority of humans engage in demeritorious activities that are harmful to the doer as well as to others.

Nibbana

103.

'*The destruction of lust, the destruction of hatred, the destruction of illusion, friend, is called nibbana.*'
'*But is there, friend, any path, any approach to the realisation of this nibbana?*'
'*There is such a path, friend, there is such an approach.*'
'*And what is that path, friend, and what is that approach to the realisation of this nibbana?*'
'*It is this noble eightfold path, friend, for the realisation of nibbana.*'
Samyutta Nikaya, Vol. IV, page 170

Nibbana, the ultimate goal, is beyond description. It is the complete destruction of craving which is the root of samsara (the cycles of birth and death). Due to ignorance of the true nature of things our minds are dominated by lust, hatred and delusion, which fuel the kammic force. By following the noble eightfold path, ignorance vanishes to be replaced by wisdom (see no. 96). Through wisdom and understanding we can attain that which cannot be defined or described; we do not know what it is but we do know that it is not pain, hatred, illusion, lust or ignorance. It is called the quenching of desires.

Arahant (The Perfect One)

104.

Ah! happy saints! In them no craving seen.
The 'I' conceit is rooted up: delusion's net is burst.
Lust-free they have attained; translucent is the heart of them.
These godlike beings, drug-immune, unspotted in the world,
Knowing the fivefold mass, they roam the seven domains of good.
Worthy of praise and worthy they – sons of the Enlightened One
The wearers of the sevenfold gem, in the threefold training trained.
These mighty heroes follow on, exempt from fear and dread:
Lords of the tenfold potency, great sages tranquillised:
Best beings they in all the world; in them no craving is seen.
They have won the knowledge of adepts. This compound is their last.
The essence of the holy life, that have they made their own.
Unshaken by the triple modes, set free from birth to come,
The plane of self-control they have won, victorious in the world.
Upward or crossways or below – no lure is found in them.
They sound aloud their lion's roar: 'Supreme are they that wake.'
Samyutta Nikaya, Vol. III, pages 69–70

The arahant is neither attached to the world nor repelled by it. Through the noble eightfold path he or she has suppressed lust, hatred and delusion and developed their opposites: detachment, loving kindness and objectivity. Through wisdom the arahant knows all things to be impermanent, full of misery, essenceless, and dependent in origination. The arahant is free of attachment and repulsion – the conditions that lead to all psychological conflicts – and experiences supreme peace. The arahant has attained the fourth or highest stage in the realisation of nibbana. The third stage in this development is called anagami (never-returner), the second stage is called sakadagami (once-returner) and the first stage is called sotapanna (stream-enterer).

A man or a woman who has become an arahant continues to live and work in the world and inspire others until, after death, he or she is born no more.

The Buddha

105.

The Tathagata, brethren, who, being arahant, is fully enlightened, he it is who doth cause a way to arise which had not arisen before; who doth bring about a way not brought about before; who doth proclaim a way not proclaimed before; who is the knower of a way, who understandeth a way, who is skilled in a way. And now, brethren, his disciples are wayfarers who follow after him. That, brethren, is the distinction, the specific feature which distinguishes the Tathagata, who, being arahant, is fully enlightened, from the disciple who is freed by insight.

Samyutta Nikaya, Vol. III, page 66

In this sermon the Buddha discusses why he was called a Buddha and the essential distinction between himself and his disciples who have become perfected ones or arahants. The Buddha is called the Enlightened One since, through personal initiative, he has fully understood the nature of the constituent parts of the human personality and has completely freed himself from attachment to them. He realised this unblemished true knowledge through the noble eightfold path (see no. 96) and so attained complete release from the bonds of samsara (the cycles of birth and death). After accepting the Buddha as their teacher and guide the arahants followed this path, first rediscovered by the Buddha, and they too attained enlightenment.

106.

The asavas whereby would be
A deva-birth or airy sprite,
Gandharva, or whereby myself
Would reach the state of Yakkahood
Or go to birth in human womb.
Those inflows now by myself
Are slain, destroyed and rooted out.

As a lotus, fair and lovely
By the water is not soiled,
By the world am I not soiled;
Therefore, brahmin, am I Buddha.

Anguttura Nikaya, Vol. II, page 45

Through complete understanding and realisation of the true nature of things we can completely free ourselves from samsara (the cycles of birth and death). When the asavas (impurities of mind) that regenerate the kammic process cease to exist we are no longer born into any sphere. Like the lotus with its roots buried in the mud but its blossom above the water, the Buddha was born into this world of suffering but, through wisdom, he was released from the bonds of ignorance, suffering and delusion while still on earth. A yakka is a ghost or sprite.

107.

I quarrel not with the world, brethren. It is the world which quarrels with me. No preacher of the norm, brethren, quarrels with anyone in the world. That which is not upheld, brethren, in the world of sages, of that I declare, 'It is not'.

What, brethren, is upheld in the world of sages, of that I declare, 'It is so'?

And what, brethren, is not upheld in the world of sages, of which I declare, 'It is not'?

That body is permanent, stable, eternal, not subject to decay. That is not upheld in the world of the sages, and of that I declare, 'It is not'. Feeling, perception, the activities, consciousness are permanent, stable, eternal, not subject to decay. That is not upheld in the world of sages, and of that I declare, 'It is not'.

But what, brethren, is upheld in the world of sages? Of what do I declare that 'It is so'?

Body is impermanent, woeful and subject to decay. That, brethren, is upheld in the world of the sages, and of that do I declare, 'It is so'. Likewise with regard to feeling, perception, the activity and consciousness. This, brethren, is upheld in the world of the sages, and of that do I declare, 'It is so'.

Samyutta Nikaya, Vol. III, page 117

In this discussion the Buddha frankly admits that he teaches no new doctrine or ethical system. He says that he does not dispute with the world, but that the world comes to dispute with him. What he teaches and upholds as true and beneficial is that taught by sages and wise men of old, and what he rejects as untrue and not conducive to well-being and happiness was also rejected by the sages and wise men of old. In this respect it is worthwhile remembering that the Buddha himself declared in another context that the noble eightfold path is not his creation, but that it is an ancient path followed by sages of old. The path was there but it was concealed from the world due to ignorance. Through his own initiative and endeavour the Buddha rediscovered the path and made it known to the world (see no. 96).

The Five Precepts

108.

The noble disciple is one who has overcome or mastered the fivefold dread.

1. The taker of life, conditioned by his lifetaking, engenders guilty dread even in this life. He also engenders guilty dread for a future state, mental suffering too, and the sorrow which he experiences; he who abstains from taking life has overcome and mastered this dread.

2. The taker of what is not given, conditioned by that taking, engenders guilty dread even in this life. He also engenders guilty dread for a future state, mental suffering too, the sorrow which he experiences; he who abstains from taking that which is not given has overcome and mastered this guilty dread.

3. He who acts wrongly in sense desires, conditioned by that wrong action, engenders guilty dread even in this life. He also engenders guilty dread for a future state, mental suffering too, the sorrow which he experiences; he who abstains from wrongful action in sense-desires has overcome and mastered this guilty dread.

4. The liar, conditioned by lying, engenders guilty dread even in this life. He also engenders guilty dread for a future state, mental suffering too, the sorrow which he experiences; he who abstains from lying has overcome and mastered this guilty dread.

5. He who persists in indulging in strong drink, conditioned by that indulging, engenders guilty dread even in this life. He also engenders guilty dread for a future state, mental suffering too, the sorrow which he experiences; he who abstains from that indulgence has mastered this guilty dread.

He has mastered this fivefold guilty dread.

Samyutta Nikaya, Vol. II, page 48

The five precepts are the fundamental ethical injunctions recommended for the followers of the Buddha.

To abide by the first precept, a follower of the Buddha should not only refrain from causing death or injury to living beings but should also be sympathetic and helpful to all living beings. To abide by the second precept, a follower of the Buddha should refrain from theft and from taking what is not voluntarily given away by its legitimate owner, and at the same time should be generous to those in needy circumstances. To abide by the third precept a follower of the Buddha should be moderate and restrained in the pursuit of sense pleasures. To abide by the fourth precept, a follower of the Buddha avoids the four categories of wrong speech: lies, slander, harsh speech and gossip. A true follower of the Buddha should not only avoid all four types but also practise their four opposites: speaking the truth, speaking in a way that encourages peace, speaking refined and gentle words, speaking relevant words at the appropriate time and place. The fifth precept encourages physical and psychological well-being needed to perform duties and obligations.

Criteria for Good and Bad

109.

'What do you think about this, Rahula? What is the purpose of a mirror?'

'Its purpose is reflection, reverend sir.'

'Even so, Rahula, a deed is to be done with the body only after repeated reflection; a deed is to be done with the speech only after repeated reflection; a deed is to be done with the mind only after repeated reflection. If you, Rahula, are desirous of doing with the body, you should reflect on that deed of your body thus: "That deed which I am desirous of doing with the body is a deed of my body that might conduce to the harm of self, and that might conduce to the harm of others, and that might conduce to the harm of both; this deed of body is unskilled, its yield is anguish, its result is anguish."... But if you, Rahula, while reflecting thus, should find, "That deed which I am desirous of doing with the body is a deed of my body that would conduce neither to the harm of self nor to the harm of others nor to the harm of both; this deed of body is skilled, its yield is happy, its result is happy" –

a deed of body like this, Rahula, may be done by you.'
                    Majjhima Nikaya, Vol. II, pages 89–90

The Buddha has offered young Rahula a practical criterion to
differentiate good from bad, right action from wrong action. What
becomes clear even in this discussion is the superior position that the
Buddha gives to humans. We have the intelligence to reflect before we act
and if, in the course of such reflection, we see that the contemplated act is
beneficial to ourselves as well as to others, this act should be pursued as
something good. If, in the course of reflection, we see that the
contemplated act is harmful to ourselves and to others, that act should not
be pursued. The Buddha offers us guidance but we are ultimately the
judge of our own actions.

The Importance of Life

110.

The whole wide world we traverse with our thought,
And nothing find to man more dear than self.
Since aye so dear the self to others is
Let the self-lover harm no other being.
                    Samyutta Nikaya, Vol. I, page 102

After taking refuge in the Buddha, the Dhamma (the Buddha's teachings)
and the Sangha (the community of monks and nuns), a Buddhist
undertakes the first of the five precepts and tries to refrain from
destroying, being the cause of destruction or sanctioning the destruction
of a sentient being, since the most precious thing for a being is its own life.
The *Dhammapada* says: 'Everyone fears violence, everyone likes life.
Comparing oneself with others, one should never slay or cause to slay.'
(verse 130).

The Highest Wealth

111.

What here is the best wealth a man can have?
What well-performed things bring happiness along?
What in good sooth is of all tastes most sweet?
How do they say that our life can best be lived?

Faith here is the best wealth a man can have,

Right deeds well done bring happiness along.
Truth in good sooth is of all tastes most sweet,
Life lived by wisdom, it is said, is best.

Samyutta Nikaya, Vol. I, page 59

Rational faith in the Buddha, in his teachings, and in his worthy disciples is considered the highest wealth we can possess. But it should be kept in mind that blind faith in the Buddha, in his teachings, and in his disciples is not encouraged. Truthfulness is considered the sweetest of all things, since the speaker of truth will never suffer mental conflicts and irritations. We are wise, we have the knowledge to differentiate between honesty and deception, compassion and cruelty, self and non-self. It is this psychological strength that enables us to lead a life beneficial to ourselves as well as others.

Blessings

112.

Thus have I heard:
    The Blessed One was once living at the monastery of Anathapinidika in Jeta's grove, near Savatthi. Now when the night was far advanced, a certain deity, whose surpassing splendour illuminated the entire Jeta Grove, came into the presence of the Blessed One and, drawing near, respectfully saluted him and stood on one side. Standing thus, he addressed the Blessed One in verse:

    'Many deities and men, yearning after happiness, have pondered on blessings. Pray tell me the highest blessing.'
    'Not to associate with fools, to associate with the wise and to honour those who are worthy of honour – this is the highest blessing.
    'To reside in a suitable locality, to have done meritorious actions in the past, and to set oneself in the right course – this is the highest blessing.
    'Vast learning, [skill in] handicraft, a highly trained discipline and pleasant speech – this is the highest blessing.
    'Supporting one's father and mother, cherishing wife and children, and peaceful occupation – this is the highest blessing.
    'Liberality, righteous conduct, the helping of relatives, and blameless actions – this is the highest blessing.
    'To cease and abstain from evil, abstention from intoxicating drinks, and diligence in virtue – this is the highest blessing.
    'Reverence, humility, contentment, gratitude, and the opportune hearing of the Dhamma – this is the highest blessing.
    'Patience, obedience, seeing the samanas [holy men] and [taking part in] religious discussion at proper times – this is the highest blessing.

'*Self-control, holy life, perception of the noble truths, and the
realisation of nibbana – this is the highest blessing.*

'*If a man's mind is sorrowless, stainless and secure, and does not
shake when touched by worldly vicissitudes – this is the highest blessing.*

'*Those who act thus are everywhere unconquered, attain happiness
everywhere – to them these are the highest blessings.*'

Sutta Nipata, Vol. II, verse 4

Over the centuries certain discourses of the Buddha assumed a place of
special importance as they were considered to possess psychic and
spiritual powers of their own. The Mangala Sutta or the Discourse on
Blessings is one such discourse and many devout Buddhists recite it daily
to protect themselves from misfortune.

Universal Love

113.

*He who is skilled in good and who wishes to attain that state of calm
should act [thus]:*

*He should be able, upright, perfectly upright, compliant, gentle and
humble.*

*Contented, easily supported, with few duties, of simple livelihood,
controlled in senses, discreet, not impudent, he should not be greedily
attached to families.*

*He should not commit any slight wrong such that otherwise men might
censure him.*

[Then he should cultivate his thoughts thus:]

May all beings be happy and secure, may their minds be contented.

*Whatever living beings there may be, feeble or strong, long or tall,
stout or medium, short, small or large, seen or unseen, those dwelling far
or near, those who are born, those who are yet to be born. May all beings
without exception be happy-minded.*

*Let no one deceive another or despise any person whatever in any
place. In anger or ill will do not let one wish any harm to another.*

*Just as a mother would protect her only child even at the risk of her
own life, so let one cultivate a boundless heart towards all beings.*

*Let one's thoughts of boundless love pervade the whole world, above,
below and across, without any obstruction, without any hatred, without
any enmity.*

*Whether one stands, walks, sits or lies down, as long as one is awake
one should maintain this mindfulness. This, they say, is the sublime
state in this life.*

Not falling into wrong views, virtuous and endowed with insight, one gives up attachment to sense-desires. Verily such a man does not return to enter a womb again.

Sutta Nipata, Vol. I, verse 8

This famous Discourse on Loving Kindness (Karaniyamettasutta) expresses the very core of the Buddha's teachings and outlines the Buddhist way of life. In many Buddhist homes both the young and the old recite these verses almost daily, especially before retiring to sleep as a sort of spiritual night-cap. This discourse is also used for meditative reflection to develop mindfulness and wisdom.

The Parable of the Raft

114.

'*O bhikkhus, a man is on a journey. He comes to a vast stretch of water... He says to himself,*

'*"This sea of water is vast and the shore on this side is full of danger, but on the other shore it is safe and without danger. No boat goes to the other side, nor is there a bridge for crossing over. It would be good, therefore, if I were to gather grass, wood, branches and leaves to make a raft..."*

'*Then that man, O bhikkhus, gathers grass, wood, branches and leaves and makes a raft and with the help of that raft crosses over safely to the other side, exerting himself with his hands and feet. Having crossed over and got to the other side, he thinks,*

'*"This raft was of great help to me. With its aid I have crossed safely over to this side... It would be good if I were to carry this raft on my head or on my back wherever I go."*

'*What do you think, O bhikkhus, if he acted in this way. Would that man be acting properly with regard to the raft?'*

'*No, sir.'*

'*In what way would he be acting properly with regard to the raft? Having crossed and gone over to the other side, suppose that man should think, "This raft was a great help to me... It would be good if I beached this raft on the shore or moored it afloat and then went on my way wherever it may be."*

'*Acting in this way, would that man act properly with regard to the raft?*

'*In the same manner, O bhikkhus, I have taught a doctrine similar to a raft – it is for crossing over and not for carrying. You, O bhikkhus, who understand that the teaching is similar to a raft, should give up even good things, how much more, then, should you give up evil things?'*

Majjhima Nikaya, Vol. I, pages 134–5

This beautiful parable clearly illustrates how the Buddha's teachings are not intended to carry selected human beings to the 'safety' of peace, happiness and nibbana. They should be made available to others so that they, too, can cross the vast ocean of samsara (the cycles of birth and death).

Kisagotami and the Mustard Seed

115.

A woman dove-eyed, young, with tearful face
And lifted hands, saluted, bending low:
'Lord, thou art he who yesterday
Had pity on me in the fig-grove here,
Where I lived alone and reared my child; but he
Straying amid the blossoms found a snake,
Which twined about his wrist, whilst he did laugh
And tease the quick-forked tongue and open mouth
Of that cold playmate. But, alas!, ere long
He turned so pale and still, I could not think
Why he should cease to play and let my breast
Fall from his lips. And one said, "He is sick
Of poison," and another, "He will die."
But I, who could not lose my precious boy,
Prayed of them physic, which might bring the light
Back to his eyes; it was so very small,
That kiss-mark of the serpent, and I think
It could not hate him, gracious as he was,
Nor hurt him in his sport. And someone said,
"There is a holy man upon the hill –
Lo! Now he passeth in the yellow robe –
Ask of the rishi if there be a cure
For that which ails thy son." Whereupon I came
Trembling to thee, whose brow is like a god's,
And wept and drew the face cloth from my babe,
Praying thee tell what simples might be good.
And thou, great sir, did spurn me not, but gaze
With gentle eyes and touch with patient hand;
Then drew the face cloth back, saying to me,
"Yea, little sister, there is that might heal
Thee first and him, if thou couldst fetch the thing:
For they who seek physicians bring to them
What is ordained. Therefore, I must pray thee, find
Black mustard seed, a tola; only mark thou,

Take it not from any hand or house
Where a father, mother, child or slave hath died;
It shall be well if one can find such seed."
Thus didst thou speak, my Lord.'
   The Master smiled,
Exceedingly tenderly. 'Yea, I spoke thus,
Dear Kisagotami. But didst thou find
The seed?'
   'I went, Lord, clasping to my breast
The babe grown colder, asking at each hut –
Here in the jungle and towards the town –
"I pray you, give me mustard, of your grace,
A tola – black", and each who had it gave,
For all the poor are piteous to the poor;
But when I asked, "In my friend's household here
Hath any, peradventure, ever died –
Husband or wife or child or slave?" they said,
"O Sister, what is this you ask? The dead
Are very many, and the living few!"
So with sad thanks I gave the mustard seed back,
And prayed of others, but the others said,
"Here is the seed, but we have lost our slave!"
"Here is the seed, but our good man is dead!"
"Here is some, but he that sowed it died
Between the rain time and the harvesting!"
Ah, sir! I could not find a single house
Where there was mustard seed and none had died!
Ah, sir! I could not find a single house,
Therefore I left my child who would not suck
Nor smile beneath the wild vines by the stream,
To seek thy face and kiss thy feet, and pray
Where I might find this seed and find no death,
If now indeed my baby be not dead,
As I do fear, and as they said to me.'
'My Sister! Thou has found,' the master said,
'Searching for what none finds – that bitter balm
I had to give thee. He thou lovest slept
Dead on thy bosom yesterday: today
Thou knowest the whole world weeps with thy woe:
The grief which all hearts share grows less for one.
Lo! I would pour my blood if it could stay
Thy tears and win the secret of that curse
Which makes sweet love our anguish and which drives
O'er flowers and pastures to the sacrifice –
As these dumb beasts are driven; men their lords.
I seek that secret; bury thou thy child.'

                   The Light of Asia, **pages 81-3**

The story of Kisagotami is one of the most deeply moving episodes in the life of Buddha and is a lesson to all humanity. It is a story heard in all Buddhist lands and often beyond. Here it is related by Sir Edwin Arnold in his epic *The Light of Asia*.

II MAHAYANA

3 India

Compiled with commentary by Stephen Hodge

Though many of its ideas no doubt date from the very beginnings of Buddhism, Mahayana probably arose as a consciously distinct school during the last century BCE and went from strength to strength until the last days of Buddhism in India, as well as spreading throughout much of North and East Asia. The reasons for its emergence are complex, but seem to have been primarily a restatement of the basic aims of Buddhism in reaction to the increasing stagnation of Buddhist thought and practice at that time. In contrast to the earliest times, Buddhism had become side-tracked into a sterile intellectualism in monastic enclaves.

During most of the thousand years of its existence in India, Mahayana continued to be innovative and did not hesitate to introduce new and controversial ideas. One product of this process is the vast amount of scriptural writings. (It is generally accepted that writing was only coming into significant use shortly before the appearance of Mahayana sutras in the first century BCE.) One of the first things we notice about these texts is their literary style. In contrast to the simple, almost prosaic dialogues of the scriptures which preceded them, the Mahayana sutras are often highly polished works of art which present us with dramas on a cosmic scale. Moreover, they are frequently of great length, and some of them are known to have undergone a number of revisions, further adding to their length. Though this book introduces a good selection of these texts, it must be remembered that they are only a fraction of the total, which runs to many hundreds. Although the majority of the Mahayana sutras (as literary works) are now dated by many scholars to the period between the first and sixth centuries CE, the traditional criterion for canonical acceptance maintained that whatever is well spoken (true and apposite) was spoken by the Buddha. So if a text upheld a certain number of basic principles such as impermanence and the absence of self in all phenomena, then in principle there was no reason to reject its claims to be Buddhist. Furthermore, detailed study shows that many Mahayana doctrines have their roots in the pre-Mahayana schools of Buddhism. Hence all Mahayana sutras may be considered as authentic, although some sail fairly close to the wind of heresy. It seems that as various ideas, which had probably existed as oral traditions for centuries, became of special interest, a selection of sutras was produced to expound and elaborate them.

The reader should note that there are specific groups of texts associated with the various viewpoints that arose within Mahayana, though it is quite beyond the scope of this book to give a full account of them. Though all Mahayana sutras deal to a greater or lesser extent with such key themes as the bodhisattva path, nothingness (shunyata) and the perfection of insight (prajna paramita), we find a wide range of scriptures catering for all shades of opinion from popular faith and devotion to abstruse philosophy. Through this process of continuous revelation, Mahayana Buddhism was largely able to avoid the stagnation and lack of relevance to changing social conditions that have beset many other religious movements.

I present a selection here of passages from a few of the most important scriptures which have been influential in all Mahayana countries over the centuries, arranged in approximate chronological order (100 BCE–600 CE).

The Doctrine of Nothingness

116.

It is better to believe in the reality of a self as great as Mount Sumeru than to cling stubbornly to a belief in nothingness. Why is that? If it is nothingness that frees you from all opinions, what then can free you from attachment to nothingness?

Kashyapa-parivarta

The doctrine of nothingness (shunyata) forms a key element of all Mahayana sutras. Though it was re-interpreted by various schools within Mahayana, this doctrine basically implies that all methods of analysing and describing phenomena are merely conventional and do not ultimately refer to anything real. It was therefore taught as an antidote to the mistaken belief that 'the map is the territory'. However, it seems that certain people merely replaced one set of mistaken beliefs with another that was far more pernicious, and came to believe that nothingness itself was somehow real. But even the doctrine of nothingness is only skilful means (upaya), to be abandoned in its turn like a raft when one has crossed the river.

Generating Insight

117.

When two pieces of wood are rubbed together by the wind, fire is produced and this fire then consumes the wood. In the same way, the faculty of insight is generated in dependence upon thorough investigation. Then when it has been generated, even that thorough investigation is burnt up.

Kashyapa-parivarta

Insight is produced by a detailed investigation into the true nature of phenomena. Though this process of investigation naturally involves an observer and an observed, this is eventually transcended by the resultant insight which is free from all duality. Hence, even the means that produces enlightenment must be abandoned.

In Search of the Mind

118.

> *The mind cannot be found even after a thorough search. What cannot be found has no objective basis. That which has no objective basis is not past, present or future. What is not past, present or future lacks any inherent existence. What lacks any inherent existence does not have any origin. What does not have any point of origin has no cessation.*
>
> *Kashyapa-parivarta*

Although we may find it easier to accept the idea that all external phenomena lack autonomous existence and are nothing in themselves, it is far harder for us to realise that even our subjective minds also lack any real existence. One of the ways in which this belief is eradicated is through an exhaustive search for the mind, that is, for the perceiving subject. But even after such a search, we find that we cannot pinpoint or locate the mind. Essentially, it is also a conventional way of speaking, which derives from the dualistic split we have imposed upon reality.

The Bodhisattva Commitment to Benefit Others

119.

> *Anyone who strives to benefit just himself and abandons the welfare of others, may gain all material things but he will never achieve the ultimate purpose of life.*
>
> *Ratnakuta Sutra*

This states in a concise form one of the most important Mahayana doctrines – the fact that true progress on the religious path also involves working for the benefit of others, both materially and spiritually. This viewpoint is especially stressed in Mahayana sutras to counteract escapist tendencies that may arise. Indeed, the ideal for Mahayana practice is to be 'in the world but not of it', for the bodhisattva vows to forgo his or her own final liberation and remain in the world until all other beings have been liberated.

Training for Samadhi, the Holistic State

120.

*How are you to enter into the holistic state (samadhi) wherein the
Buddha comes directly into your presence? If you wish to enter into this
holistic state, you should always turn your thoughts to the Buddha and
strive without over-excitedness or slackness. You should cultivate
insight, engage in the good, and be ever diligent. You should avoid evil
companions, but associate with the good. You should train yourself to
consider all phenomena to be empty, and cut off all lethargy and
apathy. Avoid getting involved in useless gossip, and control the
involvement of your senses in physical objects. You should eat
moderately, not go to bed early in the evening or rise late in the morning.
Do not be attached to your clothes, food, seat, bedding, medicine or the
various things around you. It is preferable for you to live in the woods,
away from settlements. You should cease to cosset your body and think
that you alone are special, nor should you have any attachments to
particular people or places, just because these are your relatives or your
birthplace.*

Pratyutpanna-samadhi Sutra

In this sutra, which belongs to the earliest phase of Mahayana, we find
practical advice for those who have entered the spiritual life. Samadhi is a
state in which the mind is fixed one-pointedly upon its object, where
duality is eventually overcome and the two become identical. In order to
achieve this state, it is first necessary to simplify one's life to remove
distractions. But here, as in Buddhism generally, the key word is
moderation. The extremes of hedonism and asceticism are both to be
avoided.

Beholding Amitabha

121.

*When you wake up, you vividly remember the things you dreamt in your
sleep, and you may tell others about them as though you were actually
seeing these things again and feel joy or sorrow in them once more. In the
same way, if a monk or a house-holder sits straight and calms his
thoughts and constantly imagines the Buddha Amitabha's western
realm and also Amitabha Himself teaching the Dharma for the space of
a single day and night up to a whole week, eventually he will behold
vividly the Buddha Amitabha. If he does not directly encounter the*

Buddha during his waking hours, then he will definitely do so during his
sleep.

                                                    Pratyutpanna-samadhi Sutra

Through constant devotion and the use of creative imagination, you can
even transform your waking experience of the world so that it becomes
the paradisical Pure Land. The function of the mind has always been
central to Buddhist teachings, for it is the focal point for both liberation
and bondage, and so many techniques were developed to re-fashion the
mind and its outlook. Furthermore, the kind of meditational practice
mentioned here became especially important in the tantras later, as will be
seen from other sections in this book.

The Insubstantiality of the World

122.

Once upon a time, there was a traveller who was lost in a desolate place.
Tormented by hunger and thirst, he collapsed and fainted. In his dreams
he imagined he had obtained various kinds of delicious food and feasted
upon this until his hunger was satisfied. Yet when he awoke, he was still
as hungry and thirsty as ever. Due to this, he realised that all things in
the world are empty like dreams and thenceforth he tirelessly sought out
the true awakening of his mind.

                                                    Pratyutpanna-samadhi Sutra

Mahayana Buddhist teachings are full of stories and similes to show us the
insubstantiality of the world, as in this example. However, there is an
important point to be understood here regarding the nature of the world
as we normally perceive it. Buddhism is sometimes thought to teach that
'everything is an illusion''. It does not. What it actually teaches is that
'everything is *like* an illusion', which is quite different. Dreams and
illusions are given as models for us to understand how we construct or
superimpose a false picture upon reality due to our basic misunderstanding of the true nature of things.

Even Enlightenment is like an Illusion

123.

Subhuti said, 'Even the enlightenment of a Buddha is like an illusion,
like a dream!' The gods said, 'Subhuti! Is even nirvana like an illusion,
like a dream?' Subhuti answered, 'Even nirvana is like an illusion, like

*a dream. Were there anything more distinguished than nirvana, then I
would say that it too is like an illusion, like a dream!'*

Prajna Paramita Sutra in 8000 verses

It is bad enough to be told that the everyday world as we experience it,
together with our expectations and beliefs about it, is like a dream or an
illusion, but even more shocking to hear that enlightenment and nirvana,
the cherished aims of Buddhists, are also thus. Yet the intention here is to
prevent us from falling into the trap of imagining we think and talk about
enlightenment because, by definition, it lies beyond all dualistic activities.
It is all too easy for us to believe we understand something if we can talk
about it, but unfortunately we often mistake the words for the reality!

Faith and Insight

124.

*We know that when someone carries water in an unfired pot, the pot will
quickly break because it is unfit to hold water. But when water is carried
in a fired pot, there is no fear that the pot will break on the way, and you
can carry it safely home. Although a bodhisattva may have much faith,
he is soon destroyed if he lacks insight. But when he is upheld by both
faith and insight, he will transcend the two levels and attain supreme
enlightenment.*

Ratna-guna-samcaya, verse 287

The importance of insight has always been stressed in Buddhism from the
earliest days. Without insight can there be enlightenment? The general
answer would seem to be no. Yet the role of faith is not denied, for this too
is necessary. However, when Buddhist scriptures talk of 'faith', it does not
convey quite the same meaning as in Christianity for example. Buddhist
faith is said to be a calm state of mind akin to trust which serves as the
basis for the development of insight. In principle, there is nothing taught
in Buddhism which you cannot experience and verify for yourself – faith
merely provides the motivation for the acquisition of insight.

Without Inherent Existence

125.

*O Subhuti, You should know that all phenomena [dharmas] are without
inherent existence. Even the six perfections are without inherent*

*existence. Neither the observer nor the observed can be found. They
cannot be taken as real, nor can they be seen. However, this Teaching
should not be mentioned to those who have newly entered the Way, nor
in the presence of shravakas [heroes/disciples] and pratyekabuddhas
[solitary Buddhas]. Why is that? Because they may reject this
perfection of insight, saying it terrifies them and makes their hair stand
on end.*

Prajna Paramita Sutra in 8000 verses

The early Mahayana sutras constantly pound in the idea that our world
view is a mental construction superimposed upon and completely
concealing reality. Everything we believe in is brought into question, even
our religious practices such as the six perfections (generosity, morality,
strenuousness, patience, meditation and insight). Yet so powerful is this
doctrine, it must be taught with care for there are many who, in their
ignorance, will confuse it with nihilism and shun it. The sword of insight
must be used with compassion.

Those People Do Not See Me

126.

*They who see me as a physical body,
And who follow me by my voice,
Are devoted to perverse efforts:
Those people do not see me!*

Vajracchedika Prajna Paramita Sutra

Look at the contents not the container!

The Spell of Ignorance

127.

*Magicians conjure up various forms
Of horses, elephants and chariots.
Though they appear as such,
They do not really exist:
Understand all phenomena to be thus.*

Samadhi-raja Sutra

As we have already seen, the illusory creations of magic are often taken as a simile for the way we create and experience the world. Indian magicians were thought to take a piece of wood or stone and caused the spectator to see it as a horse or elephant by the use of spells or drugs. In the same way, under the spell of ignorance (avidya), we are duped by a false image that is thus projected upon reality. Note that in both cases there is *something* underlying the illusion; it is just that it is not what it seems to be.

Manifested Reality

128.

Do not distress yourself, Ananda! Do not lament, Ananda! In later times I shall manifest myself a spiritual friend and act for the benefit of you and others!

Mahabheri Sutra

A common idea in Mahayana scriptures is that Shakyamuni, the historical Buddha, was manifested from a deeper level of reality (the Dharmakaya) in order to teach and guide beings to enlightenment. At the same time, it is said that this manifestation was not a once-only event, but is happening continuously. Indeed, many sutras state that all teachers, whoever or whatever they are, are similar manifestations and as such may be seen as embodiments of enlightenment.

The Pure and Luminous Mind

129.

Nobly born ones! The natural state of the mind is intrinsically luminous, intrinsically devoid of inherent existence.

Nirvana Sutra

As we have already mentioned, the status and function of the mind was always a central concern of Buddhism, and this was of particular interest to the Yogacara and the Tathagata-garbha schools of Mahayana. This passage states the basic position of Buddhism regarding the mind. In its natural state it is pure and luminous. It is unaffected and unconnected with all obscuring defilements, which are said to be like the clouds that hide the sun. Consequently, Buddhism has an optimistic view of human nature, due to the presence of this intrinsically pure mind in all beings. At the same time, the mind cannot be objectified as a thing, for reasons already given (see no. 118 above). What we normally call the 'mind' is only one part of the true nature of mind which is the indivisible unity of that 'mind' and its external objects.

The Graded Path

130.

You should study and apply my profound teachings in sequence, like a flight of stairs. Just as children grow up in stages, so also this teaching from the beginner's level up to complete perfection.

Nirvana Sutra

The Buddhist path is carefully graded according to the ability and interests of the devotee. There are simple teachings and there are difficult teachings. But if we are at a higher level, we are not to sneer at or dismiss the beliefs and practices of those below us. In any case, there will always be somebody at a higher level than ourselves. Mature Mahayana regards all teachings within Buddhism, and many of those without, as being worthy of respect. After all, a flight of stairs is not much use if all the lower steps are removed.

The Wrestler and the Diamond

131.

There was a champion wrestler, and upon his forehead he wore a diamond. While wrestling with another champion, he was struck by the other's head, and though the jewel on his forehead had become embedded in his flesh, he was not aware of this. As he was wounded a doctor was called in to heal him, but the doctor did not apply salves to the wound because of the presence of the jewel within it.

The doctor said to the wrestler, 'O mighty one, where is the jewel from your forehead?'

[Finding it missing], the wrestler became angry and replied, 'The jewel on my forehead should still be there, but as it is not there, I think you must have tricked me and I am very annoyed about this.'

Then the doctor said, 'Don't worry and fret! When you were wrestling, the jewel became embedded in your flesh and now only its shape shows on the surface. While you were wrestling, you were excited and did not feel it enter your flesh.'

But even then the wrestler did not believe the doctor and he said, 'Don't tell me lies! If it has become embedded in my flesh as you say, how could its shape be visible for the wound is dirty with pus and blood?'

So the doctor took out a mirror and held it up for the wrestler, who then to his surprise saw it glinting there in the wound.

All beings are also like that. Since they do not trust spiritual friends, they are unable to see they have the nature of Buddhas. They are deluded and oppressed by attachment, hatred, and stupidity, so they wander lost and tormented through the many states of existence.

Nirvana Sutra

This is one of the many examples given in Mahayana sutras to illustrate the unknown presence of the Buddha-nature, the potentiality for enlightenment, known as Tathagata-garbha. Although it lies within us, tragically we are unable to perceive it. Yet if it were not there, there would be no possibility for enlightenment at all.

The Bitter Bile of Nothingness

132.

There was a suckling child who became ill. His mother was tormented with anxiety and so sought out a doctor for help. After having mixed the medicine with butter, milk and honey and measured it out for the child, the doctor said to the mother, 'I have given your child some medicine, but you should not breastfeed him for a while, until he digests it.'

So the woman smeared bitter bile upon her nipples so that the child would not suck, and said to the child, 'I have put poison on my nipples so you must not suck them!' Even though that child of hers felt tormented by thirst and wanted to suckle, he was unable to do so for he could not bear the bitter taste.

After the medicine had been digested, the mother washed her breasts and called the child to suck, but he would not come despite his thirst. So his mother explained that she had smeared bile on her nipples to prevent him from suckling while he was digesting the medicine and said, 'Now you have digested the medicine, I have washed the bile off, so there is no bitterness now.'

Likewise in order to save all beings, the Buddha also teaches non-self. When they have earnestly practised that and have freed themselves from the idea of a self, they are able to achieve nirvana. Just as the mother smeared bile on her nipples for the sake of her child, so also does the Buddha say that all phenomena (dharmas) are without self for beings to cultivate nothingness (shunyata) in order to clear away evil

*materialistic views. Just as the mother later cleaned her breasts and
suckled the child, so also does the Buddha now teach Tathagata-garbha
to beings.*

Nirvana Sutra

The notion of a 'self' has always been anathema to Buddhists. In this
parable, the Buddha explains the reason why he denied the existence of a
'self' or autonomous existence in phenomena – it was as a remedy against
a specific view of the world. When the medicine has done its work, he can
teach the existence of an inherent Tathagata-garbha (Buddha-nature
potentiality). But so strong an aversion did his listeners have to anything
that even resembled a 'self', they also rejected this Buddha-nature or
Tathagata potentiality.

The Potential Buddha-nature

133.

*If there were no Tathagata potentiality, there would be neither aversion
towards suffering nor longing for nirvana. Why? The seven kinds of
consciousness are momentary and unabiding, and so cannot retain the
experience of suffering. Therefore they are unable to be averse to
suffering or long for nirvana.*

Sutra of the Goddess Shrimala

*The existence of something like the Tathagata potentiality is necessary as
the ultimate basis for our moral actions and experiences. Without this
potentiality or Buddha-nature, we would be unable to strive for
enlightenment and nirvana. We can only seek the good if we already have
some affinity with it.*

The Receptacle of All Actions

134.

*The receptacle consciousness is profound and subtle;
like a raging current, it carries along all seeds.
Yet I have not taught this to the foolish,
for fear that they may imagine it is a self.*

Sandhi-nirmocana Sutra

With the passage of time, certain difficulties were encountered with Mahayana regarding the nature of the mind. These particularly concerned the question of rebirth and the continuity of karmic impressions. Sutras connected with the Yogacara school taught the existence of a substratum consciousness underlying the sensory awarenesses and the ideational processes. This consciousness was thought to be like a receptacle into which the impressions (seeds) of karmic actions are implanted, awaiting a suitable time for their fruition in the future. However, like the Tathagata-garbha (Buddha-nature potentiality), there is a danger that some people will mistake this consciousness for a kind of 'self'.

The Obscured, but Unsullied Buddha-nature

135.

Though ignorant beings imagine the moon to wax and wane, it does not actually do so, but just appears thus continent by continent. Likewise though ignorant beings imagine the substratum consciousness to grow and decrease, it is actually unsullied Buddhahood. When one transforms the substratum of all phenomena which has been made turbid by the bloating dispositions and false concepts, it is unsullied. If its natural unsullied state is reached, they become unchanging and stable.

Ghanavyuha Sutra

We have already read about the Tathagata-garbha (Buddha-nature potentiality) and the substratum consciousness, which were originally quite distinct theories. But in scriptures such as the *Ghanavyuha* which emerged during the late phase of Mahayana, the attributes of the Tathagata potentiality were merged with those of the substratum consciousness. Now the substratum consciousness is viewed as the inherent enlightenment of Buddha-nature which has merely been obscured by our basic misunderstanding and the predispositions which it gives rise to. When we are involved in samsara (the cycle of births and deaths), this consciousness seems to be affected by the amount of impurity it is encumbered with, but in fact it is unchanging and unaffected in itself. This point of view was taken up by the tantras, as will be seen in the section dealing with the Japanese Shingon tradition.

4   Tibet

Compiled with commentary by James Belither

Buddhism was introduced into Tibet in the seventh century and
became firmly established over the next hundred years, principally
through the efforts of the great Indian teachers, Shantarakshita and
Padmasambhava. The latter is particularly revered by Tibetans, and is
known as Guru Rinpoche or 'Precious Teacher'. In the ninth century
Buddhism was suppressed by the Tibetan king Langdarma; many
monks were killed and monasteries destroyed. In the following
century, Buddhism revived rapidly to become the predominant
religion of Tibet, although Bon, the indigenous religion, was and still is
practised in Tibet.

The key figures in the restoration of Buddhism at this time included
Rinchen Zangpo, Atisha, Drogmi and Marpa. Atisha and his disciples,
notably Dromtonpa, founded the Kadam tradition, Marpa founded
the Kagyu tradition and Drogmi's disciples founded the Sakya
tradition. In the fourteenth century Je Tsongkhapa founded the
tradition known as the New Kadam or Gelug, basing his approach
mainly on that of Atisha but incorporating teachings from the other
traditions. These later traditions are known as Sarma (or 'New')
traditions, whereas the tradition based on the earlier translations of the
Buddha's teachings, made before Langdarma's persecution, is known
as Nyingma (or 'Old').

To help people discover and develop their own potentialities, the
Buddha taught many ways of practice suited to individuals' differing
needs. Although there are now four main traditions of Tibetan
Buddhism (Nyingma, Sakya, Kagyu and Gelug) which transmit the
different lineages of Buddhist practice inherited from India and which
differ slightly in their approach to the Buddha's teachings, all are
respected equally since each encapsulates the essence of Buddhism.

The sequence of these readings loosely follows that of the 'stages of
the path' or *lamrim* in Tibetan. The prototype lamrim text was written
by Atisha, and this influenced later writings in all Tibetan traditions.
Je Tsongkhapa and his successors in particular enriched the lamrim
tradition and this forms the backbone of study and practice in the
Gelug tradition.

The lamrim refers to a graduated sequence of meditation practices for training the mind on the path of enlightenment. Atisha's genius was to reconcile the apparent contradictions between Buddha's teachings, for instance between sutra and tantra, by showing how all Buddha's teachings are necessary at certain stages of an individual's growth. The basic motivation of all beings is to gain happiness. At first desire for happiness is limited to this life, but with a deep recognition of rebirth and the operation of cause and effect (karma), our motivation grows to wishing for happiness in future lives also. With a deeper understanding of the fundamental causes of suffering and happiness – delusions and deluded actions – the practitioner's motivation grows to seeking to remove these underlying causes and thus attain liberation from all possibility of future suffering. Up to this point the practitioner is following the Hinayana ('small vehicle') path, 'small' because the practitioner's motivation is principally for self-liberation. However, in his Mahayana ('great vehicle') teachings, the Buddha encouraged his followers to work not just for self-liberation but to attain the fully perfected qualities of a Buddha, in order to help guide the greatest number of beings to enlightenment. Just as we cannot honestly help others if we are unable to help ourselves, we need to follow the Hinayana path before we can truly enter the Mahayana.

The principal feature of Mahayana is compassion, since this is what motivates the practitioner at this stage to continue on the spiritual path. In his tantric teachings the Buddha taught methods which, if practised correctly, can lead the practitioner to enlightenment very quickly. Out of the deepest compassion, wishing to attain enlightenment quickly in order to help all beings more immediately, the Mahayana practitioner enters the tantric or vajrayana path. Tantra is the post-sutra vehicle of Buddhism capable of leading the practitioner to full enlightenment within one lifetime.

By incorporating the essential teachings of Hinayana and Mahayana, including tantra, in this way, Atisha laid down a basic approach to spiritual practice which has been followed by most Tibetan Buddhists ever since.

I have attempted to select these readings from sources recognised and respected by all traditions of Tibetan Buddhism, for instance, those of the great Indian masters, such as Shantideva. Because my teachers are from the Gelug tradition, I chose a lamrim outline in order to present the teachings in a coherent sequence and also included many readings from texts written by Je Tsongkhapa and later Gelug masters. This was not out of disrespect for other traditions, but simply reflects my greater familiarity with works of this tradition than with those of any other. Furthermore, a number of readings and commentaries have been extracted from *Joyful Path of Good Fortune,* a commentary to stages of the path by Geshe Kelsang Gyatso.

My choice has tried to reflect the differing ways Buddhadharma was presented in Tibet, with selections from philosophical texts, oral teachings, spiritual poems, biographies and letters of personal advice. Many of the great writings of Tibetan Buddhism are written in poetic verse to aid memorisation. Even today, songs of the twelfth-century poet-saint Milarepa are chanted and sung in Tibetan homes as people go about their domestic duties. Buddhism permeated every aspect of Tibetan life and until the Chinese invasion in 1959 was a dynamic, living spiritual tradition. Since the Chinese invasion, Buddhism has suffered tremendous persecution. However, many Tibetans escaped with HH the Dalai Lama, to refound monasteries and centres first in India and later in many countries throughout the world.

Through the efforts of the great masters of the four traditions, it is hoped that the teachings of the Buddha, transmitted through the lineages of realised Indian and Tibetan masters, will continue to enrich the spiritual life of the world, helping to bring greater peace and well-being in these troubled times.

Praise to Shakyamuni Buddha, the Source of All Teachings

136.

I bow to him who attained Buddhahood,
peaceful, without beginning, middle or end;
and who from his realisation taught the path,
fearless and firm, to enlighten the unawakened;
and who holds the supreme sword of wisdom
and who wields the thunderbolt of compassion,
cutting through all the weeds of suffering,
smashing the great barrier of perplexity,
buried deep in the jungle of various views.

> Maitreya Asanga, *Analysis of the Jewel Matrix*

Just as a river can be traced back to its source, all Tibetan Buddhist teachings and practices find their source in the sutras and tantras of Shakyamuni Buddha who was born in northern India 2500 years ago. According to the Mahayana Buddhism of Tibet he was already fully enlightened and appeared with the sole purpose of guiding beings on the path to liberation from suffering and the attainment of Buddhahood. His life in itself provides inspiration and guidance. Out of his boundless wisdom and compassion he gave teachings that were multi-faceted and which skilfully matched the capacities and inclinations of his followers.

In essence the Buddha's teachings are not conditioned by any one culture or age, and they naturally find different forms of expression suited to each new milieu. Introduced into Tibet in the eighth century, Buddhism gradually came to influence the whole society and its practice permeated every feature of Tibetan life. Even the Tibetan script was developed and adapted specifically to enable the translation of the Sanskrit Buddhist scriptures. In the process of establishing Buddhism, the Tibetan and Indian translators took great pains to ensure that the textual traditions were maintained with the utmost purity. Thus, when Buddhism declined in India, Tibet became the centre of Buddhist learning for much of central Asia.

Praises such as this are often found at the beginning of Indian and Tibetan Buddhist commentaries. This one is taken from a work by the great Indian Buddhist master, Asanga, who wrote under the direct inspiration of Buddha Maitreya. Works written by such masters were highly revered and widely studied in Tibet. Even though there is a vast corpus of commentaries by later Tibetan masters, reference is always made to the Buddha's sutras and tantras and to works by Indian Buddhist masters to show the authenticity of the commentaries.

Relying on a Qualified Spiritual Guide: the Root of the Path

137.

The foundation of all excellence is the kind and venerable guru. By seeing clearly that correct reliance on the guru is the root of the path, may I follow my guru with great devotion and joyful effort.
      Je Tsongkhapa, *The Foundation of All Excellence,* verse 1

A central feature of all traditions of Tibetan Buddhism is the acknowledgement of the vital role played by the spiritual guide or guru (Tib. *lama*) in spiritual development. As the teacher who initially instructs the practitioner in spiritual practice, the guru is considered 'the root of the path', but the guru's role is considered greater than just that of an imparter of knowledge. Since the guru performs the same function as the Buddha he or she is shown the same respect as the Buddha, and in the advanced practices of tantra the guru is viewed as having the form and attributes of the Buddha. With this awareness, the practitioner is able to receive the blessings and inspiration of the Buddha directly through contact with his or her guru. This is essential for successful progress on the spiritual path.

Following and relying upon the guru requires that we first develop greater receptivity to the instructions and example provided by the guru, and put his or her teachings into practice. On a deeper level, becoming closer to the guru, or guru yoga, which is the essence of tantric practice, means attaining the same level of realisation as one's guru, the state of Buddhahood.

Relying on the Spiritual Guide is More Important than Relying on Scriptures

138.

When Atisha arrived in Tibet, his three disciples, Ku, Noke and Drom, asked him, 'To attain the high state of liberation and omniscience, which is more important, to follow the precept of the Lama or to follow the scriptures and commentaries?'

Atisha replied, 'The precept of the Lama is more important than scriptures and commentaries.'

'Why is that?' they asked.

'Even if you know that the primary characteristic of all phenomena is voidness, and can recite the Tripitaka as well, you and the teaching will be completely separate if you do not apply the precept of the Lama at the time of practice.'

Precepts of the Kadampa Masters

In Tibetan Buddhism, great respect is shown to the Tripitaka or Three Baskets (collections) of Buddha's teachings, and to the commentaries by later Indian and Tibetan masters. However, spiritual development is not just a matter of gaining intellectual knowledge. Whatever understanding of the scriptures we acquire must be put into practice. It is only by following the skilful advice of a qualified spiritual guide that we learn to transform our understanding of Buddha's teachings into practical methods for uprooting deluded and confused states of mind, which are the source of all problems, and for gaining clarity and peace of mind. Even though we intellectually understand voidness, or emptiness, the ultimate way in which all phenomena exist – the most profound teaching within Buddhism – we will be unable to utilise this understanding as a method of gaining liberation from suffering or enlightenment without the advice and inspiration of our spiritual guide.

This dialogue between the great Indian master Atisha (who revitalised Buddhism in Tibet in the eleventh century) and three of his main disciples, in itself shows how important the personal guru–disciple relationship was considered in Tibet.

Through Relying on Our Spiritual Guide We Receive the Buddha's Blessings

139.

Although the rays of the sun are hot,
Without a magnifying glass they cannot be used to make a fire.
Even though the blessings of Vajradhara are powerful,
We cannot receive them without our spiritual guide.

Sakya Pandita

Faith and respect in the spiritual guide do not develop automatically. Because following a spiritual guide is so crucial in spiritual terms it is very important to follow one who is qualified, and it may take time for the student to appreciate fully the qualities of a particular spiritual guide. There are a number of meditation practices presented in the Tibetan commentaries which help the student develop greater faith and respect for his or her spiritual guide.

One such method involves contemplation of various points which lead to the conviction that the spiritual guide is a Buddha. In the sutras the Buddha told his followers that in the future he would appear as gurus, abbots and preceptors. In the tantras, Buddha Vajradhara, the form the Buddha took when delivering the tantras, also spoke of appearing for the benefit of beings in future times. Since Buddhas attained enlightenment with the sole intention of benefiting others, it is impossible that they are not helping beings in this age. We have not attained a sufficiently advanced spiritual level to see Buddhas and be benefited by them directly. When we consider who at this present time is the emanation of Buddha Vajradhara who is benefiting us, we conclude that it can be none other than our own spiritual guide, no matter how humble he or she may appear.

By guiding us on the path through teaching, example and inspiration, our spiritual guide is acting in precisely the same way as would Shakyamuni Buddha if he were to appear directly before us. Also when we view our guru as a Buddha, all the Buddhas enter his body and we receive their blessings and inspiration directly through him.

To develop faith and respect in the guru, the practitioner contemplates these and many other points, usually given in oral teachings and backed up by quotations from the sutras and commentaries by Indian and Tibetan masters.

One of the qualities of a qualified guru is being more pleased by the spiritual progress of his students than by receiving material offerings. The guru does not exploit his students but leads them to realise their own potential as human beings, guiding them in the spiritual methods that lead to Buddhahood.

Milarepa's Song of Departure for Tsang

140.

Master Buddha Vajradhara, the Immutable One,
For the first time I go to Tsang as a beggar.
For the first time I go to my home, and as a mere seeker.

By the grace of my father and compassionate lama,
At the summit of Silma Pass in Tsang,
The twelve dakinis of the mountains will come to meet me.

I invoke the Master, the Blessed One.
I put my confidence in the Three Jewels.

My escorts are the dakinis of the three stages of the path.

I go with enlightened attitude as a companion.
Eight armies of gods and their followers will welcome me.
I have nothing to fear from a hostile enemy.

Even so, it is to you I turn,
I beg you to meet and guide me in this life and the next.
Turn all danger away from me.
Protect my body, speech and mind.

Bring about the realisation of my vows.
Initiate me into the power of compassion,
Strengthen me in knowledge of the Tantra and in transmitting it.

Grant me a long life devoid of illness.
You who know the joys and sorrows of this mendicant,
Bless me that I may have the strength
To live in solitude in the mountains.

Rechungpa, *The Life of Milarepa*

Milarepa is one of the most famous of the scholar-saints of Tibetan Buddhism, whose life story is a testament to the importance and way of following the spiritual guide. On the death of his father, Milarepa and his family were dispossessed of their land and property and badly treated by his uncle. Milarepa took revenge by destroying his uncle's house and killing him and many of his family through black magic. Later, overcome with remorse, he turned to Buddhism and became the chief disciple of the great master, Marpa the Translator. As a method of purifying his negative actions, Milarepa was forced to endure tremendous hardship. Milarepa's faith never faltered and through the methods taught to him by Marpa, Milarepa finally attained Buddhahood.

This song, sung by Milarepa to Marpa just before they parted for the last time, expresses the depth of feeling between them. By this time, Milarepa had already attained a high level of spiritual development, but still invoked the assistance and protection of his guru during the difficult years of solitary retreat to which he was committing himself A dakini is a Buddha in female aspect who helps arouse blissful energy in a qualified tantric practitioner.

Milarepa is particularly revered in Tibetan Buddhism for the austerity of his spiritual practice and loved for the beauty of his poetry. Although Marpa and Milarepa are considered lineage gurus of the Kagyu tradition of Tibetan Buddhism (see p. 108) in particular, the songs of Milarepa are part of the literary heritage shared by all Tibetans, and are sung as folksongs and studied as meditation manuals.

The Guru Yoga of Padmasambhava

141.

In the northwest country of Uddiyana
Is the one born on the petal of a stem of a lotus
And endowed with the most marvellous attainments.
Renowned as the Lotus-Born One, Padmasambhava,
And surrounded by a retinue of many dakinis;
I will practise by following you;

Please come forth to grace me with your inspiration
Guru padma siddhi hum.

Nyingma prayer

One of the most important spiritual practices common to all the four major traditions of Tibetan Buddhism (Sakya, Kagyu, Nyingma and Gelug) is guru yoga. This involves the practitioner cultivating awareness of the essential oneness of his or her own guru with all the Buddhas. It includes visualisation practices in which the practitioner focuses on a mentally created image of his or her guru in the form of a particular Buddha or the founder of the tradition. This prayer focuses on Padmasambhava, also known as Guru Rinpoche, the founder of the Nyingma tradition.

This prayer can be interpreted on many different levels of meaning corresponding to the practitioner's level of development. Whilst reciting it, the practitioner recalls the oneness of his or her spiritual guide with Padmasambhava seen as the essence of all Buddhas. In this way, the practitioner opens up a channel to receive the inspiration and blessings from the Buddhas, which is essential to successful development on the spiritual path.

The Guru Yoga of Je Tsongkapa

142.

Avalokiteshvara, great treasure of unobservable compassion,
Manjushri, powerful one with stainless wisdom,
Vajrapani, destroyer of all hosts of demons,
Tsongkhapa, crown ornament of the pandits in the Land of the Snows,
O Losang Dragpa, to you I make requests.

Je Tsongkhapa/Rendawa, *The Migtsema Prayer*

The founder of the Gelug tradition of Tibetan Buddhism was the fourteenth-century enlightened master Je Tsongkhapa, whose personal name was Losang Dragpa. This prayer was originally written by Je Tsongkhapa in praise of Rendawa, who revised it and offered it back to Je Tsongkhapa. One of the guru yoga practices of the Gelug tradition is to recite this prayer while focusing on a visualised form of Tsongkhapa, seen as one with the practitioner's personal guru and all the lineage of gurus going back to Shakyamuni Buddha and embodying the Buddha's universal compassion, wisdom and spiritual power.

The practitioner may recite the prayer sitting in meditation or continuously as he or she goes about daily life. In one of the visualisation practices that accompany the recitation, he or she imagines white, red and blue light and nectar dissolving from Je Tsongkhapa's crown, throat and heart respectively. This purifies the practitioner's body, speech and mind and awakens his or her own latent compassion, wisdom and spiritual power.

'Unobservable compassion' personified as the Buddha Avalokiteshvara, is compassion suffused with the wisdom which understands the true nature of all things (see nos. 218–22).

Vajrapani is the embodiment of spiritual power which sees through delusions, referred to here as the 'hosts of demons'. Delusion is a translation of the Sanskrit word *klesha* which carries the sense of both an obscuration and an affliction. We are afflicted by anger, jealousy, attachment and so on. These afflictions also obscure our perceptions, causing us to engage in harmful emotions and actions.

The Importance of Listening, Contemplating and Meditating

143.

*Now, when we have attained this great ship of leisure and endowment
  so hard to find,*
In order to free ourself and others from the ocean of samsara
*We should listen, contemplate and meditate all day and night
  without distraction.*
This is a practice of the bodhisattvas.
Togme Zangpo, *Thirty-seven Practices of All The Bodhisattvas*, verse 3

In this verse, the thirteenth-century teacher Togme Zangpo speaks of 'this great ship of leisure and endowment', referring to our human body. This human body has all the conditions and endowments necessary to engage in the spiritual path. Now that we have attained this human body and the capacity to free ourselves and others from the ocean of samsara – the uncontrolled cycle of death and rebirth – we need to practise Dharma according to a threefold process. This is taught as the best method of bringing the teachings into our daily life and is the practice of the bodhisattvas – those intent on attaining enlightenment for all beings.

The first step is to listen to the teachings in an open and receptive way. The second is to contemplate their meaning. The third is to meditate. Meditation involves bringing the understanding we have gained through contemplation deeply within us. It is gaining familiarity with a wholesome object to the extent that it begins to transform our attitudes. For example, if we listen to the teachings on impermanence, we can intellectually accept that everything is always changing. Nevertheless, we have the attitude that we are going to last for ever. To overcome this attitude, we contemplate the fact that moment by moment we are coming closer to our death. We then meditate on this awareness until it begins to percolate deep within us, becoming second nature. Instead of viewing ourselves and all things as existing for ever, we come to believe very strongly that everything is impermanent and this changes our behaviour at all levels, stimulating us to use every moment of our life in a worthwhile and meaningful way.

Each topic of the Buddhist teachings is taken in this way. We listen to the instructions and think about them, trying to resolve our doubts and gain a clear understanding. Then we meditate on our understanding single-pointedly to take it deep within us.

The Importance of Study

144.

'Meditate! There is no need to learn by instruction,'
says the shallow-minded fool.
Contemplation without previous instruction
though diligently pursued is the way of the beast.

Sakya Pandita, *Elegant Sayings*

This verse emphasises the importance of receiving instruction. In this way we come to know what we are meditating on, and also how and why. Sitting quietly for a long period of time is not a uniquely human quality. If we are simply 'meditating' without any understanding or direction, then we are merely like a cat able to sit quietly for hours on end. Only when we contemplate and meditate with understanding of what we are doing does that contemplation and meditation become of real value.

The Importance of Reasoning

145.

Monks and scholars should
Analyse my words as one would analyse gold
Through melting, refining and polishing,
And adopt them only then –
Not for the sake of showing me respect.

Shakyamuni Buddha

In Tibetan Buddhism there is a great emphasis not only on study but on logic and reasoning to gain a clear understanding, free from doubts or hesitation, of what the Buddha was saying. Within the Tibetan monasteries, debates were a systematic way of using logic and reasoning to resolve doubts and develop true understanding of the Buddha's teachings.

Logic and reasoning are used as methods of progressing from a wrongly held view or misunderstanding to direct realisation. If, for example, we reject the idea of rebirth, we have, from the Buddhist point of view, a wrong consciousness on this point. As we listen to teachings about rebirth, we may begin to question our previously held views and then gradually develop a doubt which tends toward believing in rebirth. Through contemplating the subject further we may develop what is known as a 'correct assumption' about rebirth but at this stage there is no strength in our belief and we could easily be dissuaded from it. To strengthen the correct assumption we need to analyse, use logic and reasoning, even play devil's advocate by trying to disprove rebirth. In this way we gradually develop an inference, which is an understanding or conviction gained through the power of our own reasoning. Through our meditation on it, this inferential understanding can ripen into a direct realisation of rebirth, at which stage we have gained an indestructible conviction.

There is the same progression with many topics of meditation from wrong consciousness or doubt up to direct realisation. Logic is therefore stressed not as an end in itself but as a means of helping meditation. It is only when we have a crystal-clear conviction about something that we can effectively meditate on it.

Integrating Dharma into Daily Life

146.

> *Whenever you listen [to the Dharma] think about or recite them*
> *[Dharma teachings], undertake these for the sake of liberating your*
> *mind-stream. Whenever you write, read, memorise or teach, do so*
> *desiring only liberation. In your meditation, philosophising and conduct*
> *too, never separate your mind from being set on liberation alone. There*
> *is nothing higher than these essential oral teachings. Eating, sleeping,*
> *walking, sitting, talking, speaking, thinking and so on – in short,*
> *whatever activity you are doing – never let your mind stray from the*
> *wish to liberation.*
>
>   Longchen Rabjampa, *The Four-Themed Precious Garland*

This quote by the Nyingma (see p. 108) master, Longchen Rabjampa, emphasises the importance of putting the teachings we receive into practice. Lamas from all Tibetan traditions teach yogas (meditational practices) of eating, sleeping and so on to transform these everyday activities into the spiritual path.

For example, if we are trying to cultivate thoughts of love and compassion towards others, one way is to contemplate their kindness. Before eating or drinking, we can reflect for a moment on where this food we are about to enjoy has come from. Through realising we are dependent on the kindness of others for our food, we then eat with the motivation of strengthening our body as a means of helping others. This transforms eating into a means of enhancing attitudes of love and kindness.

Integrating Daily Life into Dharma

147.

> *Everything I see and experience is a teacher that teaches me the spiritual*
> *path. The flowing of the water teaches me impermanence . . .*
> *I don't need to have books made up of paper and ink. Everything I see*
> *around me teaches me the Dharma.*
>
>   *The Songs of Milarepa*

In these lines, Milarepa (see no. 140) reminds us that all our experiences should be viewed as teachings about ourselves and about the spiritual path. The profound impact of this view was clearly apparent in Tibet where Buddhism came to permeate every aspect of life, including music, art, drama, architecture.

The Most Profound Teaching in Buddhism

148.

*Milarepa then sent Gambopa on his journey, himself remaining where
he was. When Gambopa had crossed the river and reached a distance
from whence he could hardly hear Jetsun's voice, Milarepa called him
back, saying, 'Who else but you would deserve to receive this most
precious instruction, even though it is of too great a value to be given
away? Now come here and I will impart it to you.'*

In great joy Gambopa asked, 'Should I now offer you a mandala?'

*'No, it is not necessary to offer me one. I only hope that you will
cherish this teaching and never waste it. Now look!' Saying this,
Milarepa pulled up his robe, exposing his naked body covered with
calluses. 'There is no profounder teaching than this. See what hardships
I have undergone. The most profound teaching in Buddhism is to
practise. It has simply been due to this persistent effort that I have
earned the merits and accomplishment. You should also exert yourself
with perseverance in meditation.'*

The Songs of Milarepa

Gambopa was one of the main disciples of Milarepa (see nos. 140, 147).
When he was leaving Milarepa for the last time in that life, he asked
Milarepa for one final teaching to carry in his heart always. He wanted the
most important teaching. Milarepa refused repeatedly, saying he had
given him enough teachings. But then just as they were parting, Milarepa
called Gambopa back and gave this instruction showing his backside
covered in calluses to demonstrate that he had undergone extensive
periods of meditation. In this way, Milarepa emphasised there is nothing
profounder than consistent effort. Meditation on an occasional basis is not
enough. We need to meditate continually. To boil water we need
constantly to apply the heat of the fire. If we apply heat and then turn it
off, the water will never reach boiling point. Similarly, the only way we
can really change our attitudes and make progress is to apply constant
effort in our meditation and spiritual practices.

Importance of Mindfulness in Daily Life

149.

*Examining my continuum in all actions,
As soon as a delusion arises,
Whereby I and others act unwholesomely,*

May I firmly face and avert it.
Geshe Langri Tangpa, *Eight Verses of Training the Mind,* verse 3

All our experiences result from our attitude of mind, so awareness of our attitudes and state of mind is essential. Everything we do or say comes from what we think. If we think or act with a negative mind then suffering will inevitably follow, but if we think or act with a wholesome mind we will definitely create the cause to experience happiness.

Therefore it is essential in daily life that we are aware of what we are doing, saying and thinking so that as soon as a deluded state of mind such as anger, attachment or jealousy arises we can acknowledge it and apply methods taught by Buddha to dispel it. Acknowledging the influence of deluded states of mind in this way is the first step to being able to reduce and then remove them completely.

Prostration

150.

However many Lions of Men there are in the worlds
Of the ten directions and in the three times,
To all of them without exception,
I prostrate with body, speech and mind.
                          Prayer of Auspicious Deeds, verse 1

In Tibetan Buddhism, paying homage to the Buddhas implies 'may I become like you'. Through appreciating the qualities of those to whom we are showing respect, we develop the aspiration also to attain that level. Prostration is not humiliating ourselves in front of enlightened beings but is an acknowledgement that we must give up ordinary limited views in order to awaken our own capacity for enlightenment. All beings with a mind have the potential to awaken that mind to full Buddhahood.

Prostration is the first of the 'seven limbs of practice', preliminaries to meditation, which are necessary to ensure success in meditation. These 'limbs' are ways of opening our minds so we become receptive to the spiritual path and to the particular meditation we are doing. They also increase our positive mental strength or merit and purify our negative states of mind. This process is likened to preparing soil for successful cultivation of the crops of meditation.

In this verse, prostration is made to the 'Lions of Men', an epithet of the Buddhas. The ten directions are the four cardinal and sub-cardinal compass points as well as above and below. The three times are the past, present and future. We prostrate to them all, showing respect and appreciation while generating the aspiration 'May I and all beings attain Buddhahood.'

Prostration of the body may be anything from folding hands to a full-length physical prostration on the ground before the object of respect. Reciting a verse such as this is prostration of the speech. Developing faith and appreciation for the Buddhas and the qualities they represent is prostration of the mind.

Offering

151.

In order to seize that precious mind
I offer now to the Tathagata,
To the sacred Dharma, the stainless Jewel,
And to the bodhisattvas, the oceans of excellence,

Whatever flowers and fruits there are
And whatever kinds of medicine,
Whatever jewels exist in this world,
And whatever clean refreshing waters.

Lakes and pools adorned with lotuses
And the beautiful cry of wild geese,
Everything unowned
Within the limitless spheres of space.

> Shantideva, *Guide to the Bodhisattva's Way of Life,*
> ch. 2, verses 1, 2, 5

Through offering, the second of the seven limbs of practice (see nos. 150–56), we develop great merit as well as receptivity to the objects of respect and practice: the Buddha, the sacred Dharma (Buddha's teachings contained within the Tripitaka or Three Baskets), and the Sangha (the spiritual community including the bodhisattvas, see no. 143). There are many different ways of making offerings. The basic idea is to offer everything that is treasured as a way of expressing appreciation for, and receptivity to, the spiritual path and its guide.

When we recite this verse, written by the famous eighth-century Indian master Shantideva, we imagine making offerings of everything that is beautiful, thus demonstrating that the spiritual path taught by the Buddha is in fact more important than anything in this world that we consider valuable or beautiful.

Confession

152.

U hu lag!
[What have I done!]
O gurus, great holders of the vajra [tantric masters],
All you Buddhas, bodhisattvas and venerable Sanghas who are dwelling
in the ten directions,
I request you, please listen to me. I, whose name is [insert your own
name] have, since beginningless samsara until this present moment,
Committed great wrongs with my body, speech and mind, powered by
the delusions of desirous attachment, hatred and ignorance;
I engaged in the ten non-virtuous actions, the five actions of immediate
retribution and the five actions close to these.
I transgressed the vows of individual liberation, the training of a
bodhisattva and the commitments of secret mantra [tantra];
I showed disrespect to my father and mother, to my abbots and
preceptors, to my friends and those following pure conducts;
I harmed the Three Jewels [Buddha, Dharma, Sangha], abandoned the
holy Dharma, disparaged the superior Sangha and injured sentient
beings.
I committed these and other non-virtuous actions, commanded others to
commit them and rejoiced at their being committed.
In short, I openly confess and declare all these obstacles to my higher
status and liberation, this collection of faults and downfalls which
are the causes of samsara and lower rebirth, and I promise in the
presence of my gurus, the great holders of the vajra, all the Buddhas,
bodhisattvas and venerable Sanghas who are dwelling in the ten
directions, to avoid committing such actions in the future.
By making this confession I will gain happiness, but if I do not this will
not happen.

Ashvaghosa, *The General Confession*

Confession, the third of the seven limbs of practice (see nos. 150–56), is an open declaration of our faults and mistakes. The root of the Tibetan word for 'confession' means 'to cut open'. Just as we cut open a tree to see if it is rotten, the practice of confession involves looking into our own mind to see its state.

Buddhism teaches that every action we perform arises from mental intention and leaves an imprint upon our mind. Unless imprints of negative harmful actions are purified through open declaration, they will inevitably lead to suffering experiences. For example, the more we get angry the easier it becomes. The stronger the negative power of our mind, the more likely it is we will find ourselves in situations of pain and conflict. To prevent such negative experiences we must create stronger positive imprints on our mind which will counteract the negative imprints.

Confession begins with an open declaration that we have committed negative actions, either specific ones we can recall or even those we do not remember, including actions in previous lives. By acknowledging our negative actions through this prayer we begin to feel regret. With that attitude of regret we then choose a spiritual practice to help us purify the negative effects of such actions. This can be one of many practices – reciting mantras, making offerings, meditating or even sweeping the floor with the thought that we are trying to sweep negative imprints from the mind. Any action can purify if it is directed towards the removal of a specific negative imprint. This purification process is accompanied by a strong promise not to act in that manner again.

We often use prayers to remind ourselves about the practice of confession or purification. This well-known prayer was written by the Indian master Ashvaghosa, who was originally a persecutor of Buddhists, but later converted and, deeply regretting his previous actions, wrote this prayer.

The five actions of immediate retribution referred to are killing our father, our mother and an arhat (one who has attained personal liberation), wounding a Buddha (a Buddha cannot be killed), and causing a schism in the spiritual community. These actions are considered so negative that they lead immediately in our next life to the experience of intense suffering.

The 'vows of individual liberation' refer to the vows undertaken with the motive of personal liberation. However, in Mahayana Buddhism, the motive should be to seek the liberation of others. This is emphasised in the bodhisattva training in love and consideration for others. This later stage of spiritual development is more concerned with interaction with others and less with the discipline emphasised in the vows of individual liberation. However, such discipline aimed at helping ourselves to a certain level is necessary before we can truly benefit others.

Rejoicing

153.

Gladly do I rejoice
In the virtue that relieves the misery
Of all those in unfortunate states
And that places those with suffering in happiness.
          Shantideva, *A Guide to the Bodhisattva's Way of Life*,
                                                    ch. 3, verse 1

The fourth of the seven limbs of practice (see nos. 150–56) is developing a mind which is happy that others are happy and are practising a positive way of life. It is a mind free from any kind of jealousy. This attitude arouses feelings of warmth and nearness to others and is very close to love and compassion.

Beseeching the Buddha to Give Teachings

154.

With folded hands I beseech
The Buddhas of all directions
To shine the lamp of Dharma
For all bewildered in misery's gloom.

Shantideva, *A Guide to the Bodhisattva's Way of Life*, ch. 3, verse 5

The fifth of the seven limbs of practice (see nos. 150–56) is requesting the Buddha to continue manifesting in a form which comes into contact with ordinary beings, ourselves included, thereby giving teachings on the spiritual path. The request is made while visualising or thinking about the Buddha. By continuing to request that the Buddha give teachings, we create the causes to meet the Buddha's teachings. We also open up our mind to receive the teachings. Only then is it in a fit state to learn and meditate.

It is said that the Buddha and his followers should only give teachings to those who request them three times. The Buddha kept quiet for forty-nine days after he achieved enlightenment until he was requested to give teachings.

For the Buddhadharma to be of benefit to others it is important that those listening are receptive to it. It is not enough for the Buddhadharma to be valid, it must be fitting for each person at his or her particular stage of development. A person not ready to receive the Buddha's teachings may become very angry and antagonistic when he or she hears them and this cannot be of any help. Only when a person asks with genuine openness will teachings be given to him or her.

Beseeching the Buddhas Not to Pass Away

155.

With folded hands I beseech
The conquerors who wish to pass away
To please remain for countless aeons

And not to leave the world in darkness.
> Shantideva, *A Guide to the Bodhisattva's Way of Life,*
> ch. 3, verse 6

Beseeching the Buddhas not to pass away is the sixth of the seven limbs of practice (see nos. 150–56). According to Buddhism there are countless world systems all with sentient beings. A Buddha will only appear in a particular world system if the beings of that system are actually requesting his appearance. If people are not receptive, all the compassion and wisdom of the Buddhas will be to no avail. It is like a very skilful psychologist who has at his disposal all the drugs and facilities necessary for curing drug addicts. However, if a drug addict does not want to be cured, there is nothing the psychologist can do.

Dedication

156.

Thus by the virtue collected
Through all that I have done
May the pain of every living being created
Be completely cleared away.

May I become an inexhaustible treasure
For those who are destitute.
May I turn into all things they could need
And may these be placed close beside them.
> Shantideva, *A Guide to the Bodhisattva's Way of Life,*
> ch. 3, verses 7–8

Dedication means directing all the positive mental energy we have created through the previous six limbs of practice (see nos. 150–56), and through any virtuous activity, to a specific end. Without direction, all this positive energy is in danger of simply dissipating or of being destroyed by subsequent negative actions. Dedication is likened to a bridle on a horse. Just as the bridle directs the horse, dedication directs our meditations toward our desired goal.

In the Mahayana Buddhist traditions of Tibet, the end to which we direct ourselves is enlightenment for the benefit of others. In these verses, the dedication is towards becoming a Buddha who is able to relieve the pain and suffering of others and, through skill and wisdom, help in the most effective and lasting ways. Through their power Buddhas and bodhisattvas are able to manifest in countless ways which will bring happiness to others. As the second verse indicates, through their power of concentration Buddhas and bodhisattvas will even manifest food, drink and inanimate objects to help relieve the suffering of others and lead them to the spiritual path.

The Qualities of Our Human Life

157.

The eighteen blessings of a precious human rebirth are like gold,
Do not waste your life in meaningless ways, O people of Tingri.

Padampa Sangye,
100 Verses of Advice to the People of Tingri

In this verse to the people of the Tibetan town of Tingri, the Indian master Padampa Sangye speaks of the preciousness of our human life which has all the necessary qualities to complete successfully the spiritual path. This opportunity is extremely rare. It is rare to be born human. It is rare to be born in a country where we are free to practise the spiritual path. It is rare to be born when and where such teachings and masters are accessible. As we have all the conditions necessary for spiritual practice we should not waste our life in mundane pursuits which have no true essence or lasting meaning. We should make the best use of our opportunity by concentrating on spiritual practice.

There are eighteen qualities of our human life on which we contemplate to develop a joyful appreciation of the preciousness of our life. These include eight freedoms from states in which it would be impossible for us to practise spiritual paths, such as the state of great suffering, as an animal without power of discrimination or being born mentally handicapped. These and other states prevent us realising our latent potential for attaining enlightenment. We are also endowed with ten conditions conducive for successful spiritual practice. Realising that our life has the eight freedoms and the ten endowments, we should not waste it in meaningless activities but apply effort in spiritual practice.

The Value of Human Life

158.

Relying upon the boat of a human body,
Free yourself from the great river of pain!

As it is hard to find this boat again
This is no time to sleep, you fool.

Shantideva, *A Guide to the Bodhisattva's Way of Life,*
ch. 7, verse 14

In every moment of this human life we can create the causes to attain lasting happiness, complete freedom from suffering and the state of full enlightenment. In meditation on the preciousness of human life, we focus first on the qualities of our human life, its rarity and value, in order to generate a strong determination to make the best use of our life. This meditation arouses great energy for spiritual practice. Whenever we become tired, depressed or lazy in our spiritual practice, we recollect this meditation and remind ourselves that every moment is a great opportunity not to be wasted.

The meditation also highlights the fact that we should not start the spiritual path with the escapist attitude, 'I am terrible and I want to escape to a spiritual world.' On the contrary, we start with a healthy regard for our qualities as human beings and an appreciation for our greater potential. Realising this potential through progressing along the spiritual path gives richer purpose and meaning to our life.

The Importance of Being Aware of Death

159.

The Lord of Death who dwells in the south does not
Consider the state of your plans.
You should speak with him.
When he comes to call on you,
He will not ask if you are young or old.
High or low, rich or poor, ready or not.

All are forced to go alone,
Leaving behind their unfinished works,
The thread of life suddenly is broken
Like a rope snapping under a heavy load.

There is no time for plan-making.
To die without spiritual knowledge
Is to die in pathetic helplessness.

Lama Guntang Konchog Dronme,
Conversations with an Old Man

These verses are taken from a supposed conversation between a young man and an old man. At first, the young man is contemptuous of the old man but later acknowledges the spiritual wisdom of his elder. However, as the young man declares he will worry about spiritual practice later, the old man warns that while it is certain that death comes to all whether they are old or young, the time of death is uncertain.

Having recognised the qualities and value of human life (see nos. 157–8) and realising that we can attain so much, we then realise that we do not have a great deal of time. Awareness of death is very important because it forces us to engage in spiritual practice with a heightened sense of urgency and concentration and thus intensifies the energy generated in the previous meditations.

Meditation on Death

160.

We will be parted from close friends of long acquaintance.
Our wealth and possessions, obtained with great effort, will be left behind.
The guesthouse of our body must be left by its guest, the mind.
Casting away thoughts concerned with this life only is a practice of the bodhisattvas.

Togme Zangpo,
Thirty-seven Practices of all the Bodhisattvas, verse 8

Meditations on death, in which we reflect on our own impermanence, help us appreciate the value of every moment of our life and maximise our use of it. In one form of this meditation we first recognise that our death is certain, its time is uncertain and, by asking what can really help us at the time of death, we realise that it is not our friends, family, wealth and so on that can help but only our state of mind. At the time of death the body dies but the mind continues. The rebirth we then take is determined by our state of mind. If we have a mind which is principally influenced by anger and violence, then we will be drawn towards a life which reflects these states. We will be born into a life where we meet with violence and conflict and we will tend to be violent again. On the other hand, with a positive state of mind we are drawn towards a life and experiences of greater peace and happiness. Therefore, a positive state of mind at the time of death is extremely important and this can only be ensured by developing a positive state of mind throughout life.

Death is a traumatic time and can be one of great fear, but through training it is possible to control our mind at a very subtle level and thus determine our next rebirth. People who have chosen their rebirth can often remember their past lives. They choose a particular family to be born into which will recognise and respect Buddhism and allow them to continue teaching and practising, possibly contacting their former disciples.

In Tibet, there were many recognised reincarnations of great teachers such as the Dalai Lama who would continue reincarnating for many generations to give guidance and inspiration. In a society such as Tibet where rebirth is accepted as a fact of life, any abnormality of a child is not perceived as quirky or troublesome but is regarded as possibly indicating the child's previous life.

Rebirth

161.

When taking rebirth,
Breathing, sense faculties and mind
Do not develop from only the body
Without depending upon their own similar type,
Because [if they did it would lead to] extremely absurd consequences.

Dharmakirti,
Commentary on Dignaga's Compendium of Valid Cognition

The idea that our consciousness continues after death is generally accepted by all Tibetans. Nevertheless, to strengthen that conviction, there are teachings and lines of reasonings presented, including those in Dharmakirti's text, to establish the validity of rebirth.

One of the reasons Dharmakirti gives for rebirth is that the mind and body are of different nature and therefore the mind cannot develop from the body. Mind is defined as formless and knowing. The body is form made of matter. Mind cannot develop from something which is not the same type; it must develop from its own type. Mind can only develop from mind. Just as this moment's mind comes from the last moment's mind, there is a continuum going back from my mind now to, for example, my mind when I was five years old and to when I was in my mother's womb. In this way, we can trace our mind back to beginningless previous lives.

As we go through the death process, the mind goes from a gross to a subtle level. This is similar to falling into a deep sleep in which there is no awareness of hearing, seeing, smelling and so on. After a while in sleep the mind becomes slightly less subtle and we begin to have dreams. This activity of mind becomes grosser and grosser until we wake up and our gross sense consciousnesses begin to function. This parallels the process of rebirth. At death, the mind becomes increasingly subtle, all gross sensations and memories dissolve and, in the case of being reborn human, the subtle mind then becomes associated with a union of cells in a woman's womb. As the foetus begins to develop, the mind becomes increasingly gross as it associates more closely with the bodily senses. The mind and body are fundamentally of different natures but as they become associated thay have considerable influence over each other.

In contemplating rebirth we can also think about the different tendencies we see in children, even very young babies. Why should twins show markedly different personalities from birth? Where do these propensities come from? If it is all explained by genetic structuring or chemical reactions, then what are the factors that determine these structures and reactions? By thinking about these and other points, we begin to gain more and more conviction about the validity of rebirth.

The Lower Realms of Existence

162.

Who intentionally created
All the weapons for those in hell?
Who created the burning iron ground?
From where did all the enticing women come?
This is none other than the mind itself.
Shantideva, A Guide to the Bodhisattva's Way of Life,
ch. 5, verse 7

Buddhism teaches that there are hell-realms, states of existence in which beings experience intense suffering. This famous verse by Shantideva asks who creates these hell-realms and states that these are mentally created realms. However, this in no way diminishes the intensity of the suffering experienced. If we dream there is a murderer in our room, we feel as much fear as if there was a murderer in the room of our waking world.

Hell-realms are described using images of conflict and intense frustration. For example, there is a hell-realm of constant conflict where we are born with a sword in our hand and we have to fight a never-ending onslaught of foes. We are killed and we are immediately reborn again to continue fighting. Because of constant internal anger and conflict, the angrier we become and the more the world seems to be against us, the angrier we become and so on. In the hell-realm, there is nothing and no one to break this vicious cycle of violence. There are no family or friends to pull us out. We are in a nightmare world of our own making.

Even in the human realm, some people live in their own hell of intense suffering where everyone and everything is a cause for suffering. Even if someone tries to help them, it is interpreted as a threat.

At time of death, when we are no longer seeing, hearing, smelling and so on, our mind turns inward. The imprints or mental tendencies implanted on our mind by our previous actions then determine our experiences. If we have created largely negative actions motivated by greed or violence, we will experience 'hellish' realms of intense suffering or states of intense hunger or an animal rebirth characterised by blind instinct, fear and exploitation.

Having become aware through previous meditation of our opportunity as a human being and of how tenuous and fragile life is, we then consider the possibility of rebirth and realise that if we are not careful we could create the causes for such suffering rebirths in our future lives. We meditate on the suffering of these realms in order to develop the determination to avoid them through cultivating positive actions and states of mind. To develop such positive states of mind we turn to the Buddha, Dharma and Sangha (the enlightened one, his teachings and the spiritual community) for help and guidance.

Going for Refuge

163.

Namo Guruba
Namo Buddhaya
Namo Dharmaya
Namo Sanghaya

[*I go for refuge to the Guru*
I go for refuge to the Buddha
I go for refuge to the Dharma
I go for refuge to the Sangha]

Refuge prayer in Sanskrit

The basic motivation for going for refuge is seeking freedom from being reborn in lower states of existence. A more advanced motivation is to gain freedom from all states of existence within samsara – the cycle of uncontrolled birth, sickness, old age and death.

As well as recognising realms of great suffering, Buddhism also recognises the possibility of rebirth in realms of great pleasure or god realms. Although the causes for such rebirths are positive, they are still taken in ignorance of the true nature of things and so are not lasting states. When the positive energy which propels us into the god-realms is exhausted we descend to lower realms where our experiences are once again those of suffering. The only way to attain total liberation is to remove all delusions, especially that of ignorance.

From the Mahayana point of view, we should go for refuge motivated by the wish to gain enlightenment to help others become free from suffering and also attain enlightenment. In the above prayer we go for refuge to the Three Jewels – Buddha, Dharma, Sangha – but going for refuge to the guru also affirms the importance of the guru as embodying the Three Jewels and as the vehicle through which we receive the Dharma teachings and become Buddha and Sangha.

Going for Refuge to the Buddha

164.

The Buddha is an ultimate source of refuge, having eight good qualities such as non-produced and so forth.
                     Maitreya, *Sublime Continuum of the Great Vehicle*

The Buddha is likened to a doctor who diagnoses the problem and who is able to prescribe the correct medicine. He or she is an ultimate source of refuge because he or she has eight qualities, one of which is 'non-produced'. This refers to Buddhas being free from all faults, having freed themselves from delusions and their imprints – the source of all faults. The Tibetans translate Buddha as *Sang gya. Sang* means 'purified' and *gya* means 'to expand'. Anyone who has purified his or her mind of all delusions and harmful attitudes and who has fully expanded all positive qualities such as compassion and wisdom is a Buddha. Buddhas are free from all suffering and fears because they have removed the causes. They have the wisdom and skill to know what is the most appropriate way to help others. They have universal compassion for all without partiality. Such a person will never let us down when we go to him or her for help.

However, going for refuge does not just mean seeking the protection and guidance of enlightened beings. It also involves acknowledging that we too can attain the state of enlightenment. All Buddhist practices, from the initial stages to the attainment of enlightenment itself, are aspects of going for refuge.

The Eight Good Qualities of the Buddha – nos. 1 & 2

165.

. . . non-produced, effortlessly achieved . . .
Maitreya, *Sublime Continuum of the Great Vehicle*

'Non-produced' refers to true cessations (the fourth noble truth), which are completely free from the two forms of obstruction: 'delusion obstructions' and their imprints, which are called 'obstructions to ominscience'. Buddhas are free from all faults because they are free from these two obstructions which are the roots of all faults. True cessations are permanent and so their nature is unproduced.

'Effortlessly achieved' means that Buddhas accomplish everything effortlessly. Because they are free from conceptual thought, Buddhas do not need to motivate themselves like ordinary beings, thinking 'Now I shall do this.' When the moon shines in a clear sky its reflection appears effortlessly on the surface of all oceans, rivers, lakes and puddles of the world. Just as the moonlight needs no motivation to appear, so it is with the Buddha's activities. Whenever we need to visualise the Buddhas in front of us, our mind becomes like water on a clear moonlit night and the Buddhas appear in front of us without effort. They do not have to make up their minds to travel there from a distant place.

The Eight Good Qualities of the Buddha – no. 3

166.

. . . not realised by the conditions of others . . .
Maitreya, *Sublime Continuum of the Great Vehicle*

The Buddhas have good qualities of body, speech and mind that cannot be comprehended by sentient beings, that is, they are 'not realised by the conditions of others'. For example, Buddhas can manifest as anything, even as inanimate objects, in order to help sentient beings. They can manifest as men and women simultaneously but we cannot understand how they develop these emanations.

The Buddha's speech has qualities which also cannot be comprehended by others. If all the beings of the world were to ask Buddha questions in their own language, Buddha would be able to answer all these questions with one word which would be understood by all.

The volume of Buddha's speech remains the same at any distance.

Maudgalyanaputra, a disciple of the Buddha, once decided to test this quality of speech. While the Buddha was teaching, he first listened at his feet and then went a mile way and listened again. The voice sounded the same. He then went many miles away and listened again. The voice was exactly the same. By means of his magical power he then went to another universe and listened. The voice sounded exactly the same. As he returned closer and closer to the Buddha the voice was always at the same volume as it had been when he was sitting at the Buddha's feet. This wonderful quality of his speech is incomprehensible to other beings.

The Eight Good Qualities of the Buddha – nos. 4, 5 & 6

167.

> ... *having wisdom, compassion and power*...
> Maitreya, *Sublime Continuum of the Great Vehicle*

'Wisdom' refers to the quality of the Buddha's mind that directly perceives all phenomena clearly without confusing them. Although the mind of every being is clear in nature, its clarity is obstructed like a clear sky overcast by clouds. Until the cloud-like obstructions have been completely eliminated from our mind, it is hard for we ordinary beings to understand things clearly and precisely. For instance, it is hard for us to understand one another's state of mind, even that of a close friend or our own child. However, if our best friend were a Buddha, she or he would directly understand what was going on in our mind. Only Buddhas have this direct awareness because only Buddhas have eliminated all obstructions. With such direct intuitive awareness they are able more effectively to benefit others.

The Buddha's great compassion extends to all living beings without exception, feeling for everyone as a mother feels for her own child. Buddha's 'power' refers to the perfect ability to free all sentient beings.

The Eight Good Qualities of the Buddha – nos. 7 & 8

168.

> *Only Buddha possesses two purposes.*
> Maitreya, *Sublime Continuum of the Great Vehicle*

The 'two purposes' means that Buddhas have gained enlightenment themselves and thereby gained perfect ability to accomplish their main purpose of bringing benefit to others. Only a Buddha has accomplished both purposes. Arhats, literally 'foe-destroyers', have reached a level of development in which they have destroyed all their delusions and are thus free from suffering but they have not yet fully developed qualities to help others. Using the analogy of clouds, arhats have removed the thick layers of clouds which produce the rain, hail, sleet and snow of suffering, but they have not removed the subtler layers of cloud which obscure the full lucid quality of the sky. Arhats are free from suffering but have not awakened the full power of their minds.

Going for Refuge to the Dharma

169.

The Dharma is a perfectly purified truth in the mind continuum of a superior being which has any of the eight great qualities such as inconceivable and so forth.
> Maitreya, *Sublime Continuum of the Great Vehicle*

The Dharma usually refers to the 'teachings of the Buddha'. At one level this refers to his instructions and books, but on a deeper level Dharma refers to our own inner experiences, realisations of impermanence, wisdom and so on, which we develop as we progress along the spiritual path.

Dharma is likened to medicine and the Buddha to the doctor (see no. 164) who prescribes the medicine which cures us of our suffering and delusions.

The Eight Qualities of the Dharmas – nos. 1–6

170.

Inconceivable, non-duality, non-conceptuality,
Purity, clarity, side of the opponent.
> Maitreya, *Sublime Continuum of the Great Vehicle*

We meditate on the eight qualities of the Dharma Jewel to generate the wish to develop these qualities within our mind. Just as doctors can only help their patients if the patients actually take the prescribed medicine, we can only receive the perfect protection of the Buddha and Sangha (spiritual community) Jewels if we develop Dharma Jewel realisations. By developing Dharma Jewels within our own minds we eventually become objects of refuge for others.

At a deeper level Dharma refers to the last two of the four noble truths: true cessations and true paths. True cessations are absence of delusions and true paths are minds.

The first three qualities listed above refer to true cessations. 'Inconceivable' means that conceptual minds cannot understand true cessations exactly because these need to be directly experienced to be perfectly understood. Since true cessations are experienced mainly through the power of meditation, they cannot be correctly understood by those who gain a merely intellectual understanding of the Dharma without putting it into practice.

'Non-duality' refers to the absence of one or both of the two obstructions – delusions and their imprints. 'Non-conceptuality' means that true cessations are not endowed with conceptuality because only minds can be endowed with conceptuality and true cessations are not minds.

The next three qualities refer to true paths. 'Purity' means that a true path is a mind that is not mixed with delusions. 'Clarity' means that a true path is a mind that sees objects closely. 'Side of the opponent' means that a true path activates the opponent to the two obstructions. It is like a tool that eliminates all the mental faults and defilements that cause our problems.

The Eight Qualities of Dharma – nos. 7 & 8

171.

> *That which frees from attachment,*
> *The two truths are the definition of Dharma.*
> Maitreya, *Sublime Continuum of the Great Vehicle*

The first line mentions explicitly the fourth quality of a true path and, implicitly, the fourth quality of a true cessation. True paths are methods by which we gain true cessations which free us completely from delusions such as attachment. The second line refers to the two kinds of Dharma Jewels, conventional and ultimate. Conventional Dharma Jewels are the Buddha's scriptures and ultimate Dharma Jewels are true cessations and true paths.

Going for Refuge to the Sangha

172.

A superior being has any of the eight good qualities
Such as realisation and freedom.
Maitreya, *Sublime Continuum of the Great Vehicle*

By meditating on the good qualities of the Sangha Jewel, we develop the strong determination also to become a Sangha Jewel. A superior being is someone who has directly realised emptiness (ultimate truth) and achieved peace through the three higher trainings of moral discipline, concentration and wisdom (see no. 188).

The Sangha Jewel is likened to a nurse. By setting a good example and giving help and advice, a Sangha Jewel helps us to take the medicine of Dharma prescribed by the spiritual doctor, the Buddha.

The first four qualities of the Sangha Jewel are qualities of spiritual realisation: the first stage is realisation, and the three stages that develop from this are realising ultimate truths, realising conventional truths and realising the nature of the inner mind. The remaining four qualities are qualities of freedom: freedom from all faults, freedom from obstructions to liberation, freedom from obstructions to omniscience and freedom from obstructions of inferiority. This last quality refers to an obstruction which prevents our developing a mind wishing to achieve enlightenment for the benefit of others. Dharma practitioners motivated only by the wish for their own liberation have an obstruction of inferiority because their self-cherishing is blocking this higher aspiration.

Respect for the Ordained Sangha

173.

In order that I might be fully ordained
May I never be thwarted by hindrances coming
From clinging to family, to friends or to wealth
But rather may all the conditions which favour
Becoming a monk come about as I've wished.
Je Tsongkhapa, *Prayer of Virtuous Beginning, Middle and End*

In the *Vinaya Sutra* it is said that any group of four or more fully ordained monks is called a sangha community. In Tibetan Buddhism, monks and nuns are honoured and highly valued because their good example is a source of encouragement and inspiration for lay Buddhists.

Before the Chinese invasion, about one sixth of the male population in Tibet were monks. The government was a theocracy with the Dalai Lama, a fully ordained monk, as the head of government. There were thousands of monasteries which were centres of culture and education for the local communities. Most families had at least one member who was a monk which ensured the monasteries were fully integrated into the wider community.

Although it is accepted that a lay person can be as spiritually advanced as a monk or nun, by and large, a person living as a monk or nun is considered more able to devote his or her life to meditation and the spiritual path. The fully ordained monks observe 253 vows which control in detail the behaviour of their body, speech and mind. The purpose of such constant discipline is to develop clarity and control of mind. With pure conduct, monks and nuns can remove the gross levels of delusions as they manifest in the body, speech and mind. One benefit is that the mind is more easily focused single-pointedly during meditation.

Karma – Actions and their Consequences

174.

All of the sufferings that we have endured
In the lives we have led in the three lower states,
As well as our pains of the present and future
Are the same as the case of the forger of arrows
Who later was killed by an arrow he had made.
Our suffering is the wheel of sharp weapons returning
Full circle upon us from wrongs we have done.
Hereafter let us always have care and awareness
Never to act in non-virtuous ways.

Dharmarakshita, *The Wheel of Sharp Weapons*

To put 'going for refuge' (see nos. 163–73) into practice in our daily life, we must observe our actions and their consequences. This is called 'observing karma'.

This verse by the Indian master Dharmarakshita teaches us that everything we experience is a result of actions we have created in the past, whether recently, in our youth or in previous lives. Just as a forger of arrows can be killed later by an arrow he has made, through our actions we create imprints or propensities in our mind which will manifest at a later date as suffering or happiness.

If we are to avoid suffering in the future of this life or in later rebirths, we must understand which actions lead to such suffering and then try to avoid such actions. We should also understand which actions lead to happiness and then try to cultivate them.

Meditation on Karma

175.

For every action we perform we experience a similar result.

Vinaya Sutra

There are four main points of contemplation in the meditation on karma. The first is that our actions produce effects which are similar. If, for example, we act motivated by anger then we will later experience the anger of others.

The second point is that the results of our actions increase. From small actions great results can come, much in the way a seed can grow into a very large tree. If we do not counteract the imprint of an action on the mind, that imprint can grow and later result in a very strong experience.

The third point of contemplation is that if an action is not performed, its result cannot be experienced. If we wish to experience happiness we must create the cause.

The fourth point is that if we create an action we will definitely experience its result. If we do not wish to experience suffering we must avoid creating even the smallest negative action.

Karma in Daily Life

176.

My life is passing away moment by moment like water bubbles,
It decays and perishes so quickly
After death come results of my good and bad actions
Just like the shadow follows the body.

With a deep understanding of this
Please bless me to be conscientious at all times,
Abandoning even the slightest non-virtuous actions
And completing the accumulation of virtuous actions.

Je Tsongkhapa, *The Foundation of All Excellence*, verses 3–4

The basic practice of moral discipline, which comes from observing karma (our actions and their effects), is the avoidance of the ten non-virtuous actions. There are countless negative actions but the Buddha mentioned ten – three of body, four of speech and three of mind – which encompass them all. If we avoid these we will avoid all negative actions. All virtuous actions are also included within ten – three of body, four of speech and three of mind.

The three negative actions of body are: killing, stealing and sexual misconduct. The four of speech are: lying, slander, harsh speech and idle gossip. The three of mind are: ill-will, covetousness and wrong views.

We should avoid not only killing but causing any harm to others. Stealing is taking that which is not freely given. Sexual misconduct refers to sexual activity motivated by the desire for one's own gratification regardless of the suffering caused to others, whether to the partner or a third party.

Lying refers not simply to speaking deceptively, but to any action done with the intention to deceive. Slandering is causing division between people. Harsh speech is speech motivated by the desire to hurt. Shouting is not necessarily harsh speech, for instance, if we are warning someone of an immediate danger. Idle gossip is the slightest of the negative actions but one of the most frequent. We can spend a large portion of our life engaged in gossip, to no real benefit to anyone or even to ourself.

Ill-will is wishing others harm. Covetousness is developing attachment and craving for things which are not ours. Holding wrong views is clinging to views which prevent spiritual development.

By examining our actions we should try to avoid the ten non-virtuous actions and try to cultivate positive actions – not simply avoiding killing but trying to benefit others, not simply avoiding taking what is not given but giving to others, and so on. Avoiding harmful actions and cultivating beneficial actions is the basis of spiritual practice.

The Sufferings of Samsara

177.

Even if we take birth many times in happy realms
And enjoy their pleasures over and over again
We will die and fall down to unhappy realms
Where for aeons we will suffer unbearable pains
　　　　　Shantideva, *A Guide to the Bodhisattva's Way of Life*

In the process of development shown by these readings we recognise that we can avoid rebirth in lower realms by going for refuge to the Three Jewels (see no. 163) and by putting Dharma into practice through cultivating positive states of mind and avoiding negative states of mind. However, simply cultivating positive actions without developing wisdom which understands the root cause of delusions may lead to rebirth in a relatively better situation as a god or human but we will still be within samsara and will always experience some form of suffering. Samsara is the uncontrolled cycle of birth, sickness, old age and death fuelled by delusions and deluded actions. Within samsara the mind may go through relatively pleasant and unpleasant experiences, but since they are all conditioned by delusions, suffering will inevitably be experienced at some time. Suffering is the nature of samsara, just as heat is the nature of fire.

At this point we can meditate on the suffering of the human realm, which, compared to hell and animal realms, is relatively fortunate. For example, we can think of the extreme discomfort of birth itself, all the problems of growing up, getting sick, growing old and all the difficulties we encounter in life. By contemplating these we realise that the basic condition of our lives is not one of lasting happiness and satisfaction. In fact, it is only a relatively good state within samsara but still something to be avoided rather than sought after. By cultivating positive actions and experiencing their good results we may enjoy temporary happiness but we are like a prisoner who is given a week's reprieve to visit his family and friends. The prisoner enjoys his holiday but his happiness is not perfect because he knows that before long he must return to prison. The pleasures of a human being are like the tainted enjoyments of this prisoner. To enjoy perfect happiness, we must be completely free from the prison of samsara.

The Suffering of Choice

178.

Contemplating the suffering of change
Is seeing how beings travel from heavens to unhappy worlds.
The god Shakra falls to a common rebirth,
The sun and moon grow dark
And the universal emperor is reborn a servant.

> Jetsun Dragpa Gyaltsan,
> *Path Instructions on Parting from the Four Desires*

No matter how happy or exalted a position we may have, since we are within samsara (the cycle of uncontrolled birth and death), this experience will change into suffering. In reality, pleasurable experiences arise because of change from an extreme state of suffering to one of less suffering. For example, we may be hungry and be given a plate of tasty food. Our experience will begin as a very pleasant one, but if we continue to have more and more of the food, the experience will change to one of suffering. It is not the nature of the food to give happiness. Food is a condition for a temporary arising of happiness, but the more we experience it, the more suffering we begin to feel. On the other hand, if we take a suffering experience, such as being pricked by a pin, continuing the experience does not change it to one of happiness. The suffering simply increases.

Suffering is the nature of cyclic existence. Our apparent happiness is only a temporary respite from extreme suffering. We can see this both in our daily lives and from life to life in various realms of samsara. Those born in heavenly realms fall to lower realms, universal emperors become servants, even the sun and moon grow dark. All things are in the nature of change. By reflecting on this we see there is no abiding state or situation in samsara to which we should be attached. To experience lasting happiness we must gain liberation from samsara, the vicious cycle of suffering.

The Suffering of Pervasiveness

179.

*By realising that samsara's pleasures
Bring no satisfaction,
Are deceptive and the door to all suffering
Please bless me to cultivate great interest
In the bliss of liberation.*
Je Tsongkhapa, The Foundation of All Excellence, verse 5

Because our births in samsara are conditioned by delusion, misery, whether on a gross or subtle level, is inherent in every situation. Even positive actions done in ignorance of the true nature of things are deluded actions. Only when we are strongly motivated to attain liberation or enlightenment for the benefit of others will our every action become a cause for liberation or enlightenment. But, without that motivation, even giving thousands of pounds away, a good action leading to a good experience, is an action contaminated by delusion. It is like food mixed with poison which will temporarily sustain us but, because of the poison, will eventually lead to problems.

The suffering of pervasiveness is likened to having an open wound. If it is left untouched the suffering is less, but as soon as it touches anything, it is extremely painful. Recognising how suffering pervades every situation and state within samsara, we develop the wish to free ourselves from all the causes of samsara and to attain nirvana, the state beyond sorrow. In the meditations on observing karma (see nos. 175–6), the main emphasis is on trying to avoid negative actions, but here the motivation is more profound. We are trying to remove all delusions from the mind.

Renunciation

180.

If one clings to this life, one is not a follower of the Dharma.
If one clings to the wheel of rebirth, one does not have the aspiration for
liberation.
If one clings to one's own well-being, one does not have the enlightened
attitude.
If there is grasping [to the independent self-existence of any
phenomenon], one does not have the [realistic] view.

> Buddha Manjushri/Lama Kunga Nyingpo,
> *Parting from the Four Desires*

Before we attain nirvana we must develop the strong wish to attain it. By
repeatedly contemplating the nature of samsara – the sufferings of misery,
change and pervasiveness – and of each realm of existence within samsara,
our mind will completely turn towards trying to remove all delusions so
we can attain lasting happiness. This mind wishing to emerge from
suffering, conditioned existence is called 'renunciation' or 'definite
emergence' (Tib. *nge jung*). Only with this attitude motivating us will our
actions lead to liberation.

This reading was spoken directly by the Buddha Manjushri to Kunga
Nyingpo, one of the great teachers of the Sakya tradition.

Overcoming Worldly Concerns

181.

One day an old gentleman was walking around Radreng monastery.
Geshe Dromtonpa said to him: 'Sir, I am happy to see you walking
around, but wouldn't you rather be practising the Dharma?'
   Thinking this over, the old man felt he might be better to read the
Mahayana sutras. While he was reading in the temple courtyard, Geshe
Drom said: 'I am happy to see you reciting sutras, but wouldn't you
rather be practising Dharma?'
   At this the old gentleman thought that perhaps he should meditate.
He sat crosslegged on a cushion with his eyes half-closed. Geshe Drom
said again: 'I am happy to see you meditating, but wouldn't it be better
to practise the Dharma?'
   Now totally confused, the old gentleman asked: 'Geshe, please tell me
what should I do to practise the Dharma.'
   Drom replied: 'Renounce attraction to this life, renounce it now. For

*if you do not renounce attraction to this life, whatever you do will not be
the practice of Dharma as you have not passed beyond the eight worldly
concerns. Once you have renounced this life's habitual thoughts and are
no longer distracted by the eight worldly concerns, whatever you do will
advance you on the path to liberation.'*

Precepts of the Kadampa Master

'Renouncing attraction to this life' refers to relinquishing our attachments
to things. It does not mean we have to give up eating nice food or living
comfortably. What we have to do is to give up the attitude that these
things are a source of happiness in themselves. There are eight worldly
attitudes we must renounce:

(1) elation when receiving resources and respect
(2) depression when not receiving resources and respect
(3) elation when experiencing pleasure
(4) depression when not experiencing pleasure
(5) elation when enjoying a good reputation
(6) depression when not enjoying a good reputation
(7) elation when receiving praise
(8) depression when not receiving praise.

As long as we are attached to resources and respect, pleasure, good
reputation and praise, we are prone to over-excitement when we possess
them and dejection when we lose them. We remain unstable, vulnerable
and emotionally dependent on these things. Most of our energy goes into
securing them and guarding against their loss. When we practise Dharma
in this state, our motivation is strongly influenced by attachment so that
our practice, like all our other activities, is only in the interest of enjoying
this life and its apparent pleasures.

To overcome attachment to the welfare of this life we meditate: 'It
makes no difference whether or not I receive respect or good reputation or
praise. I do not receive any great benefit from these and when I lose them
I am not greatly harmed. Words of blame cannot hurt me. Wealth is easily
lost. The pleasures of this life are transient. I do not need to be so
interested in these things or overly concerned about them.'

If we meet good things in life we should accept them without becoming
attached. If we do not meet them we should not be overly concerned. In
all situations we should try to have a balanced mind. As long as our mind
is tied with attachment to the eight worldly concerns, all our energy and
effort will be expended in satisfying these attachments and we will never
have the interest in transforming our inner attitudes and overcoming
deluded states of mind, thus denying ourselves the possibility of gaining
true happiness.

Overcoming Pride

182.

Although we are famous, have a good reputation, are
  highly respected by many and
Have attained riches like those of the god of wealth,
By seeing that the rewards of samsara have no essence,
  remaining without arrogance
Is the practice of the bodhisattvas.

> Togme Zangpo, *Thirty-seven Practices of All the Bodhisattvas,*
> verse 21

Pride is considered one of the six root delusions, along with anger,
attachment, ignorance, deluded doubt and wrong views (see nos. 183–6).
People afflicted with pride are restricted from making progress on the
spiritual path because, for example, they think they are already fully
developed and know everything. Consequently, they are not receptive to
new knowledge and insights. A proud mind is like a mountain peak. Just
as water cannot gather on top of a mountain peak, wisdom and
understanding will never gather in a proud mind. By considering ourself
above others we hinder the possibility of collecting an ocean of spiritual
realisations.

Overcoming Anger

183.

If we do not subdue the inner enemy of our own hatred,
Trying instead to subdue external enemies will only cause them to
  increase.
Therefore taming your mind with the forces of love and compassion
Is a practice of the bodhisattvas.

> Togme Zangpo, *Thirty-seven Practices of All the Bodhisattvas,*
> verse 22

Anger is another of the six root delusions (see nos. 182–7) and is
considered one of the worst. Driven by anger we can engage in very
negative and harmful actions which, by process of cause and effect, will
lead us to experience extreme suffering in the future. Even in the moment
anger arises we experience unhappiness. We cannot enjoy anything –
food, beautiful things, the company of others. Furthermore, it is

impossible to meditate with a mind of anger. Anger is like a fire which burns up all our positive energy, previous realisations and understanding. It is an extremely destructive state of mind.

Overcoming Attachment

184.

The objects of desire are like salt water,
The more we enjoy them the more our craving will increase.
Abandoning immediately whatever objects give rise to attachment
Is a practice of the bodhisattvas.
    Togme Zangpo, *Thirty-seven Practices of All the Bodhisattvas,*
                                           verse 23

Attachment, another of the six root delusions (see nos. 180–81), is defined as a disturbed state of mind that focuses only on the good qualities of any contaminated object and wishes always to be close and never separate from the object. This will lead us to create negative actions because, in order to acquire desired objects or to keep hold of them, we may hurt others and even the object of our attachment itself.

With our mind in this state, we are unable to recognise that happiness does not come from objects but from our own peace of mind. Furthermore, the more clinging and craving we have, the more inevitable and greater is our suffering when our object of desire decays or dies. All things are impermanent. Everything and everyone evolves, moves on, decays.

The more attachment and craving we have towards things, the greater is our belief that these things will give us happiness, and therefore the more dissatisfied we are when we discover this is not so. This dissatisfaction will lead us to crave something else and in this way we become locked into a vicious cycle of craving, expectation, consumption, dissatisfaction.

Overcoming Ignorance

185.

Ignorance is the root of all the faults of this world system.
                               Je Tsongkhapa, *Praise to Dependent Arising*

If we abandon ignorance we will understand the conventional and ultimate nature of all objects of knowledge and will no longer be confused as to what are correct spiritual paths leading to liberation and what are incorrect spiritual paths leading us to samsara. Ignorance is like a darkness in our mind which prevents clear understanding. Two main kinds of ignorance can be distinguished: ignorance of the conventional nature of objects and ignorance of the ultimate nature of objects. The former refers specifically to ignorance of karma. As long as we remain confused about our actions and their effects, we continue to engage in unwholesome actions which cause lower rebirth. (see nos. 174-6). Ignorance of the ultimate nature of all objects induces self-grasping, which is the root of all other delusions and all cyclic rebirth.

Buddha taught conventional truths to lead us to understand ultimate truths. Therefore, when we study emptiness we begin by studying conventional truths. These are presented differently by each Buddhist school. By studying each presentation we are gradually led to understand the correct and perfect view presented by the Madhyamaka-Prasangika (Middle Way Consequentialists), which is recognised by all four Tibetan traditions as the supreme school.

The tenets of the Vaibhashika, Sautrantrika, Chittamatra and Madhyamaka-Prasangika schools differ in the subtleties of their views regarding conventional and ultimate truths. The Buddha taught all three to lead us progressively to perfect understanding. For example, to help us overcome desirous attachment, he taught the view presented by the Chittamatra school that the objects we perceive are in the nature of our own mind and do not exist separately from it. They are mental appearances arising from their 'seeds' carried by the 'mind basis of all'. Although the objects and the mind that perceives them arise simultaneously, we have mistaken appearances of the objects as existing external to our mind and we grasp at them as existing in this way. Since we grasp at the objects as existing externally we develop desirous attachment for those that seem attractive. By understanding conventional and ultimate truths as they are presented by the Chittamatra school, we reduce our desirous attachment and come closer to realising the correct view of emptiness presented by the Madhyamaka-Prasangika school (see nos. 219-20).

How to Overcome Delusions – the Four Noble Truths

186.

Just as diseases are to be known,
Their causes are to be abandoned.
Health is to be achieved

And the cures are to be applied.
So true sufferings are to be known,
True sources are to be abandoned,
True cessations are to be achieved
And true paths are to be practised.

Maitreya, *Sublime Continuum of the Great Vehicle*

When someone is ill the doctor does not immediately write a prescription. He first examines the patient to diagnose the illness correctly. He takes time and care to examine the symptoms closely because he knows the success of his cure depends upon an accurate diagnosis. Similarly, we need to meditate repeatedly on true sufferings (the first noble truth) because our freedom depends on a complete and certain knowledge of them. Once we fully understand that our mind and body, contaminated by delusions, have the nature of suffering we will easily develop renunciation.

Renunciation is not simply the wish to be free from suffering itself for every living being naturally and spontaneously has this wish without any special effort. Renunciation is a heartfelt determination to become completely free from everything that has the nature of suffering. This determination arises in our mind only when we have thoroughly considered and realised the dangers of samsara (the cycle of uncontrolled birth and death).

If we want to remove a poisonous plant it is not enough just to prune it. We have to dig up its entire root. In the same way, when we have realised renunciation we need to uproot true sources (the second noble truth) which are the causes of true sufferings. When we understand how true sufferings can definitely be removed by removing their causes, we will develop confidence that we ourselves are capable of experiencing true cessations (the third noble truth). If we consider what is the method for achieving true cessations we realise that it is to meditate on the true paths (the fourth noble truth).

This understanding will help us to make greater effort in all our practices and meditations. Although our present meditations are not yet true paths, they are the basis for them and if we put effort into them they will gradually transform into true paths of a superior being. Through them we will attain true cessations and thus gain freedom from all delusion and suffering.

The Wheel of Life

187.

Start with [virtuous works], give up [worldly activities],
Thus [one] enters the Buddhadharma,

The army of the lord of death will be destroyed
As an elephant in a swamp.
If any one with complete conscientiousness
Practises this Dharma discipline,
Cyclic rebirth will be abandoned fully,
And thus the sufferings [of this life] will be the last.

Verse accompanying *The Wheel of Life* paintings

This verse is found on the illustration called *The Wheel of Life* which depicts the nature and causes of samsara. At the hub of the wheel are three animals: a pig, a cock and a snake, which represent the delusions of ignorance, attachment and hatred respectively. The inner rim of the wheel is divided into six segments representing the six realms of existence: gods, demi-gods, humans, animals, hungry ghosts and hell-beings.

The outer rim of the wheel is divided into twelve segments, depicting the twelve dependent-related links. These are like links of a circular chain that binds us within samsara.

(1) The first link is dependent-related ignorance. Ignorance is confused about the real nature of people and phenomena and is depicted as a blind man.

(2) The second link, dependent-related compositional actions, refers to those actions that are rooted in ignorance and cause us to take rebirth in samsara. These actions throw us into cyclic rebirth by bringing together (or composing) all the causes, just as a potter makes pots by bringing together all the materials that are needed.

(3) Dependent-related consciousness refers to potentialities left on our consciousness as soon as any compositional action is complete.

(4) Dependent-related name and form refers to the body and mind of a being at conception.

(5) Dependent-related six sources refers to the six sense powers before the sense consciousnesses have begun to function, like an empty house waiting to be occupied.

(6) Dependent-related contact refers to the mental factor that knows its object as pleasant, unpleasant or neutral when the sense power, sense consciousness and the object come together.

(7) Dependent-related feeling arises from dependent-related contact and is the actual experience of objects as pleasant, unpleasant or neutral.

(8) Dependent-related craving is a specific kind of attachment that arises at the time of death. When ordinary beings die they develop craving not to be separated from their body and so forth, and they crave freedom from unpleasant experiences.

(9) Dependent-related grasping is an intensified form of craving that

arises at the time of death. Together, dependent-related craving and dependent-related grasping activate the potentialities, created in the mind by compositional action, that throw us into our next cyclic rebirth.

(10) Dependent-related existence is the mental action or intention that has the power immediately to produce the next rebirth.

(11) Dependent-related birth is the first moment of any cyclic rebirth when consciousness first enters the newly developed form.

(12) Dependent-related ageing begins the second moment after birth and continues until the moment of death when the consciousness leaves the body.

The Three Higher Trainings

188.

> *Superior moral discipline, superior concentration, superior wisdom, always practise these.*
>
> Nagarjuna, *Friendly Letter*

With the motivation of renunciation the practice of moral discipline becomes a cause for liberation, so any practice of moral discipline done with this motivation is known as a higher training of moral discipline. With such discipline we begin to control the grosser levels of delusion afflicting our mind. This is essential if we are to subdue the subtler levels of delusion that obstruct our concentration. Only with a fully concentrated mind can we then develop the wisdom-insight needed to understand the true nature of things.

The three higher trainings together are the methods for removing ignorance. With a strong body of moral discipline we develop the strong arm of concentration, and with the sharp axe of wisdom we can cut all the roots of ignorance from which arise delusion and suffering.

Developing Bodhichitta — Mind of Enlightenment

189.

> *Seeing that all living beings, my kind mothers,*
> *Are like myself drowning in samsara's ocean,*
> *Please bless me to train in supreme bodhichitta*
> *The mind that assumes the burden of releasing all migrators.*
>
> Je Tsongkhapa, *The Foundation of All Excellence*, verse 7

Through practising the three higher trainings (see no. 188) with the motivation of renunciation, the practitioner is able to remove delusions and suffering. However, to attain full enlightenment, renunciation alone is not enough. We need a mind motivated to perfect our wisdom and compassion so that we can lead others from suffering and towards perfect happiness. The attitude of mind wishing to attain enlightenment motivated by compassion is known as 'bodhichitta' and is the gateway through which we enter Mahayana Buddhism.

Seeking liberation for our self alone is essentially selfish because it does not take into account the kindness others have shown us over countless lifetimes. Without others helping us, both materially and spiritually, we would not be in a position to attain liberation. Experiencing the bliss of liberation whilst leaving others to experience suffering is like being a prisoner who escapes from a prison but leaves his own parents behind. 'My kind mothers' is a reference to all beings who have been our mothers at some time in our past lives, and therefore showed us great kindness (see no. 193). To repay their kindness we should develop the wish to help release these kind mothers from the prison of samsara. 'Migrators' refers to sentient beings who 'migrate' from realm to realm with samsara.

Benefits of Bodhichitta

190.

All the Buddhas who have contemplated for many aeons
Have seen it [the bodhichitta] to be beneficial.
For by it the limitless masses of being
Will quickly attain the supreme state of bliss.

Those who wish to destroy the many sorrows of their
*   conditioned existence*
Those who wish [all beings] to experience a multitude of joys
And those who wish to experience much happiness
Should never forsake the mind of enlightenment.

It is like the supreme gold-making elixir
For it transforms the unclean body we have taken
Into the priceless jewel of a Buddha-form.
Therefore firmly seize this awakening mind.

Shantideva, *A Guide to the Bodhisattva's Way of Life,*
ch. 1, verses 7, 8, 10

To help encourage us to develop strong bodhichitta, or awakening mind, we can contemplate the many benefits of such a mind. Only through bodhichitta can we transform our present contaminated body and mind into the body and mind of a Buddha. We will experience the sublime happiness of enlightenment and will then be able to help others most effectively to experience freedom from suffering and a lasting state of happiness.

Divisions of Bodhichitta

191.

> *In brief, the awakening mind*
> *Should be understood to be of two types:*
> *The mind that aspires to awaken*
> *And the mind that ventures to do so.*
> *As is understood by the distinction*
> *Between aspiring to go and actually going,*
> *So the wise understand in turn*
> *The distinction between the two.*
>
> Shantideva, *A Guide to the Bodhisattva's Way of Life*,
> ch. 1, verses 15–16

The aspiring mind of bodhichitta is a mind that wishes to attain enlightenment in order to be equipped with the perfect means for benefiting others most effectively. The engaging mind of bodhichitta is a mind which is actively engaged in the methods of achieving enlightenment with this motivation. So first we develop the aspiration – the wish to travel – and then we develop the engaging mind, which is actively travelling toward the destination, Buddhahood.

Equanimity

192.

> *It is only by narrow-minded men that such distinctions are made as to*
> *friend and enemy. A liberal man is affectionate towards all.*
>
> Sakya Pandita

Bodhichitta is the result of two wishes, the wish to attain Buddhahood, generated by recognising the qualities of this state, and the wish to benefit others. To develop this second wish we need to develop great love and great compassion. The basis for developing these is equanimity, since great love and compassion must be extended to all beings without exception, whether or not they are friend or enemy, helper or harmer.

Great love is defined as the mind wishing for the happiness of all beings. It is not simply limited to those whom we find pleasant, but extends equally even to those who have harmed us. To do this we must make our mind balanced, reducing strong feelings of hostility and attachment so that we do not make biased distinctions between 'friend' and 'enemy' but recognise both as valid objects for our love and compassion.

To this end we can contemplate, for example, that there is nothing permanent in relationships. Friends can become enemies, enemies become friends. These relationships are dependent on causes and conditions which are constantly changing. Because of this there is no reason to be strongly attached or repulsed by a particular person. Especially, taking the perspective of our numerous lifetimes, we recognise that we have had many relationships with many different people. The number of times each person has been our friend or enemy is equal. Therefore, there is no good reason to distinguish one as friend and another as enemy. Through this contemplation and many others the practitioner can reduce attachment and hatred and develop a sense of the equality of all beings.

Recognising All Beings as Our Mother

193.

All these suffering beings have been my mother...
> Panchen Lama Losang Chokyi Gyaltsan,
> *Offering to the Spiritual Guide*

By this stage in our meditation we should have developed a diamond-hard conviction in rebirth and understand that all beings, ourself included, have taken countless rebirths. It follows that whenever we have taken rebirth in a womb, or even in an egg, there was one being who was our mother. Thinking in this way, we recognise that there is no one being we can point to and say, 'This being has not been my mother.' All beings have been in countless different relationships with us – as father, brothers, sisters, friends and so – but the relationship which is generally considered the closest bond and in which the greatest kindness is shown by one being for another is that of mother and child.

If the meditator had problems with his or her mother, then it may be better to take another person as an example. However, just the fact that we are alive is a testimony to the kindness of our mother. Even if she died at our birth, she gave us life and nourished us for nine months with her own body. This is a great kindness.

Through contemplating our countless rebirths in the wombs of countless beings, we conclude that we cannot point to anyone who has definitely never been our mother. In this way, we bring our mind to the conviction that every single being has been our mother at some time in a previous life.

Recognising and Repaying the Kindness of All Beings

194.

> *... repeatedly caring for me with great kindness*
> *Reflecting on this like a loving mother for her child*
> *Let me develop authentic compassion.*
>
> Panchen Lama Losang Chokyi Gyaltsan,
Offering to the Spiritual Guide

Having recognised all beings as our mother (see no. 193) we then reflect upon their kindness by taking the example of a mother in this life. Generally speaking, she is the one who has shown us the greatest kindness, giving us life, sustaining us with nourishment from her own body for nine months and suffering great discomfort or pain through pregnancy and birth. When we were young she was intimately concerned with every moment of our lives, going without sleep and, if necessary, without food to ensure our comfort, and even defending us with her own life. By reflecting upon all of this kindness which has been shown to us at every stage of our life by our mother we will develop a sense of gratitude and great warmth.

We can also reflect on all the kindnesses shown by others in every aspect of our lives. Our physical health, our ability to read, write, understand, communicate, have healthy relations with others – all these abilities are not something we were born with. They were taught through interaction with other beings. We are fed, clothed, sheltered, educated, employed and looked after by others. At every stage of our life, we are the recipient of the kindness of others.

Through this reflection on the kindness of others when they were our mother in this and past lives and on the general kindness of others, we develop a feeling of warmth and closeness towards all beings, and the wish to repay their kindness will naturally arise. By reflecting on their lack of happiness we will then develop the strong wish to help them find happiness, and by reflecting on their suffering we will naturally develop the strong wish to free them from suffering. The best way to repay the kindness of others is to enable them to experience pure happiness and attain lasting freedom from suffering.

Developing Great Love

195.

All mother sentient beings desire happiness
And most of them do not know that the cause of happiness is virtue.
Of those who do, most do not practise virtue
And even those who try are unable to practise it because of their mental
    afflictions.

Since results are not encountered from deeds not performed,
The beings in unfortunate realms are always devoid of happiness
And although the beings in happy realms perceive their suffering as
    happiness,
Even they lack true happiness.

How wonderful it would be if all sentient beings
Possessed the supreme bliss of the omniscient Buddhas and its cause,
    the noble paths.
May they possess these. O spiritual masters,
Please bestow inspiring strength so that I may bring this about.
Geshe Tsondru, The Essence of Nectar

Love is the mind wishing others happiness, and great love is this wish extended to *all* beings without exception. Having developed affectionate love – the feeling of closeness and warmth towards others – we recognise that, although all beings wish for happiness, there is no being within samsara who experiences pure happiness. On the basis of this recognition and our affectionate love we then develop the strong wish to be able to help all beings experience happiness.

Great Compassion (1)

196.

Because for this bountiful harvest of the conquerors
Mercy itself is found to be like a seed
Like water for growth
And like ripening for long enjoyment
Therefore at the beginning I praise compassion.
Chandrakirti, Guide to the Middle Way, ch. 1, verse 2

Great compassion is the wish that *all* beings without exception be free from suffering. In the Mahayana teachings, it is considered the most important factor for successful development on the path to attaining full enlightenment. For this reason, at the beginning of his famous text on developing wisdom, Chandrakirti departs from convention and praises compassion to indicate its importance. Compassion is the seed because through it we are motivated to attain enlightenment as the perfect, most effective means of benefiting others. It strengthens our mind continually on the path like water nurturing crops. It is the ripening of these crops for, when bodhisattvas (those who seek enlightenment not only for themselves but for all beings) become Buddhas they could simply abide in the state of pure happiness, but their great compassion compels them to work for the sake of others. Therefore, great compassion is important at the beginning of our practice, throughout our practice and also at the end of our practice.

On the basis of affectionate love and contemplating again and again the suffering of others, compassion will arise naturally. By increasing our compassion we become closer to Avalokiteshvara, the embodiment of the universal compassion of all Buddhas.

Great Compassion (2)

197.

How astounding that you, O mind of great compassion,
Are devoted exclusively to the welfare of others,
But how much more astounding that you do this
Without longing and without hope of reward.

There is no better example to demonstrate how it is
That you desire to protect all beings from suffering
Than the pity that an honourable mother feels
For her beloved son.

Just as the mother, though she has many children,
Worries most about the one who is sick,
You feel the greatest pity
For the being who is tormented.

The only thing that an ordinary being like myself
Can either cherish or be preoccupied with is his own self
Hence there can be no comparison with you [great compassion]
Who cherish and are preoccupied with all beings.
        Losang Tayang, *A Precious Crystal Rosary*, verses 30–33

Great compassion is not easy to generate. We have to cultivate it gradually. We can begin by enhancing the compassion we naturally feel for our friends and families and then expand this compassion to embrace all living beings. If we find it hard to develop compassion for people who are not obviously suffering but appear to be enjoying good fortune, we can recall earlier meditations on death and the pervasive sufferings of samsara (the cycle of uncontrolled birth and death). All beings within samsara must eventually fall to lower states no matter how great their present good fortune, just as the bird must eventually return to the ground no matter how high or far it may soar. Awareness of this certainty helps us to develop compassion towards all. An animal that will be slaughtered next year should be as much an object of compassion as one who is to be slaughtered tomorrow.

We may also find it hard to develop compassion for those who are committing extremely destructive actions. In fact, these people are in a worse situation than those who are presently suffering for they are creating the causes for future suffering. Those who are presently suffering are exhausting the fruits of their past negative actions and so have a happier future to look forward to.

The sign of having realised great compassion is that whenever we see another living being we have the spontaneous wish for him or her to be free from his or her suffering and its causes.

Equalising Self and Others

198.

There is no difference between ourselves and others.
None of us wishes even the slightest of sufferings,
Nor is even content with the happiness we have.
Realising this, we seek your blessings, O Buddhas,
That we may enhance the bliss and joy of others.

Panchen Lama Losang Chokyi Gyaltsan,
Offering to the Spiritual Guide

There are two principal methods for developing great love and great compassion and for developing the bodhichitta mind – the mind wishing to attain enlightenment for the benefit of others.

The first is known as the sevenfold cause-and-effect instructions. We begin by reflecting that: (1) all beings have been our mother and (2) have shown us great kindness (see nos. 193–4). Through this meditation we (3) seek to repay this kindness and (4) develop affectionate love (see no. 195) and then (5) great compassion (see nos. 196–7) which expresses itself in (6) superior intention (see no. 205) and (7) the bodhichitta attitude (see no. 206).

The second method, called 'equalising and exchanging self for others', involves changing the object of our concern and cherishing from self to others. This method begins with the recognition of the fundamental equality between ourselves and others. Just as we wish for happiness and freedom from suffering so too do all beings. We meditate: 'I myself do not have the slightest wish to experience suffering and I am not content with the happiness I enjoy, but exactly the same goes for everyone else. Therefore it is inappropriate for me to consider myself to be more important than everyone else. I want happiness, but so do others. I want freedom from misery, but so do others. Since we all want the same thing, I shall regard others in the same way as I regard myself.'

The Dangers of Self-cherishing

199.

This chronic disease of cherishing ourselves
Is the cause giving rise to our unwanted suffering.
Perceiving this we seek your blessings, O Buddha,
To blame, begrudge and destroy the monstrous demon of selfishness.
                    Panchen Lama Losang Chokyi Gyaltsan,
                          Offering to the Spiritual Guide

Having gained an understanding of the equality between self and others (see no. 198), we then begin to recognise the faults and dangers of cherishing ourselves more than others.

Self-cherishing is a mind which attributes supreme importance to itself. Considering ourselves to be so important, we have a strong desire to secure our own welfare, but to do this we sometimes have to commit unwholesome actions which cause us to experience future suffering and dissatisfaction. In this way, all our problems, external and internal, arise directly or indirectly from our attitude of self-cherishing and cannot be traced to any other source. What is it that causes a criminal to experience all the miseries of imprisonment? The real criminal is the self-cherishing mind that drove him to commit his crime. Similarly, when a mouse is caught in a trap, its own self-cherishing is what really catches it, because self-cherishing drives the mouse to seize the cheese.

The reason why all beings are reborn within samsara is due to past actions committed out of self-cherishing. We have been pursuing our own welfare since beginningless time, but all we have succeeded in obtaining is suffering. Because of self-cherishing we have wasted countless lives.

To become convinced of the great dangers of self-cherishing, we need to check thoroughly to see if we can find any example of physical or mental suffering that is not directly or indirectly caused by self-cherishing. If we cannot, we should recognise clearly that all problems, miseries and faults, both internal and external, arise from self-cherishing. With this recognition we can make a firm decision to abandon self-cherishing. When we have made this decision we take it as our object of single-pointed meditation. Whenever we encounter problems we should think, 'This very problem is a result of my self-cherishing' and then strengthen our resolution to abandon it.

The Benefits of Cherishing Others

200.

The mind that cherishes all the motherly beings
And seeks to secure them in bliss is a gateway leading to
infinite virtue.
Seeing this, we seek your blessings, O Buddhas, to cherish
these beings more than our lives,
Even should they rise up as our enemies.

Panchen Lama Losang Chokyi Gyaltsan,
Offering to the Spiritual Guide

On the basis of understanding the equality of self and others, and having seen the dangers of self-cherishing (see nos. 198–9), we then look at the benefits of cherishing others.

When we cherish others, we will want to benefit them. With this motivation we will engage in positive actions and create the cause for future happiness. All the happiness of this world comes from the mind desiring others to be happy. If others now regard us with affection, love and concern, it is because we have cherished them in the past.

All the temporary happiness and possessions of this life, including our very life, are due to the kindness of others. Our food, shelter, clothing, and means of livelihood all arise from their kindness, both now and in the past. Even our money comes from the kindness of others. We think it is ours and has nothing to do with anyone else because we earned it. But who provided us with a job to earn the money? Who is it that makes sure our work is in demand? Who educated us to be able to get the job? It is others who employ us and create our jobs. All the happiness of our future lives also depends upon the kindness of others because it is through our relationships with others that we practise generosity, moral discipline, patience and joyous effort, which are the causes of higher rebirth. Furthermore, all ultimate happiness depends upon the kindness of others because we need others to develop great compassion and bodhichitta, the causes of full enlightenment. We can develop bodhichitta (a mind wishing to attain enlightenment for the benefit of all beings) only by taking all other living beings as our objects of cherishing. Since others are of supreme benefit to us, we should cherish them most dearly.

Exchanging Self with Others

201.

In brief, the childish work only for their own benefit
While Buddhas work solely for others.
With a mind understanding the distinctions between the
*   faults of one*
And the advantages of the other,
We seek your blessings, O Buddhas,
To enable us to equalise and exchange our self for others.

Since cherishing ourselves is a doorway to all torment,
While cherishing our mothers is the foundation for all that is good,
We seek your blessings, O Buddhas, to make our core practice
The yoga of exchanging self for others.

                              Panchen Lama Losang Chokyi Gyaltsan,
                                    Offerings to the Spiritual Guide

If we know why we need to cherish others and we are convinced that we are able to do it, we will arrive at a firm decision and it will be easy to engage in the actual practice of changing the object of cherishing from self to others. However, we cannot expect instant success. At first, there will be many people whom we find difficult to cherish. We need to train gradually, starting with those who are close to us, then expanding our cherishing to more and more people. When we are actually in meditation, we take all living beings as our object and develop a mind that cherishes all of them, but we need to meditate like this over and over again without expectation of quick results.

The sign of completing this training is that whenever we see others we spontaneously cherish them in the same way we used to cherish ourselves. With this realisation, whenever we see someone suffering we feel it is unbearable in the way we would if we were experiencing it ourselves, and whenever we see someone with happiness we feel love, wishing them to enjoy their happiness for ever.

Taking and Giving

202.

O venerable and compassionate guru,
Bless me to take all the negativities and suffering
Of mother sentient beings upon myself
And give to others my happiness and virtuous actions.
May all sentient beings be happy!

> Panchen Lama Losang Chokyi Gyaltsan,
> *Offering to the Spiritual Guide*

It is not unusual to be able to exchange self for others for a short time – a few minutes or even a few days. But what we are aiming for is a lasting experience or stable realisation. Once we have some familiarity with exchanging self for others, we can engage in the practice of taking and giving to increase and stablise our experience. The main purpose of this practice is to improve our compassion and love. It also transforms our misfortunes into the spiritual path and accumulates great and powerful merit.

We first practise taking away the miseries and suffering of others and then we practise giving them our happiness and health. We practise taking before giving because it is impossible for others to receive happiness while they are over-burdened with suffering.

There are various ways to practise taking. We begin by imagining that we are surrounded by all living beings and then we contemplate their suffering. In this way we generate compassion, thinking, 'How wonderful it would be if all these living beings were free from their sufferings right now. I, myself, will make it happen.' Then we can imagine all the sufferings of living beings in the form of black smoke which we draw into our heart where our self-cherishing mind is concentrated. As it dissolves in our heart, this black light consumes our self-cherishing. When we have taken all the black light of others' suffering, we think, 'Now this black light has completely extinguished my self-cherishing and all other living beings are released from suffering. Their bodies have become pure and their minds have been transformed into uncontaminated great bliss.'

Then we meditate single-pointedly on the feeling of having taken away the suffering of others. In this way, we generate the willingness to take the suffering of others upon ourselves. The purpose of this meditation is not to burden ourselves with an intolerable weight of suffering but to increase our compassion, stablise our experience of exchanging self for others and accumulate merit. Although we should not expect to relieve others' suffering directly and immediately, we can be sure that our practice of taking enriches our compassion, which, in turn, will enable us more effectively to help others gain freedom from suffering.

The practice of giving is motivated by the love that wishes all living beings happiness. We again visualise all living beings surrounding us and we consider how everyone wants pure happiness but no one in samsara experiences it. We think, 'How wonderful it would be if everyone had pure happiness. I myself will make this happen.' We imagine our body transformed into a jewel which radiates light to every single living being. When it touches those suffering in the hot hells, it is like cooling water; when it touches those suffering in the cold hells, it is like the warm sun; when it touches human beings, it becomes all the objects they desire; when it touches those who are hungry, it becomes food and drink, and so on.

When we have completed this visualisation, we meditate on the feeling that we have given all beings lasting satisfaction and joy. By doing this meditation every day, we will develop warm and loving regard for all the people we meet and eventually we will generate spontaneous love, compassion and bodhichitta (the mind wishing to attain enlightenment for the benefit of all beings). No greater qualities are needed to become a bodhisattva – one who is solely motivated to attain enlightenment for the benefit of others.

Transforming Adverse Conditions through Taking and Giving

203.

Whenever a physical illness arises, we usually multiply our suffering by worrying and by pressing mental anxiety on top of it. One should understand that the human body is a composite of elements and agents that constantly are struggling with one another. When these elements and agents fall into disharmony or when external forces such as the many types of evil powers are affected, the various diseases naturally arise with intensity and for long periods of time. Therefore one might as well face up to the fact that during the course of one's life a certain amount of disease is inevitable. When one does fall painfully ill, one should not be concerned with one's own situation. Instead consider the inconceivable sufferings of the hell denizens, the hungry ghosts, animals and so forth whose anguish is infinitely greater than one's own. Ask yourself, 'If they must bear such immense pain, how can I not bear this suffering which by comparison is so small? If I am so weakened by my suffering, how must they feel whose anguish is so much greater? May their afflictions be alleviated by this illness of mine.'

Thinking in this way, visualise that you are surrounded by all sentient beings experiencing every type of suffering. As you inhale, visualise that all their negativities and obscurations, sicknesses and pain ripen upon you, freeing them from all misery, and as you exhale, visualise all good things going to them in the form of white nectar giving them happiness. Repeat this process again and again.

As the benefits of even one moment of this contemplation surpass the effects of any other virtuous action, any illness should be seen as an excellent opportunity to practice Dharma. Think, 'Even if I never recover, I can continue to practise the meditation of taking others' suffering upon myself and giving others peace – a powerful practice unsurpassed by all. Therefore I am perfectly happy to lie here with this illness.'

If you can practise this advice from the depth of your heart, there is no doubt that you will be benefited in both this and future lives, hence keep it in mind.

Seventh Dalai Lama, *Using Illness to Train the Mind*

A very important theme in the meditations of exchanging self and others and in the practice of taking and giving is to try to use all our experiences, especially those which are bad, as a means of enhancing our spiritual practice. Whenever a good situation arises, we should think, 'This is a result of my virtue', and instead of being distracted by the pleasurable situation, we should motivate ourselves to increase our virtuous actions. Whenever we experience suffering, we should consider that this arises from our non-virtue and strengthen our determination to avoid negative actions. We can also use our own suffering to help us develop compassion for others, imagining taking away other people's suffering with a mind of compassion and giving them happiness with a mind of love. In this way we transform every situation, even severe pain and terminal illness, into methods of enhancing love and compassion.

Offering the Victory and Accepting the Defeat

204.

When others out of jealousy
Treat me unreasonably with abuse, insults and the like
May I accept the defeat
And offer the victory to others.
Geshe Langri Tangpa, *Eight Verses of Training the Mind*, verse 6

Defeat and victory are closely linked to self-cherishing. Practising love and compassion means giving up all self-concern even to the extent of relinquishing notions of personal victory and defeat. We should train our mind to accept defeat and offer the victory to others with love and compassion. This does not necessarily mean giving in to everybody all the time as this may not be best for them. Compassion must always be balanced with wisdom, knowing what is the most appropriate thing to do according to time and place.

This verse is famous in Tibetan Buddhism because it was after reading it, that the great bodhisattva Geshe Chekgawa became inspired to seek the teachings of love and compassion and put them into practice. Geshe Chekgawa eventually attained enlightenment and promoted the practice of equalising and exchanging self for others. These practices became known as mind-training (Tib. *lojong*).

Superior Intention

205.

It is not sufficient merely to wish for all sentient beings to be separated from suffering and possess happiness.
I myself must bring this about.

For this reason I must dispel the suffering of all sentient beings and bring them happiness,
Just as I must dispel the suffering of my mother in this life and bring her happiness.

All sentient beings want to be happy and never to suffer.
They have all been my mother and have all been equally kind to me.
Thus they are all the same.

I shall therefore take the great responsibility
Of liberating every sentient being from all
The troubles of cyclic existence and solitary peace
And of leading them to the supreme state of omniscience.
                      Geshe Tsondru, *The Essence of Nectar*

If a mother were to see her child fall into a fire, she would not rest content merely wishing for her child's safety; she would instantly, without a second thought, act to rescue her child. If a mother is experiencing pain, her children do not simply hope and pray for her to be relieved of pain; they do everything they can to ease her suffering. Similarly, having generated great compassion for all beings, we recognise the insufficiency of merely wishing that others are free from suffering. We must take responsibility ourselves for liberating all beings from suffering and leading them to perfect happiness. This is called the 'superior intention'.

Superior intention is more advanced than the wish to repay the kindness of others (see no. 194), which is motivated by the recognition of how kind others have been to us in the past, because it is motivated by great compassion. Wanting to repay the kindness of others is likened to developing the wish for something we see in the shop. Superior intention is the decision to buy.

Bodhichitta

206.

The Buddhas, reflecting with love upon all beings
And wishing to help them,
Ask, 'By what means might we help?'
They see only this, the supreme awakening mind of bodhichitta.

Converging waters form the ocean
And from these oceans clouds arise
And by these clouds is the earth made fertile
And in like manner are beings made beautiful through bodhichitta.

Out of the precepts 'All beings are our mother'
And 'Mindfulness of their kindness' is bodhichitta born.
Out of the precepts 'Intent to repay their kindness',
*   'Genial love', 'Compassion' and 'Exceptional resolve' is*
*   bodhichitta born.*
Thus assiduously strive to engender them.
  Kuna Lama Rinpoche, *A Precious Lamp in Praise of Bodhichitta*

With superior intention (see no. 205) we are like a parent who, seeing their child drowning, personally undertakes to rescue the child. However, such a thing is only possible if the parent is able to swim. We may wish to liberate all beings but are we able to accomplish this task? By checking we will recognise that even bodhisattvas (those who seek enlightenment for all beings) do not have the ability. Only those who have realised Buddhahood themselves have all the necessary qualities.

Through meditating in this way we develop bodhichitta, the mind wishing to attain enlightenment for the benefit of all beings, as the only perfectly effective means of fulfilling our wish to help all beings. Seeking enlightenment for ourselves is like searching for a cup when we want a cup of tea. The cup is the necessary means for achieving the end of drinking tea. Similarly, we need to attain enlightenment as the necessary means for achieving the end of helping all beings attain lasting happiness.

The sign that we have realised bodhichitta is that in every moment of our lives we have the strong wish to attain enlightenment for the sake of others.

Kuna Lama Rinpoche, a famous teacher who died in 1976, was born in the Kuna area of the Indian Himalayas and was educated in Tibet.

Maintaining and Strengthening Bodhichitta

207.

> *May the precious bodhichitta grow*
> *Where it has not yet grown,*
> *Where it has grown, may it not decrease*
> *But flourish for ever.*

Tibetan prayer

This verse encapsulates the whole practice of bodhichitta (the mind wishing to attain enlightenment for the benefit of all beings). In the first two lines we pray that all beings, including ourselves, who have not yet given birth to true bodhichitta, may do so. In the next line, we pray that those who have already given birth to the altruistic mind of bodhichitta may be able to maintain it, and in the final line we pray that those who have cultivated and stabilised bodhichitta may be able to bring it to its full completion.

The way to increase our bodhichitta is to engage in the six perfections of the bodhisattva path. These practices are called 'perfections' because they are undertaken with the compassionate motivation of bodhichitta. These are the main methods through which a bodhisattva attains enlightenment.

The Perfection of Giving (1)

208.

> *Giving is a wish-granting gem, fulfilling the hopes of beings,*
> *The best weapon to sever the knots of miserliness,*
> *A bodhisattva's deed that generates undaunting courage,*
> *Foundation for one's good reputation to spread afar.*
>
> *Knowing this, the wise relied on this excellent path*
> *Of giving their body, possessions and merits,*
> *I, a yogi, practised this way,*
> *You, who seek liberation, please do the same.*

Je Tsongkhapa,
Condensed Exposition on the Stages of the Path, verse 23

Giving is a wholesome mind that decides to give and motivates physical and verbal acts of giving. All giving motivated by bodhichitta (the mind wishing to attain enlightenment for the benefit of all beings) is the perfection of giving because it is a path that leads to enlightenment. There are three kinds of giving: giving of material things, giving of Dharma and giving of fearlessness.

Giving material things is a wholesome mind wishing to give either our possessions or our own body to others. However, it is not possible to develop the wish to give away our body until we have first trained in developing the wish to give away our possessions and enjoyments. First we need to contemplate the benefits of giving and the disadvantages of miserliness and then put giving material things into practice.

There are many factors which affect the amount of merit or positive spiritual energy we accumulate through giving. For instance, the most powerful objects of our generosity are Buddhas, spiritual guides, our parents and those who are in great need.

The purity and strength of our motivation is also important in determining the merit of our giving. When we give, our minds should be free from strong delusions such as pride and we should have a beneficial intention. A single crumb given with pure compassion to an insect is more virtuous than a diamond given to someone whilst taking pride in the great rarity of the gift.

Also, our actions of giving are less powerful if they are attended by a feeling of loss or we later regret our generosity. Actions of so-called giving prompted by unwholesome motivations can never be actions of giving because giving is necessarily a wholesome state of mind. For instance, when large and powerful nations motivated by arrogance, greed or the desire to dominate internationally give arms and aid to smaller countries, these are not real acts of giving.

The Perfection of Giving (2)

209.

If those who wish for enlightenment give up even their own body,
What need is there to speak of giving up external things?
Thus offering gifts with no thought of return or fully ripening effects
Is a practice of the bodhisattvas.

Togme Zangpo,
Thirty-seven Practices of All the Bodhisattvas, verse 27

As well as giving material things (see no. 208), the perfection of giving also refers to the giving of Dharma and of fearlessness.

There are many ways to give Dharma. Whenever we dedicate our virtues to the peace and happiness of all beings, give helpful advice, express pleasant thoughts, or simply whisper mantras into the ears of animals, we are giving Dharma. Just one sentence of Dharma teachings offered with good motivation to someone else will give more benefit than all our worldly possessions. This is because material gifts help others only in this life whereas the gift of Dharma helps them in all their future lives.

To give fearlessness is to protect other beings from fear and danger, either through physically rescuing them or praying and making offerings for their safety. We can also give fearlessness by praying for others to be free from their delusions, especially the delusion of self-grasping which is the source of all their fear.

This verse tells us that bodhisattvas are willing to give up even their own body on the path to enlightenment. One of the stories of Buddha Shakyamuni's previous lives tells how he gave up his own body to a hungry tigress when he saw that she was so crazed by hunger and thirst she was about to kill her own cubs. The bodhisattva cut his own body and allowed the tigress to lick his blood so she could gain the strength to devour him. This shows the great power of a bodhisattva's compassion. However, those who have not yet attained this level of wisdom and compassion should not attempt such a selfless action. There is no point in giving up our own body if this will not be of great benefit to others, or if it causes us pain or to regret our action later. The power of the bodhisattvas' compassion is so great that they generate tremendous joy at being able to give their bodies.

The Perfection of Moral Discipline (1)

210.

> *Moral discipline is water to cleanse the stains of faults,*
> *A ray of moonlight to cool the scorching heat of delusions,*
> *Splendour towering as a mountain in the midst of beings,*
> *Force subjugating all without recourse to intimidation.*
>
> *Knowing this, the holy ones, guarded as they would their own eyes*
> *Their perfectly adopted discipline.*
> *I, a yogi, practised this way,*
> *You, who seek liberation, please do the same.*

Je Tsongkhapa,
Condensed Exposition on the Stages of the Path, verse 25

Moral discipline is a wholesome mind that decides to abandon any faults and motivates physical or verbal actions of moral discipline. There are three kinds of moral discipline: restraint, gathering virtuous Dharma and benefiting others.

To practise the moral discipline of restraint, we need to understand the dangers of committing negative actions such as the ten unwholesome actions (see no. 176) and keep the promise to refrain from them. Those on the bodhisattva path also take bodhisattva vows to abandon actions motivated by self-cherishing. For example, the first of the eighteen root bodhisattva vows is to avoid praising oneself and belittling others. Bodhisattvas see clearly that self-cherishing is the principal opponent to developing bodhichitta (the mind wishing to attain enlightenment for the benefit of all beings) and the main obstacle to progressing to enlightenment.

The Perfection of Moral Discipline (2)

211.

If without the practice of moral discipline
It is not possible to fulfil our own purpose
Then wishing to fulfil the purpose is a joke.
Therefore, observing moral discipline without samsaric aspiration
Is a practice of the bodhisattvas.

Togme Zangpo,
Thirty-Seven Practices of All the Bodhisattvas, verse 28

As well as refraining from unwholesome actions (see no. 176), moral discipline also includes gathering Dharma virtue and benefiting others.

The moral discipline of gathering Dharma virtue includes engaging in the ten Dharma activities, which are: writing and reading Dharma books, memorising and reciting words of Dharma, making offerings to the Dharma, giving Dharma books, explaining the meaning of Dharma, listening to the Dharma, contemplating and meditating on the meaning of Dharma. Even if we do not fully understand what we hear or read, our actions of listening to and reading the Dharma are never wasted time because they create positive potentialities in the mind. Gathering Dharma virtue can also include engaging in the practice of the six perfections. Indeed, all spiritual practice with a wholesome motivation is an aspect of this moral discipline.

The moral discipline of benefiting living beings refers not only to practical acts of helping others but to the continuous intention to offer help to others whenever possible. The Indian master Asanga enumerated eleven ways of benefiting others: (1) alleviating the suffering of others and offering others assistance in their work; (2) teaching others skills, both worldly ones, such as how to read and write, as well as spiritual ones, such as how to meditate; (3) returning kindness we have received or, if this is not possible, remembering it and paying due respect; (4) removing dangers that threaten others as well as their causes and the fear they arouse, or, if we cannot do anything practical, at least praying for those in danger; (5) consoling others in their grief; (6) giving material aid to the destitute; (7) helping those who experience problems arising from strong delusions, such as anger or desirous attachment; (8) helping others in a way that is appropriate to their own views and customs. We cannot help people if we make an assault on their values and beliefs or if we completely ignore their temperament and personal circumstances. We need flexibility of mind and behaviour, sensitivity and tact. Bodhisattvas will do whatever needs to be done to make others happy and at ease, for only then will their minds be receptive to advice and example. Just as a mother will play with a child to keep it happy, so a bodhisattva will go along with others to keep them happy and provide the opportunity to help them whenever they can; (9) praising, encouraging and respecting those who have entered correct spiritual paths and helping them to continue their practice in the best way posible; (10) helping those who have entered wrong paths to see their error and to enter correct spiritual paths; (11) using whatever psychic or miracle powers we possess to help others, particularly to help those engaged in negative actions to abandon such actions.

The Perfection of Patience (1)

212.

Patience is the finest ornament for the powerful,
The best austerity to [overcome] the torments [of] delusions,
The high soaring eagle, enemy to the snake of hatred,
A solid armour [to protect from] the weapons of abuse.

Knowing this, [the wise] familiarised themselves in various ways,
With the supreme armour of patience.
I, a yogi, practised this way,
You, who seek liberation, please do the same.

Je Tsongkhapa,
Condensed Stages of the Spiritual Path, verses 27—28

Patience is a wholesome and peaceful mind which can bear any kind of suffering or harm. It is an antidote to anger, which is the true enemy of all living beings since it has been causing them pain and distress since beginningless time. If we ask who created the countless wars in which so many human beings have suffered, we have to say that all wars have been created by angry minds. If nations were full of calm and peace-loving people, how could any conflict arise? If we do not overcome it, this inner enemy will defeat us over and over again. It is like a blazing fire which quickly consumes our happiness and all the virtuous potentialities of our mind. Therefore, as soon as the match of anger is struck, we must extinguish it with patience. Patience helps us to experience happiness in this life and in all future lives.

There are three kinds of patience. The first is the patience of not retaliating. To practise this, we need to be continuously mindful of the dangers of anger and the benefits of patient acceptance. If we are attacked physically or verbally by others we should not respond with anger. When a mentally disturbed person abuses a doctor, the doctor does not lose his temper because he understands the patient's mind is out of control. Instead he shows compassion and seeks a cure for the illness. Similarly, whenever someone becomes angry he or she falls completely under the control of delusions and so is temporarily insane. There is no reason for us to respond by becoming insane ourselves.

There are many other lines of reasoning we can also use when putting this patience into practice. For example, when someone hits us with a stick, we do not get angry with the stick because we understand the stick is held in the hands of our attacker and has no freedom. Nor do we get angry with his hands because we know they are not in control of their own movements. Similarly, we should feel no anger towards the person who is attacking because he also has no choice. He is driven by anger and is not in charge of his own actions.

If we are going to get angry at anything, we should get angry with anger itself.

If someone tries to harm us physically or interfere with our life, we should try to solve such problems skilfully without anger. If, for example, we feel anger rising in response to harsh or mocking words, we should ask ourselves, 'Why am I getting angry? These words cannot hurt my body, nor can they hurt my mind. It is the anger I am generating that will hurt my mind.' In themselves the words are empty and cannot affect us. If someone calls us a cow we are not thereby transformed into a cow.

We should also remember that we ourselves have directly or indirectly created the causes for the anger shown to us. Just as without fuel there could be no fire, so without our previous negative actions there could be no anger in this person's mind. Therefore, we have no reason to get angry or to blame the other person.

By meditating on these lines of thought over and over again, we will develop wisdom. If we then combine our wisdom with mindfulness, never forgetting what we have understood, we will find it easy to be patient.

The Perfection of Patience (2)

213.

For the bodhisattva wishes for the wealth of virtue.
All those who harm him are like a precious treasure.
Therefore, meditating on patience without hatred for anyone

Is a practice of the bodhisattvas.

Togme Zangpo,
Thirty-seven Practices of All the Bodhisattvas, verse 29

As well as the patience of not retaliating (see no. 212) there is also the patience of voluntarily enduring suffering and the patience of definitely thinking about the Dharma.

The essence of patiently enduring suffering is to transform experiences of pain and frustration into a method of enriching our spiritual practice. With such a practice we remain happy in the very midst of circumstances that others would regard as unbearable. Furthermore, we are able to accomplish both our temporary worldly wishes and our ultimate, spiritual wishes. If there is a way of changing adverse conditions we should change them, but if there is not then we should patiently endure such situations and try to use them in a positive way.

Without the patience of voluntarily enduring suffering, we easily become discouraged whenever we encounter obstacles and so find it hard to complete our tasks. Our impatience actually aggravates our miseries and frustrations. Patient acceptance of suffering will diminish our suffering. For example, if someone sticks a large needle into our flesh, we usually find it intolerable, but if the needle contains a vaccine we want to receive, our tolerance increases considerably.

Patience of definitely thinking about Dharma includes listening, studying, contemplating and meditating on the Buddha's teachings with joyful application. With this attitude of mind we will definitely gain special Dharma wisdom.

The Perfection of Joyous Effort (1)

214.

Relying upon the boat of a human [body],
Free yourself from the great river of pain!
As it is hard to find this boat again,
This is no time for sleep, you fool!

Having rejected the supreme joy of the sacred Dharma
That is a boundless source of delight,
Why am I distracted by the causes of pain?
Why do I enjoy frivolous amusements and the like?

Without indulging in despondency I should gather the supports
*   [for enthusiasm]*
And earnestly take control of myself.

[*Then by seeing*] *the equality between self and others,*
I shall practise exchanging self for others.

Shantideva,
Guide to the Bodhisattva's Way of Life, ch. 7, verses 14–16

Joyous effort is a mind that delights in wholesome actions. With joyous effort we can gain all temporary worldly happiness as well as ultimate spiritual happiness. Without effort, even if we possess wisdom, we are unable to complete our spiritual practice. To generate effort we have to abandon its main opponent, laziness. There are three kinds of laziness: procrastination, being attracted to what is meaningless or unwholesome, and discouragement.

If we are interested in Dharma, believe it to be worthwhile and intend to practise it, but think that the time to practise it is some time in the future, we are suffering from the laziness of procrastination. This laziness is very harmful because time passes quickly and, as our lifespan is uncertain, our opportunities are soon lost.

Most of us are very familiar with the laziness of being attracted to what is meaningless or unwholesome. We give in to it whenever we watch television for hours on end without caring what comes on, indulge in prolonged and pointless conversations or become engrossed in sport or business ventures just for the sake of it. Activities such as these dissipate the energy we have for practising Dharma. Indeed, our spiritual practice begins to feel like an obstacle to our pleasures. If we do not overcome this laziness, we can gradually become so involved in meaningless activities that we give up our Dharma practices completely. To prevent this we need to meditate again and again on the dangers of samsara (the cycle of uncontrolled birth and death), reminding ourselves that all the entertainments of worldly life are deceptive. They bind us within samsara and are the basis for future suffering.

There are many things that can induce the laziness of discouragement. Since we cannot see living examples of Buddhas with our own eyes, we may doubt whether such a state is possible or conclude that it must be so rare there is no hope that we ourselves can attain it. We may also see faults in our spiritual guide and in those who are practising Dharma and conclude that they have no realisations, and therefore efforts put into Dharma practice are wasted. If we find we are becoming discouraged in this way, we need to remember that to the minds of ordinary beings every appearance is mistaken because it is contaminated by ignorance.

We can also reflect upon our own potential as human beings. By gradually increasing the qualities of our mind we will know from our own experience how we gain greater happiness. With effort, everything can be achieved. We gain experience of the Dharma and our problems become fewer, our progress towards enlightenment is easier and we are able to accomplish tasks such as the bodhisattva's giving of his or her own body. We have the seed of enlightenment and we have found the perfect methods for gaining enlightenment. All we need is to apply it. It is not necessary to undergo unusual hardships, so what reason is there to become discouraged?

The Perfection of Joyous Effort (2)

215.

If one wears the armour of resolute, irreversible joyous effort,
Knowledge of scriptures and insight will increase like the waxing moon,
All actions one engages in will come to have meaning
And whatever task is undertaken will reach its intended conclusion.

Knowing this, the bodhisattvas exerted great waves of joyous effort
To dispel laziness [in all its forms].
I, a yogi, practised this way,
You, who seek liberation, please do the same.

Je Tsongkhapa,
Condensed Stages on the Path to Enlightenment, verses 29—30

There are three kinds of effort: strong armour-like effort; the effort of gathering virtuous Dharma; and the effort of benefiting living beings.

Strong armour-like effort arises from the confidence that whatever difficulties we encounter we shall achieve our aim of Buddahood for the sake of others. When we get up in the morning or at the beginning of any spiritual activity we need to put on this strong armour-like effort to protect us from the enemy laziness, deciding to persevere throughout the day or activity, and not be overwhelmed or depressed by setbacks or apparent lack of results.

The effort of gathering virtuous Dharma is the energy we put into wholesome actions. The moral discipline of gathering Dharma virtue (see no. 211) is principally the wish to engage in positive actions, whereas this effort is the actual exertion of effort towards any wholesome action. Likewise, the effort of benefiting others is the exertion of effort to fulfil the moral discipline of benefiting others.

Once we have generated effort we need to maintain it continuously if we are to accomplish our goal. There are four powers that increase our effort: aspiration, steadfastness, joy and relaxation. The stronger our aspiration to do something, the greater our effort to do it. We generate aspiration to engage in wholesome actions by seeing their benefits.

Steadfastness is the power of consistency which is essential to maintain steady, continuous effort. Our practice should be like the gentle flow of a broad river, not like the erratic flow of a mountain stream.

Joy is a power because it enables us to accomplish our spiritual tasks quickly and easily. It makes our efforts strong and courageous. If we are anxious or depressed, our efforts will be blocked and frustrated. When we practise Dharma we should be like a child at play. When children are engrossed in their play they are totally contented and cannot be distracted.

At times, when our mind becomes over-excited, we need to calm it down by doing meditations such as those on death, impermanence and the truth of suffering. However, it would be a mistake to apply these methods when we are feeling sad or depressed. At such times we need to encourage ourselves by meditating on the qualities and fortune of our precious human life, which provides us with the opportunity to gain the ultimate happiness of enlightenment.

Relaxation is a power because it protects and supports our constant effort. If we neglect the need for rest and become over-tired, we are not able to exert effort again with joy, but if we relax at the right time, we will soon be able to apply fresh effort.

The Perfection of Mental Stabilisation (Concentration) (1)

216.

Concentration is the king to rule the mind.
When fixed, it is immovable as a vast mountain.
When directed, it can engage in any object of virtue,
Inducing great bliss of physical and mental flexibility.

Knowing this, the powerful yogis have always relied
On the concentration which destroys the enemy of mental wandering.
I, a yogi, practised this way,
You, who seek liberation, please do the same.

Je Tsongkhapa,
Condensed Stages on the Path to Enlightenment, verses 31—2

Mental stabilisation or concentration is a wholesome mind that remains on its object single-pointedly. It controls and prevents conceptual thoughts and other distractions. Without the power of concentration our mind is weak like a candle-flame in the wind, and we are unable to muster much strength of mind when we engage in wholesome actions.

If we have perfect concentration, we will experience joy continuously and all our meditations will be successful. We will easily and powerfully eliminate mental hindrances and quickly apprehend the nature of any object we set ourselves to understand. Mental stabilisation brings the mind closer and closer to its object until they mix inseparably. In this way, concentration induces realisations at all stages of the spiritual path.

Since concentration is necessarily a wholesome mind, if we have a bad motivation it is impossible to develop real concentration. Our main aim always should be to achieve full enlightenment for the sake of others. There are many different kinds of concentration, such as mundane and supermundane. Mundane concentrations are motivated by the wish to achieve miracle powers, clairvoyance, rebirth in the god realms or greater worldly happiness. Supermundane concentrations are motivated either by a wish to gain liberation from samsara or by bodhichitta (the mind wishing to attain enlightenment for the benefit of all beings).

The Perfection of Mental Stabilisation (Concentration) (2)

217.

*Having understood that delusions can be completely destroyed
By superior seeing endowed with tranquil abiding,
Meditating on the concentration that completely surpasses the four
    formless absorptions
Is a practice of the bodhisattvas.*

Togme Zangpo,
Thirty-seven Practices of All the Bodhisattvas, verse 29

According to Buddhism, developing concentration is not an end in itself, but a means of developing greater wisdom and understanding. Specifically, we need to develop the concentration of tranquil abiding and combine this with the wisdom of superior seeing. Superior seeing is the insight into the ultimate nature of all phenomena which is developed in dependence upon tranquil abiding. Tranquil abiding (Tib. *zhine*, Sanskrit. *shamatha*) is a mind that remains single-pointedly on its object and possesses the special bliss of suppleness.

Tranquil abiding is attained in dependence upon completing nine stages of concentration or mental abidings. We first need to choose an object upon which to focus our mind. Training in tranquil abiding is the method for taming and gaining control over our wild elephant-like mind. Our object of concentration is like a fixed stake to which we tie our mind. There are many objects suitable to take as our object of tranquil abiding. Visualisation of a Buddha is widely used and practised within the Tibetan traditions and was recommended by Shakyamuni Buddha in *The King of Concentrations Sutra.* However, we can choose another wholesome object if we wish.

We then sit in a correct posture of meditation and generate a strong motivation to train in tranquil abiding for the benefit of others. Next, we have to 'find' our chosen object of meditation by examining it in detail. For example, if our object is the visualised form of a Buddha, we find it by recollecting the various aspects of its appearance. After looking at a picture of the Buddha for a few minutes, we visualise the Buddha, thumb-sized, in front of us in the space level with our eyebrows. After checking the aspects of its appearance from the crown to the feet and then back to the crown a few times, we try to establish the image in our mind's eye.

When we are able to establish a rough generic image of the whole form, we take this as our object and focus our mind on it single-pointedly. Even if the object is very vague, we have attained the first mental abiding called 'placement'. At this stage it is more important to have the strong feeling that a real living Buddha is in front of us than it is to visualise the object clearly. When we are able to hold our object single-pointedly for about five minutes we attain the second level of tranquil abiding called 'continuous placement.' Through training we will achieve the third stage, 'replacement', when even if we lose our object we can immediately regain it without having to go through a checking process to refind it. This is like a child whose co-ordination has developed far enough for him or her to pick up the ball easily when he or she drops it.

As our concentration becomes stronger and we are able to overcome first gross and then subtle distractions of the mind, we progress through the remaining mental abidings, achieving the ninth stage known as 'spontaneous placement'. At this stage, once we have decided to practise concentration and recall our object, concentration comes effortlessly and spontaneously. We then continue training until we attain tranquil abiding, developing a special suppleness free from all mental and physical inflexibility and heaviness. Our mind becomes clear and so we do not experience obstacles to engaging in wholesome actions.

'The four formless absorptions' referred to in this reading are the meditations practised by those on the mundane paths (see no. 216). By practising with a motivation other than the wish to gain liberation or enlightenment we can attain very advanced stages of concentration, clairvoyance and miracle powers, but these are still mundane meditations. When the energy generated through these concentrations is exhausted, one is again reborn into lower realms of cyclic existence. We should put all our efforts into developing supermundane concentration and use this to cultivate wisdom which will uproot ignorance, the source of all problems.

The Perfection of Wisdom

218.

If wisdom is lacking, full enlightenment cannot be attained by the other five perfections alone.
Therefore, meditating with non-conceptual wisdom on [the nature] of the three spheres,

In conjunction with method
Is a practice of the bodhisattvas.

Togme Zangpo,
Thirty-seven Practices of All the Bodhisattvas, verse 30

Wisdom is a wholesome mind that functions principally to dispel doubt and confusion by thoroughly understanding any object of knowledge. Just as a blind man cannot reach his destination unless he has a guide, so, without wisdom, the other five perfections are blind and cannot take us to our destination of full enlightenment. Without wisdom it is impossible to perform any wholesome action because wisdom distinguishes between what is wholesome and what is unwholesome. The more wisdom we have, the greater will be our wish to do what is wholesome and so the stronger our effort in Dharma practice. Mental stabilisation brings greater wisdom. All good qualities and spiritual realisations are grounded in wisdom.

When bodhisattvas practise each of the six perfections they do so in such a way that they are able to practise the other five perfections at the same time. For instance, when they practise the perfection of giving, they abandon all self-interest, thereby combining the perfection of moral discipline. They overcome any hatred or irritation they may feel towards the person who is to receive their gift and in this way practise the perfection of patience. They also give whenever they can and with joy, thereby combining the perfection of joyous effort. When they give they concentrate their minds, thinking, 'May this gift bring real benefit to this person', and so they combine giving with the perfection of mental stabilisation. When they give, bodhisattvas know that the three spheres – the gift, the act of giving and they themselves as giver – all lack inherent existence. In this way they combine the perfection of wisdom. Practising in this way is the skilful action of a bodhisattva which hastens the completion of the two accumulations of merit and wisdom.

Superior Seeing
The Four Point Analysis (1)

219.

In the final analysis, this is the root of cyclic existence: all phenomena of cyclic existence and transcendence appear to be self-existent and are held to be [self-existent] without the understanding that [self-existence] is merely ascribed to them by conception.

Thus the object to be refuted is a self which appears to be a self-existent I, rather than I ascribed to the assemblage of my body and mind.

Geshe Tsondru, *The Essence of Nectar*

Superior seeing (Tib. *lhag tong,* Sanskrit *vipashyana*) is a superior wisdom arising in dependence upon tranquil abiding (see no. 217). The superior seeing of the perfection of wisdom is a path to full enlightenment, and it eliminates all faults and delusions.

When we have attained tranquil abiding we can examine the nature of our object of meditation. Eventually, we will discover that it has two natures, a conventional one and an ultimate one. Through further investigation we will see with increasing clarity the ultimate nature of the object is emptiness, until finally we realise it directly. We need to realise emptiness to gain liberation or full enlightenment.

Emptiness refers to the way in which all phenomena exist; that is, lacking or empty of inherent existence. If things existed inherently they would not be dependent upon causes and conditions for their existence, but because things are dependently related they do not exist inherently.

Self-grasping is the conception that grasps things as existing inherently. When we realise that the objects of the self-grasping mind, inherently existing phenomena, do not exist at all, we can completely destroy self-grasping and thereby become free of all suffering and problems.

If we first understand how a person is empty we will easily understand how other phenomena are empty. One of the methods for gaining a clear understanding of the emptiness of persons is presented in four essential steps:

(1) ascertaining the object of negation,
(2) ascertaining the pervasion,
(3) ascertaining the absence of true oneness,
(4) ascertaining the absence of true difference.

Ascertaining the object of negation

The first step in realising emptiness is to identify what inherent existence is. If we want to remove our enemy we have to identify him clearly, otherwise we may remove our friend. In realising emptiness of persons we have to identify an independent person, someone who exists inherently without depending on causes and conditions. If we cannot find such a person, then we will know that such an inherently existent person does not exist. By analogy, before we can say that rabbits do not have horns on their head, we have to know what horns on a rabbit's head would look like if they did exist.

We begin by meditating upon our 'I'. An inherently existing 'I' is always appearing to our mind and we are always grasping it, even in our sleep. We consider how we are grasping at self, what is the 'I' that appears to our mind, and in this way we try to establish a clear image of the inherently existent 'I'. If someone describes to us their holiday house we can perceive a clear image of it even though we have never seen it. This image of the house is its generic image. Similarly, by considering the 'I' that usually appears in our mind, which is the object of our self-grasping, we can gain a clear generic image of the inherently existing 'I'. We can think to ourselves 'I am reading this book' and then ask ourselves 'How does the "I" that is reading this book appear to my mind?' We will observe that this 'I' appears as different from, and independent of, our body and mind. We do not feel that 'I am reading this book' means the same as 'my body is reading this book' or 'my mind is reading this book'. The 'I' appears to exist from its own side. This independent 'I', if it exists, is the inherently existent 'I', the 'I' we cherish.

At this stage, we should deliberately cultivate a strong sense of 'I' and establish a rough generic image. Then we can concentrate on it, thinking: 'This is the "I" that I cherish. This is the "I" reading this book. This is the "I" that works and sleeps. This is the independent inherent existing "I"'.

Having established a rough generic image of the 'I', we then do placement meditation (see no. 217) to become more familiar with it. We should spend as long as necessary at this stage, even years, because it is an essential foundation for the subsequent steps of the four point meditation.

Superior Seeing(2)

220.

> *If the I exists in the [self-existent] way that it appears to exist then that [self-existent] I must be either identical with both the body and mind or separate from them for there is no third way that we can exist.*
>
> *If [there is a self-existent I that is] identical [with the body and mind] then just as the body and mind are two [entities] the I must also be two separate continuums. Or since the I is one entity, both the body and mind must likewise be an indivisible whole.*
>
> *If one says that [there is a self-existent I that is] separate [from the body and mind] then they must be individual [entities]. [Thus one must be able to say] this is the body, this is the mind, this is the I. But since [three individual entities] do not exist like this, [a self-existent I] does not exist separate [from the body and mind].*
>
> Geshe Tsondru, *The Essence of Nectar*

As a result of practising the first stage of the four point analysis (see no. 219), we have ascertained the object to be negated – the inherently existent 'I'.

Ascertaining the pervasion

When we apprehend the generic image of the object of negation, the inherently existing 'I', we proceed to investigate whether such an 'I' actually exists. The first step is to ascertain the pervasion that: if an inherently existing 'I' exists, it must be either one with or different from the aggregates of body and mind. There is no third possibility. By analogy, if we want to know if there is a fish in our house, either it is inside the aquarium or outside the aquarium. There is no third place where it could be. If we establish that there is no fish inside or outside the aquarium we can firmly conclude that there is no fish in our house.

Ascertaining the absence of true oneness

The next step in our meditation is to find out whether or not the inherently existent 'I' is one with the aggregates of body and mind. If the 'I' is one with them, it follows that one person has two 'I's. Alternatively 'I' must either be one with the body or one with the mind. If it is one with the body, it follows that when our body is cremated or decomposed, the 'I' becomes nonexistent and so there can be no rebirth. If the 'I' and the mind are one, it follows that one person is many 'I's because there are many minds: wholesome minds, unwholesome minds and so forth. Furthermore, we refer to 'my body' and 'my mind', indicating clearly that we regard the 'I' as possessing the mind and body and therefore different from them.

From these reasons it follows that the 'I' is not one with the aggregates of body and mind or with any one of them. Having firmly concluded this, we should then meditate single-pointedly on this conclusion.

Ascertaining the absence of true difference

The fourth step of the meditation is to investigate the remaining possibility that the inherently existing 'I' is different from the body and mind. If the 'I' is different from the mind and body, it would not make sense to say 'I am getting old' when our body is ageing. It would make just as much sense to say 'I am getting old' when our dog's body is ageing because both bodies would be equally different from our 'I'. Likewise if the 'I' were different from the mind and body, it would be nonsense to say 'I have a headache'.

Furthermore, if the 'I' were different from the aggregates of mind and body, we would be able to find it apart from the aggregates. For example, take someone called Peter. If Peter's 'I' were different from his body and mind, we would be able to find Peter leaving aside his body and mind. However, apart from his body and mind, it is impossible to find Peter. For these reasons, it follows that the 'I' does not exist separately from the body and mind. Once again we should meditate single-pointedly on this conclusion.

When we have ascertained the absence of true difference we are close to realising that the inherently existent 'I' does not exist at all. At this point, we need to recall the generic image of the inherently existent 'I'. Until now we have believed this 'I' to exist, but upon thorough investigation we have seen that no such 'I' exists. Having checked the two possibilities that it is one with the aggregates of body and mind or different from them, we have found it to be neither.

As a result of engaging in this analytical meditation we become aware that the inherently existent 'I' we usually perceive does not exist. We ascertain the emptiness of our 'I'. At this point, we do not need to think specifically, 'This is emptiness', we just meditate single-pointedly on the absence of an inherently existing 'I'. Through this meditation, called 'space-like meditative equipoise', we feel there is no 'I' to cherish. By repeated meditation on emptiness, our self-grasping and other delusions will lessen. Eventually we will realise emptiness directly and eliminate the root of all our problems.

The Results of Wisdom

221.

From what are pleasure and pain derived?
What is there to be happy or unhappy about?
When I search for the ultimate nature
Who is there to crave and what is there to crave for?

Upon analysis, this world of living beings [is found to have no true
*   existence]*
Therefore who can die here?
What is there to come and what has been?
Who are friends and who are relatives?

O you [who are investigating reality]
Please recognise as I have done that all is just like space.
Those who wish to be happy
Are greatly disturbed by the causes for conflict
And overjoyed by the causes for pleasure.

But not finding happiness they suffer.
And in order to find it they exert themselves.
They argue with others, cut and stab one another.
With many evil deeds they live in a state of great hardship.

Within conditioned existence the chasms [of suffering] are many
And the [liberating comprehension of] ultimate truth is absent.
Furthermore [the apprehension of true existence and the
 understanding of emptiness] mutually contradict one another.
But if, while in conditioned existence, I do not [realise] this ultimate
 truth,
I shall [continue to experience] a limitless ocean of misery
Unbearable and beyond analogy.

Shantideva,
A Guide to the Bodhisattva's Way of Life, ch. 9, verses 152–5, 157–8

Having firmly concluded that there is no inherently existent 'I', we improve our understanding so that we realise the subtle conventional 'I', the 'I' that is merely imputed by conception. We need to consider how does the 'I' exist? When we realise the 'I' exists as a mere name imputed by conception, we realise subtle conventionality and the union of the two truths, conventional and ultimate. We see that functioning things exist as mere imputations. Our 'I' is merely imputed by conception, which is a mind that conceives 'I' and clings to it. It is the merely imputed 'I' that creates karma, experiences suffering and so forth. For instance, if we dream we are being pursued by a tiger, we may become frightened in our dream, but only because we believe the tiger to be real. In fact it is a creation of our mind. Our 'I' is like this dream tiger. Whenever the 'I' appears to our mind we believe it truly exists and we develop anxiety, discontent and so forth, but apart from the conception of 'I', there is no 'I'. The same thing applies to any other object we investigate. We never find anything existing from its own side. All we ever find is emptiness.

As long as we apprehend ourselves and others to exist inherently we discriminate strongly between self and others and commit many negative actions that cause us to continue experiencing suffering within samsara (the cycle of uncontrolled birth and death). Through realising the emptiness of self and others we will cease to commit such unwholesome actions. The way to meditate on the emptiness of others is to follow the same procedure as before (see nos. 219–20) beginning by identifying the object of negation as an inherently existing friend, stranger or enemy.

When we arise from meditation in which we have realised the emptiness of the inherently existing 'I', the 'I' will still continue to appear to us as if it were inherently existent. It has appeared in this way since beginningless time and this appearance does not immediately cease as soon as we have negated inherent existence in our meditation. Therefore, our practice outside formal meditation sessions is to disbelieve this appearance. We continuously remember our realisation of emptiness and recognise the appearance of inherent existence as false. If we look into a mirror we can see our face reflected, but the face in the mirror is just a reflection and not a real face existing on the other side. Similarly, the 'I' also does not exist on the other side. Whenever any inherently existing phenomena appear to our mind, this very appearance will remind us that there are no inherently existing phenomena, thereby helping us to maintain our realisation of emptiness at all times.

Realisation of emptiness is a universal remedy because it is the only experience that alone solves all our problems. It removes the physical and mental torment of this life and all future lives because it completely destroys self-grasping, which is the root cause of all suffering.

Entering the Tantric Path

222.

When I become a suitable vessel through training in common paths
Please bless me to enter quickly
The supreme vehicle, the vajrayana,
The holy gateway for those of good fortune.
                    Je Tsongkhapa, *The Foundation of All Excellence*, verse 10

As this verse indicates, when we reach a certain level on the spiritual path through following the sutra teachings of Buddha, we should enter the vajrayana, sometimes known as tantra or secret mantra, which is the gateway for 'those of good fortune', the bodhisattvas. Vajrayana literally means 'vehicle of indestructible union'. By practising vajrayana we accumulate wisdom and merit within one concentration, whereas in sutrayana they can only be done separately.

All the tantric practices of Tibetan Buddhism have their source in the tantra teachings of Buddha. Buddha taught four sets of tantra in accordance with the different degrees of ability and wisdom amongst disciples. Action tantra stresses external actions, performance tantra places equal stress on external and internal actions, yoga tantra focuses on internal action, and the supreme class of tantra, called highest yoga tantra, is the only tantra that has complete methods for gaining full enlightenment in one lifetime.

The practice of highest yoga tantra is very extensive, but all the practices are included within five: generating bodhichitta (see no. 189), receiving empowerments, maintaining commitments and vows purely, practising the yogas of generation stage and practising the yogas of completion stage.

If we practise tantra without having the motivation of bodhichitta we cannot attain enlightenment. Bodhichitta is like the outer door to tantric practice and receiving empowerments is like the inner door. This is why the bodhisattva vows, which are trainings in love and compassion, are always granted before a tantric empowerment is given.

Maintaining Vows and Commitments Purely on the Tantric Path

223.

With a deep and genuine understanding that
The basis for achieving the two aspects of powerful attainment
Is perfect observance of my vows and commitments,
Please bless me to observe these even at the cost of my life.
        Je Tsongkhapa, *The Foundation of All Excellence*, verse. 11

After taking tantric vows we must keep vows and commitments purely. One of the misconceptions about tantra, based largely on a misunderstanding of the symbolic use of sexual imagery in tantric meditation, is that tantric practice is immoral. On the contrary, a tantric practitioner must observe very strict vows that help control and channel the subtle energies of body, speech and mind. He or she must always turn away from negative actions and cultivate positive actions and attitudes based on love and compassion, and never needlessly break vows of individual liberation. Practitioners must observe all these vows and commitments if they are to make any real progress on the tantric path. Just as when a field is filled with stones and weeds, crops do not grow easily in it, if our moral discipline is impure, it will be very difficult for us to gain the special realisations of tantra.

The Two Stages of Highest Yoga Tantra

224.

Having realised the significance of the two stages
Which are the essence of the tantras,
Please bless me to practise the four sessions of yoga without wavering
    and with joyful effort,
And achieve joyful realisations in accordance with the teachings of the
    holy ones.
        Je Tsongkhapa, *The Foundation of All Excellence*, verse. 12

The 'two stages' of the tantric path are known as the generation and completion stages. The main function of these yogas or meditation practices is to purify ordinary death, ordinary intermediate stage and ordinary rebirth, which follow one another relentlessly like a wheel spinning, keeping ordinary beings trapped within samsara. Ordinary death, ordinary intermediate stage and ordinary rebirth are also called the 'three basic bodies' because they are the basis for achieving the three bodies of a Buddha: truth body, enjoyment body and emanation body. The truth body is the omniscient mind of a Buddha. The enjoyment body is the completely purified form of a Buddha. The emanation bodies are the forms which Buddhas manifest to help beings who cannot perceive the other bodies of a Buddha.

Generation stage purifies the three basic bodies indirectly, whereas the yogas of completion stage purify them directly. To attain realisations of generation stage we need to do meditation that has the following three features:

(1) Bringing the three bodies of a Buddha into the path: namely, bringing death into the path of the truth body, bringing the intermediate stage into the path of the enjoyment body and bringing birth into the path of the emanation body.

(2) Generating ourself as a deity, that is, a tantric Buddha; holding this appearance clearly and developing divine pride, that is, strong identification with being the deity.

(3) Overcoming ordinary appearance and conception by depending on divine pride and clear appearance. Through cultivating clear appearance and divine pride of being the deity, the generation stage practitioner learns to think, speak and act now as if he or she was already a fully enlightened being. This is a particularly powerful method that brings the future result of enlightenment into the present spiritual path.

Through practising generation stage we create the conditions for the ripening of completion stage realisations. In completion stage, ordinary death, intermediate stage and rebirth are directly and completely purified and we achieve the three bodies of a Buddha.

The Final Resultant Enlightenment

225.

May beings not experience the misery of lower realms
May they never know any hardships
With a physical form superior to the gods
May they swiftly attain Buddhahood.
          A Guide to the Bodhisattva's Way of Life,   Shantideva,
                                                    ch. 10, verse 47

Buddha Shakyamuni said: 'If we realise our own mind, we are Buddha. We do not need to seek Buddha elsewhere.' To realise our own mind means to experience it as pure and free from the obstructions of delusions and their imprints. Through diligent effort in the trainings of sutra and tantra, these can be reduced and eventually removed completely. Any being who has become completely free from the two obstructions has attained Buddhahood. If we consider our peronal experience, we see that sometimes we have great and numerous faults, but at other times we have fewer faults. Since, even without applying effort, our faults and delusions sometimes decrease, this indicates that, with sufficient effort, we can abandon them completely and become a Buddha.

The extraordinary qualities of a Buddha's mind are summarised in the scriptures variously as ten powers, eighteen unmixed qualities, four fearlessnesses, four correct distinct cognisers and so on. Even very highly realised bodhisattvas cannot adequately express the good qualities of a Buddha's mind. If a bird flies high in the sky, it must eventually come down somewhere, no matter how high it soars. This is not because the bird has arrived at the end of space but because the bird has run out of energy to fly. Space is vast and endless and so the bird's power is exhausted before it has travelled throughout space. The good qualities of a Buddha are like space and our understanding is like this bird. If we were to try to describe all the good qualities of a Buddha, our wisdom and skill would run out before we could finish describing them. They are beyond our imagination.

Emptiness, Meditation and Action

An image of the sun enthroned in the heavens,
Radiating one thousand beams of light:
Were one to shower bright rays of light upon all beings,
How excellent.

An image of a kingly eagle gliding high in space:
Were one's mind to glide without grasping,
In the space of truth itself, clear and void,
How excellent.

An image of a grey wind flowing forcefully through the sky:
Were one to maintain an energy flow always beneficial to others,
The best of spiritual practices, never artificial,
How excellent.

An image of fresh white clouds,
Bright, pure and drifting freely:
Were one to build clear, blissful meditation in the perfect
* mystic mandala,*
How excellent.

An image of the vast sky, everywhere free of obstructions:
Were this song on emptiness, meditation and action
Without hindrance to benefit the world,
How excellent.

Seventh Dalai Lama

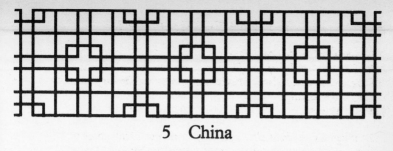

5 China

Compiled with commentary by Richard Hunn

Much has changed since the Chinese obtained their first glimpse of Buddhist sutras and relics as they made their way into China via the old Silk Road. When they beheld the *devanagari* script of Sanskrit, they fancied that they could see flying dragons therein and dubbed it 'dragon script', marvelling at the mysterious doctrine cultivated in the land to their west. However, Buddhism had to undergo a long process of absorption and adaptation before it could genuinely speak to the Chinese heart and mind. What, then, was the appeal of this rival to China's native doctrines – Taoism and Confucianism?

Taoism, already hoary with age long before Lao Tzu set down his *Tao-te-ching*, had predisposed the Chinese mind towards things spiritual, inculcating a detachment from worldly affairs fostered by yoga methods usually practised on cloud-girt peaks far from the haunts of men. Confucianism, by contrast, appealed to the Chinese sense of social duty and filial conduct, placing its main emphasis upon the right ordering of society. Both teachings exerted a strong pull on the Chinese psyche, yet they were in many ways irreconcilable or at least very divergent in their aims. However, with the appearance of Buddhism in China and its bodhisattva path, the man of affairs could also be a sage dwelling in the secret places of the spirit. This fact, more than anything else, explains how and why Buddhism could take on such far-reaching influence in the Middle Kingdom.

Of course, this did not happen overnight, for the Hinayana form of Buddhism initially introduced to China was exclusively monastic (see *Sutra of Forty-Two Sections*) and it was not until the arrival of the Mahayana scriptures in China (see *Diamond Sutra* and *Heart Sutra, Lankavatara, Surangama* and *Vimalakirti* sutras, *Lotus Sutra* etc.) that conditions were ripe for a truly Chinese form of Buddhism to emerge. The contrast, for instance, between the world angst evident in the *Sutra of Forty-Two Sections* and the confident spirit of Seng Chao's essay 'On the Immutability of Phenomena' could not be more marked. Although a monk who worked alongside the illustrious Dharma Master Kumarajiva in Chang An, Seng Chao was very much the traditional Chinese scholar-sage, well versed in both the Taoist and Confucian classics as well as Buddhist scriptures. The teaching of emptiness (*sunyata*) hinted at in

Mahayana texts endowed the phenomenal world with a magical quality reminiscent of the Taoist vision, which saw the great emptiness in all things, and when the Chinese read of layman Vimalakirti helping the Buddha to enlighten living beings, this appealed to their sense of balance, for here was a form of Buddhism which spoke to everyone. Being a practical people, the Chinese abhor abstractions and, although tantalised by Buddhist iconography and the mind-bending vision of countless world systems conveyed in the sutras, they were by nature inclined towards a concrete embodiment of spiritual values. Even the lofty *Hua Yen Ching* (*Avatamsaka Sutra*), with all its fantastic imagery, had to spell out a practical insight – the realisation of *shih shih wu ai* or the unhindered interpenetration of 'thing-events'. This is how the fruit of sunyata insight came to be interpreted through Chinese eyes. Needless to say, this preference for the direct and concrete found its ultimate form of expression in Ch'an (Zen) Buddhism. Introduced to China around 260 CE by the legendary bearded patriarch Bodhidharma, Ch'an specialised in a direct pointing to the mind which discarded all concepts – even the most sacred when necessary – in favour of a purely intuitive method. Centuries later the Ch'an masters could happily say that the Buddha was 'just an old barbarian from the West' and teach their disciples that 'the everyday mind is the Way' (see 'Ma Tsu's Talks of Instruction', Nos. 255–7). This was not, of course, a rejection of Buddhism's inner truth but a profound embodiment of its spirit, which could afford to discard the shell of external tradition and arguably, it was the Ch'an school that exerted the most creative influence upon Chinese culture. To take a graphic example, Ch'an-inspired artists often preferred to portray natural objects rather than Buddhas or celestial realms – as exemplified by Mu Chi's famous painting, *Six Persimmons* – a sure sign that the Chinese had made Buddhism pulse with their own blood and feeling, bringing form and spirit together in a sublime vision wherein seemingly ordinary objects were endowed with an extraordinary resonance and transparence, an indescribable quality which the Buddhists expediently call 'suchness'. This, then, was the ultimate message of Chinese Buddhism – just cleanse the doors of perception and even a humble collection of fruit can be seen to expound the Dharma. But of course, cultivating such a heightened spiritual awareness is no fool's play and it is paradoxical to note that such an easy, natural and spontaneous response to the flow of events is, in fact, the outcome of careful discipline (see the teachings of Ta Hui and Hsu Yun), confirming that 'all true art conceals art'. Here, in Ch'an, the native Chinese genius excelled itself and left a lasting legacy.

The Early Tradition

226.

The Buddha said, 'Those who leave the householder's life to become monks know their minds and penetrate the fundamental. With ties severed, they realise the uncreated [asamskrta] Dharma. Thus they are called sramanas. Constant in their cultivation of sila (the 250 rules of discipline), they advance to find perfect tranquillity. Practising the four correct paths, they attain the arhat stage, the arhats being able to fly and perform mysterious transformations with the ability to lengthen their life span for many kalpas. They can remain at rest or move at will wherever they wish. Next in rank are the anagamins. After a long life, they rise through the nineteen dhyana heavens and eventually realise the arhat stage. Next after these are the sakrdagamins who must advance a stage, returning once more to this world before realising arhatship. Next in rank are those called srota-appanas. They must undergo death and rebirth seven more times before realising arhatship. He who has severed himself from attachment and desire is like one who, having severed his limbs, has no further use for them.

Sutra of Forty-Two Sections, Section 2

The title 'sramana' means 'one who diligently exerts himself in pursuit of the truth'. The 'four correct paths' mentioned here are actually four aspects of one and the same path as found in primitive Buddhism. The first stage embraces diligent practice of the 'three studies' – sila (discipline), dhyana (stillness) and prajna (wisdom or insight); the second stage constitutes unimpeded progress to the point where delusion has been banished; the third stage constitutes the actual state of liberation in which realisation of the truth prevails; and the fourth stage consummate mastery of dhyana wisdom.

According to tradition, the *Sutra of Forty-Two Sections* was delivered by the Buddha in the Royal Deer Park at the beginning of his ministry; it is held to have been the first sutra translated into Chinese. Whether apocryphal or not, this is said to have taken place after the Emperor Ming Ti had a dream-like premonition in which a 'golden-bodied one' appeared in the royal palace, allegedly prompting him to send a mission to India in quest of Buddhist teachings. So the story goes, such a mission eventually resulted in the arrival of the two monks Kasyapa-matanga and Gobharana at Loyang in 69 CE (Han dynasty), riding upon white steeds and bearing sutras with them. As a consequence of this the emperor is said to have founded the Pai Ma Ssu (White Horse Monastery) in Loyang to facilitate their work. Symbolically this legend represents the birth of Chinese Buddhism.

227.

A sramana asked the Buddha, 'By what means can we attain that knowledge which puts an end to conditioned life and enables us to unite with the truth?' In reply the Buddha said, 'By purifying the mind and maintaining a determined spirit, one can unite with the truth, just as by wiping a mirror, the dust goes away and only brightness remains; so, by cutting off desire and seeking for nothing, one can put an end to conditioned life.'

Sutra of Forty-Two Sections, Section 13

The notion of 'putting an end to conditioned life' here means to practise in accordance with the three signs of being (impermanence, absence of ego and nirvana) and the four noble truths (suffering, accumulation of suffering, extinction of suffering and the path thereto). This is the ideal of the arhat, the one beyond the worldly way, who awakens to the truth of dependent origination, meditates upon the twelve nidanas or causal links in the chain of existence and turns his back on the phenomenal world. His practice is a solitary one and therefore lacking in bodhisattva wisdom and compassion. The mirror-wiping analogy used here is very characteristic of the realistic view of the skandhas (the five aggregates or heaps) – ayatana (senses), dhatu (states), etc. – found in early Buddhism, but, as we shall see in later readings, the Mahayana encouraged a quite different approach.

228.

The Buddha said, 'Those tied to wife, family and home life are even worse than prisoners. A prisoner is eventually set free but wives and children will never think of leaving [to set us free], so why the fear of casting off attraction and affection? While you have the misfortune of being in a tiger's mouth, your heart nevertheless cherishes sweet delights. Thus you voluntarily fall and drown in the quagmire [of desire] and are therefore called common worldlings. [But just] by entering this Dharma door of mine, you can forsake the world's dust and become arhats.

Sutra of Forty-Two Sections, Section 23

While noble enough in its own way, this somewhat cold outlook reflects the other-worldly view of primitive Buddhism and offers little solace to lay folk. Not entirely without reason, this early teaching points to the dangers of a life wholly given over to worldly pursuits. But however futile it may be to engage in a vain quest for greater and greater material pleasures, such a sour-grapes philosophy seemed especially repugnant to the Chinese. Its exclusively monastic (or at least antisocial) formulation militated against Confucian feeling for social values and on more than one occasion the Chinese authorities threatened to banish Buddhism from China because of it. These days some modern readers (especially women) are likely to find the *Forty-Two Sections* equally repugnant, reflecting as it does in places a kind of patriarchal prejudice against womenfolk and lay life.

The Still Centre of the Turning World

229.

That things move between birth and death, that summer and winter follow on one another, and that all things flow in their courses is a common sentiment, but I cannot agree with such a view. Why so? The Fang Kuang Sutra *says, 'The dharmas [phenomena] neither come nor go, nor do they change places with one another.' Looking at what this sutra means by the 'non-movement' of things, it does not mean that movement must be arrested in order to find quiescence, but that quiescence must be sought within movement. As quiescence must be sought within movement, it follows that while things move [in their courses], they are always at rest. This being so, movement and quiescence are inseparable from the very beginning.*

Seng Chao, *On the Immutability of Phenomena*, Part I

There is an unmistakable difference of mood between Seng Chao's approach and the spirit displayed in the *Sutra of Forty-Two Sections*. While the latter speaks of 'stopping' or 'putting an end to conditioned existence' in the phenomenal world, Seng Chao's vision is by contrast concerned with finding the still point at the centre of the turning world – a kind of Copernican revolution stimulated by contact with the new Mahayana texts being translated at Chang An. The world angst typical of primitive Buddhism has been replaced by a confident insight into the inherent emptiness of the 'ten thousand things'. Before joining the Sangha, Seng Chao had worked as a copyist of Taoist and Confucian texts and in his essays Taoist and Buddhist intuitions blend together. Working alongside the great translator Kumarajiva at Chang An as he did, Seng Chao became thoroughly versed in the prajna-sunyata (wisdom of inherent emptiness of all things) teaching of Mahayana Buddhism and the noticeable shift of emphasis present in his essays owed its inspiration to this development.

230.

The Tao Hsing Sutra *says, 'The dharma [phenomena] have neither whence to come nor whither to go.' The* Chuang Kuan *says, 'Observing a vacant place, one knows that something has departed, but what has gone away does not go to another place.' Both texts show that motion and quiescence are identical and clearly show that phenomenal events do not move as we conventionally hold them to. Most people assume that things move into the past by virtue of the fact that past events cannot return to the present. This is why they say that things are in motion and not at rest. But on the contrary, I maintain that things are at rest just because they cannot return to the present . . . the principle of experience is the same in each case, it is just the interpretation of events which differs.*

> Seng Chao, *On the Immutability of Phenomena*, Part I

What did Seng Chao mean by saying that 'phenomenal events are at rest'? To get into the feel of this, it helps to consider a simple observation: does the young boy or girl of ten literally become a teenager? Does the teenager literally become an adult? And does the fully grown adult literally become an old man or woman? Does spring become summer, summer become autumn, or autumn winter? The famous Ming dynasty master Han Shan (1546–1623 CE) gained a sudden insight into the meaning of Seng Chao's words when he chanced to read his reference to the tale of the brahmin elder who had returned home after an absence of years. In this story a neighbour of old saw the brahmin and exclaimed, 'So, the man who used to reside here lives yet!' The brahmin elder replied, 'I look like that man but I am not he.'

231.

The Dharmadhatu has the wish-fulfilling gem,
But people have always sealed it up in themselves.
It bears an inscription which says:
The ancients disciplined their minds,
So guard it well, guard it well.
Much knowledge and many deeds
Are not as good as putting an end to thought.
Do away with all preoccupations,
For they are not as good as preserving oneness . . .

> Seng Wang Ming, 'Hsi Hsin Ming' ('An Inscription on Stilling the Mind'), *Chuan Teng Lu*, Chuan 30

This first part of this gatha alludes to a well-known Buddhist parable which likens the mind's inner wisdom to a hidden treasure concealed on our person. The mind is, therefore, like the fabled cintamani or wish-fulfilling gem because it responds exactly in accordance with our thoughts. When we are deluded it shrinks to the confinement of our bodily selves; when we are awakened it expands and manifests to embrace everything in the Dharmadhatu (totality of Dharma realms). The suggestion that we should rid ourselves of knowledge is reminiscent of Lao Tzu's dictum that 'in learning, one daily increases knowledge; when practising the way of Tao, one daily diminishes knowledge' (*Tao-te-ching*, 481). The term 'preserving the one' also has Taoist origins and was borrowed by Chinese Buddhists as an equivalent to dhyana samadhi.

232.

An endless trickle of water
Will soon fill the four oceans!
If you do not shake off the world's ensnaring dust,
It soon heaps up like the five [sacred] mountains of China!
Be on your guard in all things great or small,
Even a small hindrance should not be slighted.
Shut fast the seven openings [senses],
Block out the six sense objects,
Pay no regard to attractions;
Disregard what you hear, hearing deafens the ear,
Gazing at things blinds the eye . . .
    Seng Wang Ming, 'Hsi Hsin Ming' ('An Inscription on Stilling the Mind'), *Chuan Teng Lu*, Chuan 30

This is clear enough: seemingly inconsequential habits and actions have an accumulative karmic effect. Allusions to Lao Tsu are once more evident, for does not Lao Tzu say, 'The five colours blind the eye, the five tones deafen the ear' (*Tao-te-ching*, 12). The Taoist idea of diminishing desire and casting off encumbrances is not foreign to Buddhism, so it was only natural that Chinese Buddhists should allude to Lao Tzu's ideas. The point here, of course, is not that we should literally dull our senses, but we should learn to see things in the great emptiness and vice versa.

233.

When contemplating mind, emptiness is supreme,
But its marvellous profoundity is hard to explain.
Without form or fixed characteristics,
Yet within it there is great spiritual power.
It can avert a thousand calamities,
Bring to completion countless spiritual virtues.
Although it is in essence void,
It can inculcate the Dharma's pattern.

Observing it, you see that it is formless,
Yet it is there in the sound of a shout!
It can serve as if it were a great Dharma general
Like the mind sila [discipline] transmitted in the sutras.
All-pervading like the flavour of salt in water,
Clear just like colourless gum,
It is there for sure – but you can't see its form . . .

> Fu Ta Shih, 'Hsin Wang Ming' ('An Inscription on the Sovereign Mind'), *Fu Tsu Hsin Yao*, Chuan 1, page 10

Fu Ta Shih (497–569 CE) was a contemporary of Bodhidharma and, like him, tried to enlighten the Emperor Liang Wu Ti. His gatha points directly to the mind, hinting at the presence of this well-nigh indescribable source. When we look for it it seems as if it were not there, yet it is the sustainer of all. Though immaterial and formless it is there, even in the sound of a shout, all-pervading like the taste of salt in water. A 'Dharma general' is a fierce guardian or protector of the Dharma, and he who recognises the mind's inherent emptiness is as strong as a general who can marshal his forces against delusion. Fu Ta Shih likens this mind to the colourless gum used in Chinese painting for, while it is colourless itself, it enables colours to be used. So too all phenomenal forms and manifestations actually arise within the clear-light of the mind.

The Diamond Wisdom

234.

'Although immeasurable, uncountable and limitless numbers of living beings are thus led [to the final nirvana for] the extinction of reincarnation, it is true that not a living being is led there. Why so, Subhuti? [Because] if a bodhisattva [still] clings to the false notion of an ego, a personality, a being and a life, he is not [a true] bodhisattva. Furthermore, Subhuti, a bodhisattva's mind should not abide anywhere when giving alms; that is to say, he should give [alms] without a mind abiding in form, or he should give without a mind abiding in sound, or in smell, or in taste, in touch or in things. Subhuti, thus, a bodhisattva should give alms without a mind abiding in false notions of form. Why? Because if a bodhisattva's mind does not abide in form when practising charity, his merit will be inconceivable and immeasurable.'

> *Vajracchedika Sutra*, Part 1

In the Far East Buddhists talk about 'cultivating secret virtue,' which is not the same as ostentatiously trying to appear like a do-gooder. The *Vajracchedika Sutra* hints at what the Mahayana calls 'inconceivable liberation'. The sutra opens with Subhuti, a leading disciple, asking the Buddha how the minds of disciples should abide. Instead of teaching Subhuti and the other disciples to cultivate an abode for the mind, the Buddha urges them to cultivate a non-abiding mind, and the whole sutra is an elaboration of this theme. As the sutra teaches, there is a vast difference between a bodhisattva whose good works (*dana*) are offered without clinging to notions of a giver, recipient and gift and those who still cling to such notions – known as the three-wheeled condition in Buddhism – because it is still bound up with karmic retribution. The Buddha's words were therefore intended to break up Subhuti's dualistic ideas about the bestowal of Dharma based on attachment to the four forms (laksana) of an ego, a personality, a being and a life.

235.

'Subhuti, in a like manner, if a bodhisattva says, "I should lead uncountable living beings to put a stop to reincarnation and escape from suffering," he cannot be called a bodhisattva. Why? Because there is really no dharma called the bodhisattva stage. Therefore the Buddha says, "Of all dharmas, there is not a single one which possesses an ego, a personality, a being and a life." Subhuti, if a bodhisattva says, "I should adorn Buddha lands," he cannot be called a bodhisattva. Why? Because when the Tathagata speaks of such adornment it is not, but is expediently called adornment.'

Vajracchedika Sutra, Part 2

Previously Subhuti had been hindered by his coarse views about the liberation of living beings, so the Buddha taught him not to cling to the objective notion of liberating them in order to avoid getting entangled with the four forms (laksana) of an ego, a being, a personality and a life, for living beings were fundamentally already in the nirvanic state and only appeared to be held in bondage because of their wrong thinking. Here the Buddha teaches Subhuti to keep away from the subtle, subjective notion of Dharma, practice and realisation, for if there is attachment to the practice of Dharma, there is again entanglement in the four forms, with the corresponding notions of self and other, gain and loss, etc. This was the ultimate purpose of expounding the non-abiding mind, for when the mind abides nowhere, it not only overleaps attachment to forms in the worldly realm, but also attachment to the sravakas' and pratyekas' idea of adorning a Buddha-land by abiding in Dharma. When the mind abides nowhere it expands and returns to its inherently still condition, enabling things to appear in the light of sunyata (emptiness). The Sixth Ch'an Patriarch, Hui Neng, realised his complete enlightenment when hearing the Fifth Patriarch say, 'One should cultivate a mind which abides nowhere.'

236.

'Subhuti, if you have [in your mind] this thought: "The Tathagata does not rely on his possession of characteristics to obtain supreme enlightenment," Subhuti, banish that thought. Subhuti, if you think it while developing the perfect enlightenment mind, you will advocate the annihilation of things. Do not have such a thought. Why? Because one who develops the supreme enlightenment mind does not advocate the annihilation of things.'

Vajracchedika Sutra, Part 2

Earlier the Buddha had said, 'He who seeks me by outward appearance and seeks me in sound treads the heterodox path and cannot perceive the Tathagata [lakshana]'. This was in order to prevent Subhuti from mistaking the Buddha's Dharmakaya or immaterial body for one with form or characteristic marks. However, now that the Buddha had stripped away Subhuti's attachment to forms, the Buddha was apprehensive that he would then cling to the idea of holding on to the nonexistence of the Buddha's thirty-two characteristic marks (form), thereby falling into the false view that the nirvanic emptiness expounded by the Buddha meant the annihilation of things. The Buddha's aim, however, had only been to point out that there was no inherent selfhood in things, not that they would be annihilated in the light of sunyata (emptiness). This is what Hui Neng meant when he said that 'there never was a mirror' to collect defiling dust (see no. 251).

237.

'When bodhisattva Avalokiteshvara practised the profound prajna-paramita, he investigated and perceived that the skandhas [the five aggregates] were nonexistent, thus securing his deliverance from all distress and sufferings. Sariputra! Form does not differ from void, nor void from form. Form is identical to void and void to form. So also are reception, conception, mental function and consciousness in relation to the void.'

Hrdaya Sutra

The tiny *Heart Sutra (HsinChing)* is very popular in the Far East and even the Ch'an (Zen) monks recite it daily. Avalokiteshvara's method of practice consisted of investigating and examining the five aggregates by means of the prajnaparamita. 'Prajna' means 'wisdom' and 'paramita' means 'perfection' or 'a means of arriving at the other shore of enlightenment'. By looking into and perceiving the inherent emptiness of the five skandhas or aggregates which make up the body-mind, we no longer identify with the self or the ego which arises through a combination of causes and conditions, thus securing deliverance from all suffering. If the first aggregate (form) can be correctly perceived as empty, so too will the remaining four (reception, conception, mental function and consciousness). By saying that 'form is void,' the sutra is pointing out that form is inherently void; it is not referring to the negative or relative void upheld by annihilationists or by sravakas and pratyekas who are one-sidedly bent on keeping away from the phenomenal world.

238.

'Sariputra, the void of all things is not created, not annihiliated, not impure, not pure, not increasing and not decreasing. Therefore, with void, there is no form and no reception, conception, mental function and consciousness; there is no eye, ear, nose, tongue, body or mind; there is no form, sound, smell, taste, touch or idea; there are no such things as the eighteen realms of sense from the realm of sight up to that of the faculty of consciousness; there are no such things as the nidanas [the twelve links in the chain of existence] from ignorance and the end of ignorance up to the end of old age and death; there are no such things as the four noble truths and there is no wisdom and also no gain.'

Hrdaya Sutra

Because prajna is the wisdom of non-duality it not only transcends the dharma of worldly men, but also transcends the dharma of the aryas (saints). For instance, the sravaka and pratyeka Buddhas heed the four noble truths, observe the nidanas (the twelve links in the chain of existence) and cultivate themselves, keeping away from worldly causes in quest of the holy fruit. According to the *Hrdaya* with its prajna (wisdom) insight, however, birth and death, purity and impurity, increase and decrease, etc., are inherently empty and the chain of dependent origination is fundamentally quiescent. The position here was neatly summed up by Master Ma Tsu when he said: 'When the dharmas arise, do not say that a self arises with them, and when they dissolve, do not say that a self dissolves with them.' Thus the absolute 'thatness' of prajna transcends the worldlings' idea of being or existence (creation) just as it transcends the sravakas' and pratyekas' notion of the nonexistence of selfhood (or extinction) and therefore, the sutra says: 'there is no wisdom and no gain.'

239.

Because of gainlessness, bodhisattvas who rely on the prajnaparamita, have no hindrance in their hearts, and since they have no hindrance, they have no fear, are free from contrary and delusive ideas and attain the final nirvana.

Hrdaya Sutra

However abstract the wisdom scriptures may appear, they are really based upon the wisdom of the heart, not the head, as the title of the *Hrdaya Sutra* suggests. The Sanskrit word *hrdaya* is etymologically linked to our English word 'heart' and the Chinese equivalent (*hsin*) also means 'heart', 'core', 'kernel', or 'essence' in the spiritual sense. The gainlessness of the bodhisattva is clearly different from that of worldly people who ignore the Dharma, for it is neither a product of scepticism nor a suspension of faith, but a direct result of embodying the sublime insight of prajna (wisdom). Prajna is likened to a diamond which can cut away all illusions and doubts, and it is on account of this that bodhisattvas feel unhindered and fearless, for they are free from contrary ideas about the winning or non-winning of the Buddha-fruit and the liberation or non-liberation of sentient beings. As the mantra associated with the *Heart Sutra* suggests, those who embody such wisdom have truly gone beyond all such distinctions.

A Bodhisattva in Lay Life

240.

Vimalakirti came and said, 'Hey, Purnamaitrayaniputra, you should first enter the state of samadhi to examine the minds of your listeners before expounding the Dharma to them. Do not put rotten food in precious bowls. You should know their minds and not mistake precious crystal for ordinary glass. If you do not know their propensities, do not teach them Hinayana. They have no wounds, so do not hurt them. Do not show narrow tracks to those who want to tread the wide path. Do not [try to] enclose the great ocean in the print of an ox's foot . . .'
'The Disciples', *Vimalakirti Nirdesa Sutra*, ch. 3, page 28

Often known as the *Wei-mo* or *Yuima* in the Far East, the *Vimalakirti Nirdesa Sutra* has won the hearts of many Buddhists for the simple reason that its central figure and interlocutor is the layman Vimalakirti (spotless reputation). The sutra opens with Vimalakirti appearing sick in bed so that he can help the Buddha liberate five hundred sons of the elders in Vaisali and a host of bodhisattvas and devas besides. By placing the Dharma in the hands of a layman, the *Vimalakirti Sutra* exemplifies the universality of 'inconceivable liberation'. In this extract Vimalakirti warns a bodhisattva against hurting people by foisting arbitrary teachings upon them. If disciples can directly awaken to the truth of inherent emptiness – meaning that their fundamental nature is essentially flawless – why tie them up with Hinayana teachings?

241.

'*Subhuti, if without cutting off carnality, anger and stupidity you can keep from these [three] evils . . . if you give rise to neither the four noble truths nor their opposites . . . if you do not regard yourself as a worldly or unworldly man, as a saint or not a saint; if you perfect all Dharmas while keeping away from the concept of Dharmas, then you can receive and eat the food.*'

'*Subhuti, if you neither see the Buddha nor hear the Dharma; if the six heterodox teachers are regarded impartially as your own teachers, and if, when they induce leavers of home into heterodoxy, you also fall in with the latter, then you can take away the food and eat it.*'

'The Disciples', *Vimalakirti Nirdesa Sutra*, ch. 3, page 26

The passages above are a superb exposition of what Vimalakirti calls 'inconceivable liberation'. 'Eating the food' here symbolises the 'meal of right livelihood' or the proper way to accord with the Dharma. It is interesting to note that the *Vimalakirti* text speaks of keeping from the three evils of carnality, anger and stupidity without cutting them off. However much this appears to skirt the edges of heterodoxy, it is meant to underscore the difference between the methods of the sravaka and pratyeka Buddhas, who have minds bent on keeping from the worldly in order to abide in the saintly, and the bodhisattvas, who cultivate non-abiding minds unhindered by all such dualisms. For them the underlying nature of impurity is pure, so they have no thought of gain or loss (i.e. winning or not-winning the holy fruit, etc.).

According to the eminent Ming-dynasty master Han Shan, the six heterodox teachers mentioned here symbolise the six sense data and the 'leavers of home' signify the mind bent on enlightenment – a prosaic way of saying that, without looking into the six sense data, we cannot transmute consciousness into wisdom. Thus without contact with apparent impurities we cannot discover the inherent purity of the wisdom-nature. Hence the sutra also says, 'he who does not enter the ocean of klesa [defilement] cannot retrieve the gem of wisdom.'

The Mind-Born Universe

242.

'*Further, Mahamati, those who, afraid of sufferings arising from the discrimination of birth and death, seek for nirvana do not know that birth and death and nirvana are not to be separated the one from the other; and, seeing that all things subject to discrimination have no reality, imagine that nirvana consists in the future annihilation of the senses and their fields. They are not aware, Mahamati, of the fact that nirvana is the alayavijnana [store consciousness] where paravritti [revulsion] takes place by self-realisation. Therefore, Mahamati, those who are stupid talk of the trinity of vehicles and not of the state of mind only.'*

Lankavatara Sutra, ch. 2, XVIII, pages 61–2

Closely linked with the Ch'an (Zen) school in China, the *Lanka* text presents us with the idealist doctrine of Mind Only (cittamatra). In contrast with the earlier, realistic view of primitive Buddhism, the *Lanka* teaches that all phenomenal things are mind-born, sustained by the alayavinana or store consciousness. Projected objectively, there appears to be a world of multiplicities – living beings, birth and death (samsara), and the three vehicles of Buddhism, with nirvana as the goal to be attained after wiping out the senses and their spheres of operation. But according to the *Lanka*, this is not the last word.

243.

Like an image seen in a mirror, which is not real, the mind is seen by the ignorant in a dualistic form in the mirror of habit energy . . . When it is thoroughly understood that there is nothing but what is seen of the mind itself, discrimination ceases.

Lankavatara Sutra, ch. 3, LXXIV, pages 74–5

The *Lanka* text takes the standpoint that everything is sustained by the alayavijnana (store consciousness). While neutral in itself, it is regarded as having a pure and an impure aspect according to the play of our minds. While under the influence of the perfuming effect of vikalpa (thought construction), and vasana (thought-habit-energy), a world of distinctions and multiplicities arises, but when we become conscious of the fact that nothing exists save what is born of the mind, phenomenal things lose their power to hypnotise us – even fascination with the vehicles of Buddhism. In the *Lanka* text, this discovery is said to take place through paravritti (abrupt revulsion), which would explain the popularity of the *Lanka* text with Ch'an (Zen) Buddhists.

Host and Guest

244.

I am now senior in this assembly, in which I am the only one who has acquired the art of explaining the Dharma because of my awakening to the meaning of the two words - foreign dust - which led to my attainment of the holy fruit ... World Honoured One, foreign dust is like a guest who stops at an inn where he passes the night or takes his meal and, as soon as he has done so, he packs and continues his journey because he has no time to stay longer. As to the host of the inn, he has nowhere to go. My deduction is that one who does not stay is a guest and one who does stay is a host. Consequently, a thing is foreign when it does not stay.

Surangama Sutra, ch. 1, page 22

These two terms 'host' and 'guest', coined by Ajnata Kaundinya, have played an important part in Chinese Buddhism and the Ch'an masters made extensive use of them when teaching their disciples. The analogy is simple but its meaning is profound; the underlying nature of the mind is uncreated; it neither comes nor goes for it is immutable and beyond birth and death. All phenomenal things arise within the mind but have no inherent nature of their own. When the mind discriminates, it falls into the guest position and follows the stream of birth and death; when there is no discrimination, we can take up the host position and thereby accord with the unborn mind - the non-abiding mind hinted at in earlier readings, or what the Ch'an masters called the 'fundamental face'.

Transmuting Alayavijnana for Universal Enlightenment

245.

'I still remember that long before numbers of aeons countless as sand grains in the Ganges a Buddha called Avalokiteshvara appeared in the world. When I was with him I developed the bodhi-mind, and for my entry into samadhi I was instructed by him to practise meditation by means of the hearing organ. At first by directing the organ of hearing into the stream of meditation this organ was detached from its object [sound], and by wiping out [the concepts of] both sound and stream entry, both disturbance and stillness became clearly nonexistent. Thus advancing step by step, both hearing and its object ceased completely, but I did not stop where they ended.'

Surangama Sutra, ch. 4, page 135

Avalokiteshvara (Kuan Yin) is known to every Chinese Buddhist as a compassionate bodhisattva who heeds the cries of the world, but in this extract from the *Surangama Sutra*, Manjushri explains the esoteric meaning of this bodhisattva's method of contemplation by means of the organ of hearing. This method was often utilised by Ch'an monks who would purposely sit by thundering rapids to sublimate their minds. The technique consists of turning back the sense of hearing from its object (sound) in order to enter the stream of meditation. When detached from its object (sound), the subjective hearer also vanishes, along with the notions of disturbance and stillness, which only exist in relation to one another. Hence the simultaneous disappearance of the notions of sound and stream entry.

246.

'When the awareness of this state and this state itself were realised as nonexistent, both subject and object merged into the void, the awareness of which became all-embracing. With further elimination of the void and its object, both creation and annihilation vanished, giving way to the state of nirvana which then manifested.'

Surangama Sutra, ch. 4, page 135

This completes the full meditation which had begun with (1) detachment from coarse notions of the object (sound) and subject (that which could hear); (2) detachment of the mind from the subtle idea of abiding in or holding on to the relative voidness realised after eliminating the coarse view of subject and object (hence the statement 'but I did not stop where they ended'), and (3) realisation of absolute voidness which is neither hindered by form nor awareness of the void. Neither 'existent' nor 'inexistent', it is what the Chinese Buddhists call *miao yu* or the 'marvellous existence' and understood as the mean, which is inclusive of both the real and the seeming, for the seeming springs from the real.

247.

'Suddenly I leapt over the mundane and the supramundane and realised an all-embracing brightness pervading the ten directions, acquiring two unsurpassed merits. The first one was in accord with the fundamental profound mind of all Buddhas high up in the ten directions, possessing the same merciful power as the Tathagata [Buddha]. The second was in sympathy with all living beings in the six realms of existence, here below in the ten directions, sharing with them the same imploration of pity.'

Surangama Sutra, ch. 4, page 135

The terms 'high up' and 'below' are only used as an expedient here to emphasise the benefiting function (*yung*) which all bodhisattvas must cultivate for the sake of living beings. Thus the Avalokiteshvara method is geared up for universal enlightenment and, despite what may appear to be the case, it is not an exercise in quietism or literally shunning the senses. Rather, it is intended to transmute sense data into wisdom. Hence the

Surangama Sutra refers to what it calls 'wonderful form' or 'fragrant form', meaning the wondrous appearance of phenomena after sense data have been successfully transmuted into wisdom.

The Hua Yen Ching

The Hua Yuen school represents the fruition in China of ideas inspired by the *Avatamsaka Sutra*, its Chinese masters using their own genius to convey the totalistic vision hinted at in the vast *Flower Garland Sutra*. In Tu Shun's essay 'Meditation upon the Dharmadhatu', he categorised the four Dharma-realms thus: (1) The Dharmadhatu of shih – the realm of phenomena or events; (2) the Dharmadhatu of li – the realm of noumena, or underlying principle; (3) the Dharmadhatu of non-obstruction of li against shih – the realm of principle and events in total freedom and merging; (4) the Dharmadhatu of the non-obstruction of shih against shih – the realm of events in total freedom, merging with all other events.

It is impossible to convey the multifaceted richness of Hua Yen 'round thinking' in a brief extract, but the following example from Tu Shun's essay 'Meditation on the Dharmadhatu' clearly illustrates the all-inclusive and totalistic spirit of the Hua Yen.

248.

The True Li Is Shih Itself
If the li is true, it should not be outside shih. There are two reasons for this. First, because of the principle of Dharmanairatmya [emptiness of selfhood of things]. Second, because shih must depend on li, shih itself is but hollow without any substance. Therefore only if the li is identical with shih through and through can it be considered to be the true li. [Taking the parable of water and waves], since the water is the waves themselves, no motion can be excluded from wetness. This is why we say that the water itself is the waves. Contemplate on this.

The True Li Is Not Shih
The li that is identical with shih is not shih as such. This is because the true li is different from the illusory, and the real is different from the unreal; also, that which is depended upon [object] is different from that which depends [subject]. Likewise the water that is identical with waves is not waves as such, for motion and wetness are different.
Tu Shun, 'Meditation upon the Dharmadhatu'

These seemingly antithetical statements are both true from the standpoint of the Hua Yen. Paradoxically, dualistic thinking is one-at-a-time thinking and, paradoxically again, non-dualistic thinking can embrace dualisms and harmonise opposites. Underlying Master Tu Shun's words is a profound insight into the positive nature of pratitya-samutpada (dependent arising). More often than not people only see the negative or restricting aspects of this doctrine, yet when seen in the light of sunyata (emptiness) it also embraces the fact of interdependence and interfusion. Logically we are forced to choose between alternatives and feel compelled to say that the thing-events (shih) either are or are not identical with the underlying principle (li), but in the 'round view' of the Hua Yen it is a question of 'both... and' rather than 'either.. or'.

The Ch'an Transmission

According to tradition, the Ch'an transmission drew its initial impulse from the endeavours of Bodhidharma, an Indian master reckoned to have landed in Canton around 520 CE, bringing the 'empty-handed doctrine' with him in quest of successors. The Indian patriarch is always painted with a tigerish glare and bushy eyebrows, a larger-than-life figure whose image certainly conveys the dynamic energy and strong character that one would expect to find behind a direct, mind-to-mind transmission of wisdom. Bodhidharma is said to have declared that his doctrine was:

A special transmission outside the teaching
Not relying on words and letters
Directly pointing to the mind
For perception of self-nature, attainment of Buddhahood.

Legend has it that Bodhidharma once tried to awaken the Emperor Liang Wu Ti, but, proving unsuccessful, he retired north into the state of Wei and went into seclusion at the Shao Lin Monastery. While there he is said to have met his sole successor – the monk Hui K'o. At the time of their meeting, Hui K'o is said to have asked Bodhidharma to pacify his mind for him, whereupon Bodhidharma replied, 'Bring out your mind, show it to me!' At this, Hui K'o felt nonplussed and said, 'I cannot find it!' 'There,' said Bodhidharma. 'Now I have pacified your mind for you!' This strange-seeming dialogue typifies the Ch'an tradition. The Ch'an transmission had begun in China.

249.

Though there are many Dharma doors [methods of cultivation], they are all returnable to the mind, the source of marvellous spiritual powers, countless as the Ganges' sands. The practice of sila [discipline], dhyana, [stillness] and prajna [wisdom insight] with its supernatural powers and transformations are complete in oneself and do not depart from the mind. All defilements and karmic hindrances are fundamentally void. All things produced through causation are like a dream and an illusion. There is no triple world to escape from, no bodhi to seek for. Sentient and nonsentient beings share the same universal nature. The great Tao is empty and boundless, free from thought and care.

Tao Hsin's teaching, *Chuan Teng Lu,* Chuan 4

Though the Buddha spoke of the transmigration of living beings through the triple realm of desire, form and formlessness and karmic defilements, he had ultimately taught that all such states are mind-born. Hence all teachings are really geared up to help us realise the uncreated nature or unborn mind. Once we recognise the mind's inherent emptiness, all defilements are seen to be void and then there is no difference between the phenomenal and the noumenal or the seeming and the real. The attainment of bodhi is therefore nothing other than recognition of our inherent nature.

250.

If this pure mind you would attain,
Then cultivate no-thought,
Viewing all without distinctions,
The mind is exceedingly wondrous.
Understand the Dharma of no-knowledge,
And in not-knowing, know what's essential.
Forcing the mind to remain still
Means that you are still not free from sickness;
Forget the rise and fall of things in contemplation,
Then they are the same as the fundamental nature.

Master Fa Yung of Niu T'ou Mountain, 'An Inscription on the Mind'

Master Fa Yung's gatha typifies the straightforward approach favoured by the early Chinese masters. A collateral Dharma-heir of the Fourth Patriarch along with Hung Jen, Fa Yung used simple and unadorned words to point to the self-nature. This is Chinese Ch'an as it was before the rise of the five schools (wu chia) and the kung-an (koan). Besides the teaching of no-thought (wu nien) and silent accordance with the unborn nature, there are no special contrivances to be found. Just lay down all distinctions, including the very notion of holding the mind still, and the mind will naturally return to its inherently still condition.

251.

> *In essence, bodhi has no tree*
> *And the bright mirror has no chest,*
> *In essence there is not a thing,*
> *On what then can dust gather?*
>
> > *Liu Tsu T'an Ching*, ch. 1

This verse is so well known in China that most people can recite it by heart. It was written in the T'ang dynasty when the Fifth Ch'an Patriarch, Hung Jen, was in quest of a successor at Huang Mei. Having urged likely candidates to compose a gatha or verse to testify to their attainment of the truth, Shen Hsiu, a leading monk in the community, expected by all to receive the post, wrote a verse stressing that the mind was like a mirror which needed to be wiped clean. Hui Neng's verse, by contrast, stressed that such mirror wiping was in vain, thus exemplifying the difference between the guest position and the immutable host or non-abiding mind (see no. 244). The rest is history. Hui Neng, the unlettered peasant, received the robe and bowl and became the eminent Sixth Patriarch, whereafter Ch'an flourished all over China.

252.

> *Just be straightforward and do not cling to anything. Deluded men grasp the Dharma and hold on to the samadhi of universality. They claim that the samadhi of universality consists of sitting motionless all the time without any uprise in the mind. Such an interpretation makes the meditators inanimate and hinders realisation of self-nature...*
> *Learned friends, the self-nature should pervade everywhere. How can it be obstructed? If the mind abides in Dharma, this is self-bondage. If it is claimed that motionless sitting [in meditation] is right, it is the same as when Sariputra sat in meditation in the wood and was reprimanded by Vimalakirti.*
>
> > *Liu Tsu T'an Ching*, ch. 4

Not so long ago modern scholars used to see Hui Neng's teaching as a kind of native Chinese reaction against Indian Buddhism. However, a greater familiarity with both Indian and Chinese Buddhism in the West today has challenged the correctness of that view. What Hui Neng actually taught was in complete conformity with the non-abiding mind (wu-chu hsin) hinted at in the *Vajracchedika Sutra* and the *Hrdaya Sutra*, the *Vimalakirti Sutra* and so forth. The non-abiding mind is free from all clinging and rejection and there is a vast difference between the practice of those who cling to Dharma and those whose minds abide nowhere.

253.

'Learned friends, this Dharma door of mine was established by past patriarchs with:

1. Thoughtlessness [not a thought] as its doctrine.
2. Immateriality as its substance.
3. Non-abiding as its fundamental.

'Immateriality is detachment from all forms, aspects and characteristics while in the midst of forms, aspects and characteristics. Thoughtlessness [not a thought] is the absence of all thoughts while in the process of thinking. Non-abiding is the characteristic of man's fundamental nature.'

Liu Tsu T'an Ching, ch. 4

What Hui Neng means by 'thoughtlessness . . . while in the process of thinking' may seem an impossibility from the logical point of view, but it is the key to the whole of Ch'an Buddhism. Thoughtlessness (wu nien) makes little or no sense without the corresponding notions of immateriality and non-abiding, for these are really the same thing. Because the underlying nature of the mind is empty it is ungraspable and immaterial and therefore non-abiding. As all thoughts arise within this non-abiding mind, they are also empty. There is simply the mirroring of objects and events without the play of discrimination, attachment, aversion and so forth arising in the mind.

254.

'If someone puts a question to you about the existing, mention the nonexistent in your answer. If you are asked about the nonexistent, mention the existent in your answer. If you are asked about the worldly, mention the saintly in your answer. Thus the mutual dependence of the two extremes will bring to light the significance of the mean. If all questions are answered in this way, you will not err from the principle.'

Liu Tsu T'an Ching, ch. 10

This interesting passage from Hui Neng illustrates how the Chinese masters taught their disciples to accord with the Middle Way. It is a direct application of the truth of non-abiding. The worldly only exists in contrast with the saintly, form only exists in contrast with voidness, and existence only exists in contrast with nonexistence and vice versa. As these pairs of opposites are mutually dependent, it is futile clinging to either extreme. Thus it has always been the policy of Ch'an masters to strip away their disciples' attachments to one side of a dualism so as to accord with the mean.

255.

'The great master Bodhidharma came from India to transmit the supreme vehicle's Dharma of the One Mind so that it might edify and enlighten you. He also introduced the text of the Lankavatara Sutra *in order to seal the minds of all beings. Apprehensive that you might hold inverted views and fail to believe in this mind Dharma inherent in each of you, he quoted the* Lankavatara *which states, "Mind is the source [of enlightenment], its doctrine no fixed doctrine at all." All who seek the Dharma should realise that there is nothing fixed to seek for. Outside of mind there is no other Buddha, outside of Buddha, there is no other mind.'*

> 'Ma Tsu's Talks of Instruction', *Fu Tsu Hsin Yao*, Chuan 1

This passage makes it clear that the Ch'an masters viewed their doctrine as a direct application of the Buddha's own teaching. Masters like Ma Tsu and Lin Chi have frequently been misjudged for saying that there is nothing to seek, but the *Lanka* text itself states that there is no fixed method besides pointing to the mind. The Buddha only 'turned the wheel of the law' or expounded his Dharma for forty-nine years because of the inverted views held by living beings. If there are no fixed views, the mind is already faultless. It is interesting to note that Bodhidharma, credited with being the First Ch'an Patriarch in China, was also a master of the Lanka school, which casts Ch'an in a more orthodox light.

256.

Whenever you speak of the mind, phenomenon and noumenon are [already] unhindered and interpenetrate. This is what the bodhi fruit is like. That which arises in the mind is called form, but if we understand that form has no inherent nature of its own, then birth is the same as no-birth. If you realise the meaning of this, then you can 'nurture the sacred embryo' while wearing your clothes, eating your meals and passing naturally through the daily round. What else is there to attend to?

> 'Ma Tsu's Talks of Instruction', *Fu Tsu Hsin Yao*, Chuan 1

This is a superb exposition of the doctrine of Mind Only. Once accepted and understood experientially, there need be no hindrance from the phenomenal world. If one looks into forms as they arise, one notes that they arise in the mind and have no independent existence. As mind itself is intangible, it is unborn, and when the rise and fall of things is identified with this unborn nature, birth (i.e. conditioned existence) is identified with no-birth (i.e. the unconditioned). Thus it is precisely by looking into the phenomenal that one harmonises with the noumenal. It is interesting to note the use of a Taoist term here, 'nurturing the sacred embryo', an idiom found in Taoist yoga. Here it means strengthening spiritual insight without departing from everyday activities.

257.

When these dharmas [phenomena] arise, do not say that a self arises with them, and when they dissolve, do not say that a self dissolves with them. Thus one's previous thoughts, later thoughts and intervening thoughts follow without waiting for one another. Each thought [instant] is still and quiescent. This is the ocean-seal samadhi which embraces all things like a great ocean which holds the water of a hundred thousand streams.

'Ma Tsu's Talks of Instruction', *Fu Tsu Hsin Yao*, Chuan 1

This again is a sublime exposition of the doctrine of Mind Only and non-abiding. If we rid ourselves of the thought that there is a fixed self in the five aggregates and look into the spontaneous rise and fall of phenomena, we see that each thing-event happens freely in its own instant without hindrance from other thoughts and thing-events. It is a state of intermergence and interpenetration. Thus we can see that Ch'an represents a concrete and living embodiment of what the Hua Yen school means by shih-shih wu ai (non-obstruction between thing-events).

258.

The Dharma body [Dharmakaya] is like empty space and has never been subject to birth and death. When there is an appropriate cause for it, a Buddha appears in the world to teach; when there is no further cause to stay, a Buddha enters nirvana. The Buddha's teaching influences sentient beings everywhere, yet it is like a reflection of the moon in water [and not the real moon]. There is neither permanence nor impermanence and neither birth nor death. The real nature of living beings has never been born; those that we regard as having died never really pass away. Understand clearly that there is no mind to abide in, then it naturally follows that there is no fixed Dharma to expound.

Master Ju Man Fu Kuang, *Chuan Teng Lu*, Chuan 6

This extract comes from a dialogue between Master Fu Kuang and Emperor Shen Tsung of the T'ang. The emperor had expressed uncertainty about the question of impermanence, for, having heard that the Buddha abides eternally, he wondered about the historical Buddha (Shakyamuni) who had passed away between two sala trees at Kusinagara. In his reply Master Fu Kuang points out that the real Buddha is the Dharmakaya which is unborn, whereas the nirmanakaya or transformation body is but a temporary appearance in the phenomenal, like a reflection of the moon seen in water. As the Buddha's Dharmakaya was not born, it did not die when the Buddha's Nirmanakaya passed away. Similarly, though living beings undergo birth and death in the phenomenal world, they are fundamentally unborn and, therefore, deathless, neither permanent nor impermanent. This is a direct teaching of the non-abiding mind seen in its vertical context.

259.

*Followers of the Tao, I am only talking about that which is distnctly
solitary and bright, and is listening to my expounding of the Dharma.
This one knows no obstructions and is omnipresent in the three worlds of
existence in the ten directions of space; it can enter into all different
states without being infected by them. In aksana [though instant], it
will penetrate deeply into the Dharmadhatu where it will talk about
Buddhas when meeting Buddhas, about patriarchs when meeting
patriarchs, about arhats when meeting arhats, and about hungry ghosts
when meeting hungry ghosts.*

*Lin Chi Record, Chih Yueh Lu (Record of the Finger Pointing at
the Moon)*

Master Lin Chi (d. 866 CE) was a great enlightened master who founded
one of the two main schools of Ch'an (Zen). His teaching was very direct,
pointing to what he called the 'true man of no fixed position' (wu wei chen
jen), meaning the unborn mind inherent in us all. This unborn mind can
work in all sorts of states, reflecting all without stain, be it Buddhas, arhats
or hungry ghosts. The great beauty of Lin Chi's teaching lies in his sheer
confidence and certainty that the Buddha-nature is to be found
everywhere, working in all things. Here, the unborn is seen from its
horizontal context.

260.

*Virtuous ones, there is no peace in the three worlds of existence, which
are like a house on fire. It is not a place for a long stay because the
murderous demon of impermanence will in an [instant] make no choice
between the noble and the humble or between the old and the young. If
you do not want to differ from the patriarchs and Buddhas, it will
suffice if you seek after nothing outside.*

*Lin Chi Record, Chih Yueh Lu (Record of the Finger Pointing at
the Moon)*

This sobering reminder about impermanence is a necessary thing, for
without it we would lack the motivation to look into our minds to see that
there is only the unborn. Lin Chi is convinced that 'we are enlightened
such as we are,' but how many of us see how we truly are? Thus, the
confident spirit which Lin Chi imparts is only justified if we truly look
and forsake spurious external distractions – including Buddhas.

261.

After this mountain monk has said that there is no Dharma externally,

*students who do not understand this immediately make their
interpretation of the internal . . . If you want to catch it in the moving, it
will go into the unmoving, and if you want to catch it in the unmoving, it
will go to the moving . . . Virtuous ones, the moving and unmoving are
two kinds of states but the man of Tao can make use of both the moving
and unmoving states.*

Lin Chi Record, Wu Teng Hui Yuan
(Record of the Five Lamps Meeting at the Source)

Very often Buddhists and other spiritually inclined people find difficulty
in harmonising activity with stillness. It is the old problem of reconciling
the way of Martha with the way of Mary, but from the Ch'an angle, true
activity must be rooted in stillness or a centred way of life, and true
stillness must find its expression in activity. Without this balance the
body-mind and inner nature will be upset. Lin Chi is warning us that we
need to harmonise these aspects of experience as reflected in the saying,
'To be on the road, yet to be on the mountain; to be on the mountain, yet
to be on the road.'

262.

*Sometimes the subject is snatched away but the object is not; sometimes
the object are snatched away but the subject is not; sometimes both
subject and object is snatched away; and sometimes neither subject nor
object is snatched away.*

Lin Chi Record, Wu Teng Hui Yuan
(Record of the Five Lamps Meeting at the Source)

Here we see Master Lin Chi's famous 'snatchings', used in order to teach
his disciples how to accord with the inner nature of things. Lin Chi used
to employ what he called his 'shining wisdom' to probe the obstructions
or hindrances holding back a disciple. If there was attachment to the
subject (the knower), the master would strip that away; if there was
attachment to the object (the known), that would be stripped away; if
there was attachment to both subject and object, then both would be
stripped away. But, once freed from attachment, the master would leave
things alone, for once understood to be interdependent, they cause no
further trouble.

263.

*Ch'an practice consists solely of emptying the mind; you should fix on
your foreheads the two words 'birth' and 'death', and remember them as
if you owe a debt of ten thousand strings of threaded coins which you
must repay. Day and night, while drinking and eating; when walking,*

standing, sitting or reclining; when receiving friends and chatting with them; as well as in the still or moving state, you should give rise to the hua t'ou.

'Instructions given by Master Ta Hui', quoted by Master Han Shan in his *Han Shan Meng Yu Chih (Record of Master Han Shan's Journey in Dreamland)*

Formerly Ch'an had been transmitted by direct pointing to the mind without additional expedients, but by the Sung dynasty people found it harder to pereceive their inherent nature, so masters like Ta Hui devised the hua t'ou technique to encourage a feeling of doubt about who it is that appears to undergo birth and death. The term hua t'ou originally meant the main point or gist in a literary phrase or saying, but it was borrowed by the Ch'an masters to mean 'ante-word' or 'ante-thought', a device to encourage the mind to return to its inherently still condition. It is vital to note that Ta Hui stresses the importance of maintaining the inquiry at all times.

264.

When one looks into the hua t'ou the most important thing is to give rise to a doubt. Doubt is the crux of hua t'ou. For instance, when one is asked, 'Who is repeating the Buddha's name?', everybody knows that he himself repeats it, but is it repeated by the mouth or by the mind? If the mouth repeats it, why does it not do so when one sleeps? If the mind repeats it, what does the mind look like? As the mind is intangible, one is not clear about it. Consequently some slight feeling of doubt arises about 'who'. This doubt should not be coarse; the finer it is, the better. At all times and in all places this doubt should be looked into unremittingly, like an ever-flowing stream, without giving rise to a second thought.

'Teachings of Master Hsu Yun', *Hsu Yun Ho Shang Fa Hui,*
Vol. I, pages 165–6

Master Hsu Yun (1840–1959 CE) was an unsurpassed adept at Ch'an meditation and his teaching is very clear. He emphasises that the doubt-inquiry and hua t'ou should not be coarse or violent, but subtle. Like his predecessor, Ta Hui, Hsu Yun also emphasised that the doubt-sensation and hua t'ou should be maintained at all times. In his long pilgrimages on foot the master managed to attain singleness of mind, and in his forty-third year he realised his complete awakening upon hearing the crash of a tea cup shattering on the ground. Without knowing it, the hua t'ou technique arouses one's inner potentiality and, if sustained, it will eventually burst out, exposing one's fundamental face.

265.

*We should know that what we call 'looking into hua t'ou' and 'turning
inwards to hear the self-nature' cannot be effected by means of the eye to
look or the ear to hear. If eye and ear are so used, there will be pursuit
after sound and form, with the result that one will be turned by things
[i.e. externals]. If there is singleness of thought abiding in that which is
not born and does not die without pursuing sound and form, this is going
against the stream. This is called 'looking into the hua t'ou' or 'turning
inwards the hearing to hear the self-nature'.*

'Teachings of Master Hsu Yun', *Hsu Yun Shang Fa Hui*, Vol. I,
pages 165–6

The hua t'ou technique described here by Master Hsu Yun tallies with
the meditation mentioned in the *Surangama Sutra* (see nos. 244–7). When
Hsu Yun speaks of 'going against the stream' of birth and death, he does
not mean that we should literally make our minds blank, but that we
should sublimate the senses and not be turned round by them. Hsu Yun's
instruction on hua t'ou is in line with what Hui Neng meant when he said,
'If the true immutable is sought, one seeks it above the motion,' that is, by
looking into the stream of consciousness, not by trying to shut it out, for
only then can one perceive the uncreated nature or fundamental face and
be clear about birth and death.

The T'ien T'ai School

266.

*The attainment of nirvana is realisable by many methods whose
essentials do not go beyond the practice of chih [samatha] and kuan
[vipasyana]. Chih [stilling] is the first step to untie the bonds [of desire]
and kuan [insight] is essential to root out delusion. Chih provides
nourishment for the preservation of a knowing mind and kuan is the
skilful art of promoting spiritual understanding. Chih is the
unsurpassed cause of dhyana and kuan begets wisdom. He who achieves
both chih and kuan is fully competent to work for the welfare of self and
others.*

Master Chih Yi, 'Samatha-Vipasyana For Beginners', Part I

The T'ien T'ai School acquired its name after being consolidated by
Master Chih Yi (d. 598 CE) on Mount T'ien T'ai in Chekiang. Its
teaching is based on the *Lotus* and *Mahaparinirvana* sutras and
Nagarjuna's commentary on the *Prajnaparamita Sutra*. Its chih-kuan
method aims at realising a perfect balance between chih and kuan, which

are said to be like two wings of a bird or like two wheels of a chariot which are useless when either one or the other is missing. The practice of chih begets dhyana (stillness) and the practice of kuan begets prajna (insight, wisdom).

267.

Viewed from opposite directions, contemplation of the void pertains to one side and that of the unreal [phenomenal] to another . . . When one achieves contemplation of the void, one should not cling to the void, and when one achieves contemplation of the unreal [phenomenal], one should not grasp the unreal. When one succeeds in keeping from both extremes, the void and the unreal, his non-relying, non-clinging mind will be really bright; this is called 'contemplation of the mean'. At first glance the above chih-kuan Dharma door seems to imply different successive stages. In practice the employment of either chih or kuan depends solely upon the inclination of the mind during the meditation.
Master Yin Shih Tsu, 'The Chih-Kuan Dharma Door'

The T'ien T'ai method aims at what it calls the 'combined triple insight', the threefold aspects being (1) insight into emptiness (the real or noumenal), (2) the phenomenal (the illusory or unreal), and (3) the mean, which is inclusive of both. In reality these are the same thing looked at in more and more refined ways. Initially there is only coarse perception of the phenomenal (form); next, a coarse perception of the noumenal (void aspect) which seems to fall outside or clash with the seeming; and, finally, correct harmonisation of phenomenon and noumenon, without thought of either avoiding the seeming or clinging to the real – the Middle Way. Thus, both chih and kuan are employed until this balanced triple insight has been attained.

Pure Land Buddhism

268.

Namo Amitabhaya Tathagataya Tadyatha Amrtbhave Amrtsambhave Amrtavikrante Amrtavikrantagamini Gagana Kirtichare Swaha!

[We take refuge in the Tathagata Amitabha. Be it thus: that immortality has become, that immortality has perfectly become, that immortality has progressed, that immortality is progressing, going forward in the glorious Transcendental Way – Swaha!]
'Mantra for Rebirth in the Pure Land'

This mantra is recited daily by thousands of Chinese Buddhists. It is the way of the heart, not of the head, and, as the saying goes, 'He who lacks the hand of faith cannot pick up the wish-fulfilling gem.' The Pure Land tradition is perhaps the least well understood of Buddhism's schools outside its native centres. The idea of rebirth in the Pure Land is often branded as 'superstition' in the West, an attitude which puzzles Asian Buddhists, who see nothing extraordinary in the idea of uniting faith with the power of visualisation, for Pure Land Buddhists are not alone in doing this. Recollection of the Buddha (Buddhanusmriti) is considerably more complex and multifaceted than many Western Buddhists acknowledge, ranging as it does from an almost pietistic simplicity to the virtually tantric visualisations engaged in by its more serious adherents.

269.

The Buddha then said to Ananda and Vaidehi, 'You should visualise the radiant body of Amitayus Buddha. Ananda, you should know that his body is coloured like the pure gold in a hundred, a thousand, ten thousand and a hundred thousand yamalokas [making a pile reaching the height of] as many yojanas as there are sand grains in six hundred thousand lacs of nayutas of Ganges rivers. The white hair between his eyebrows curls five times to the right like five Mount Sumerus. His eyes are like the water of four oceans with the blue and white clearly distinguishable. The pores of his body send out rays of light as great as Mount Sumeru.'

'Contemplation of Amitayus Buddha', *Sutra of the Contemplation of Amitayus*, 9

The *Sutra of the Contemplation of Amitayus* teaches sixteen methods of meditation for rebirth in the Pure Land, entailing highly complex visualisations of incredibly rich imagery – lakes and pools, crystal trees, jewelled tents, and splendid rays emanating from the Buddha and bodhisattvas – a procession of interwoven images highly suggestive of a Pure Land glittering with an unearthly beauty and radiance. However hard it may seem to reconcile such fantastic imagery with the wisdom teachings, which appear to preclude such things, the Buddhist explanation is simple: by concentrating their minds with such visualisations, the Pure Land devotees attain singleness of mind and thus realise the inherent Buddha wisdom, no less than the Ch'an adept. We must remember that the whole Buddhist teaching is cast in terms of upaya (skilful means) and, ultimately, the whole issue of self-power versus other power is a game of words, for why else did the Buddha teach 'No self, no other'?

The Lotus Sutra

270.

*Seeing seekers of the way, slacking in midcourse, unable to secure
liberation from birth and death and the hazardous path of the
defilements, by means of my expedient powers... I therefore spoke of
nirvana for the sake of a resting place, saying, 'All your sufferings are
ended, your tasks finished.' But when, knowing that you had reached
[relative] nirvana and attained arhatship, I then gathered a great
assembly in order to expound the real [absolute] Dharma. By their
expedient powers, all Buddhas distinguish between and expound [the
teaching of] the three vehicles. [But ultimately] there is only the one
Buddha-vehicle. It was only for the sake of a resting place that two
[other] vehicles were expounded.*

'The Magic [Transformation] City', *Lotus Sutra*, ch. 7

According to the T'ien T'ai school, the Buddha's teaching was divided
into five periods, the Lotus teaching being the last in the series, along with
the *Mahaparinirvana Sutra*. The key point of the *Lotus Sutra* is the
Buddha's introduction of the idea that his preliminary teaching of the
three vehicles (sravakayana, pratyekayana and bodhisattvayana) was but a
temporary expedient in order to wean living beings away from their
worldly entanglements. According to legend, five hundred bhikkhus
(monks) refused to listen any further and withdrew, a symbolic way of
expressing how difficult it was for practitioners in the sravaka and
pratyeka stages to renounce their attainments and forsake the relative
nirvana, which the Buddha likened to an 'illusion city' for temporary
refuge. If true universality and compassion are to prevail, this 'illusion
city' of nirvana also has to be renounced.

271.

*I have constantly been expounding the Dharma in this saha world [a
world of sorrows, subject to transmigration], leading and benefiting all
living beings in hundreds of thousands of myriads of kotis of nayutas of
realms beyond number. Sons of a good family, during this time I have
referred to myself as Dipamkara and other Buddhas, and I have spoken
of their entry into nirvana. Thus have I given all these expedient
teachings... I have expounded different teachings under different
names, [spoken differently] as to the length of my life, and also clearly
said that I would enter nirvana... I have expounded the wondrously
subtle Dharma, thus causing all living beings to be gladdened in heart.*

Lotus Sutra, ch. 16

It is fitting to close this series of readings by acknowledging the timelessness of the Buddha's Dharmakaya. In this extract from the *Lotus Sutra*, the Buddha testifies that he has appeared under many names and in different guises throughout countless realms and measureless aeons. Here the Dharma becomes a trans-historical phenomenon, no longer exclusively tied to the transformation body (Nirmanakaya) of Sakyamuni Buddha. The Dharma is the Buddha-potentiality of all living beings, for all inherently possess the Buddha-nature and all will eventually become Buddhas.

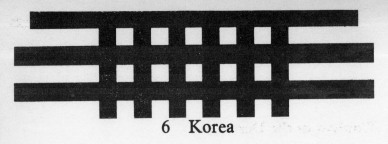

6 Korea

Compiled with commentary by Stephen Batchelor
and Martine Fages

According to tradition, Buddhism was first brought to Korea from China by a monk called Sundo in 372 CE. At this time what we now know as Korea was divided into three separate kingdoms: Koguryo in the north, Paekche in the south-west and Silla in the south-east. Over the next three centuries, Buddhism was gradually adopted in favour of the local animist and shamanist religions in all three kingdoms. A constant stream of monks and scholars travelled between China and Korea bringing with them scriptures of the different Chinese schools. In 668 CE, Silla succeeded in unifying the three kingdoms under its rule and Buddhism became the national religion of the new country.

Although Korean Buddhism is entirely Chinese in origin, it has evolved its own distinct form over the centuries. Whereas China was a large country that could accommodate several different schools, Korea was a small land that, because of a constant danger of invasion from its neighbours, had always to strengthen its sense of unity. Thus the greatest representatives of Korean Buddhism are noted for their attempts to synthesise the diverse tendencies within the religion.

Nonetheless, the Zen school has probably had the greatest influence in Korea and it continues to do so today. Yet this form of Zen is one that has absorbed many of the insights of the Huayen school of Chinese Buddhism and still keeps alive the ideal of a unity between meditation and philosophy.

Korean Zen is much closer to Chinese Chan than to the Rinzai and Soto forms of Zen practised in Japan. Korean Zen practice is much less bound by strict rules and conventions than many of its Japanese counterparts. And unlike his Japanese brethren, most of whom are bound to a single teacher and monastery for their training before they take up a post as a married priest in a village or city temple, the Korean monk is an independent figure who observes the Vinaya (body of ethics and disciplines prescribed by the Buddha) while wandering from monastery to monastery, studying under different teachers to refine his insight into Zen.

Today there are approximately eight million Buddhists in Korea, served by about 15,000 clergy, at least half of whom are nuns.

Wonhyo in the Desert

272.

*One evening as Wonhyo was crossing the desert, he stopped at a small
patch of green, where there were a few trees and some water, and went to
sleep. Towards midnight he awoke thirsty – it was pitch dark. He
groped along on all fours, searching for water. At last his hand touched
a cup on the ground. He picked it up and drank. Ah, how delicious!
Then he bowed deeply, in gratitude, to Buddha for the gift of water.
The next morning, Wonhyo woke up and saw beside him what he had
taken for a cup [during the night]. It was a shattered skull, blood-caked
and with shreds of flesh still stuck to the cheek-bones. Strange insects
crawled or floated on the surface of the filthy rainwater inside it.
Wonhyo looked at the skull and felt a great wave of nausea. He opened
his mouth. As soon as the vomit poured out, his mind opened and he
understood. Last night, because he hadn't seen and hadn't thought, the
water was delicious. This morning, seeing and thinking had made him
vomit. Ah, he said to himself, thinking makes good and bad, life and
death. And without thinking there is no universe, no Buddha, no
Dharma. All is one, and this one is empty. There was no need now to
find a master. Wonhyo already understood life and death. What more
was there to learn? So he turned and started back across the desert to
Korea.*

Mu Seong Sunim, *Thousand Peaks: Korean Zen –
Tradition and Teachers*

Wonhyo (617–686 CE) was born during the period of Korea's struggle for
political unification, which was achieved in 668 CE. Although most of the
main Buddhist schools of China were already established in the country,
Wonhyo was dissatisfied with the state of the religion and, as was
customary for ambitious young monks of his time, decided to travel with
his friend Uisang to the holy land of China to seek out deeper truths. The
episode cited here describes what happened to him on this journey. The
spiritual awakening he undergoes upon vomiting the foul water he had
drunk the night before gives him two key realisations. First, that the truth
of Buddhism does not reside in a particular country like China, but within
one's own mind. At this very moment Wonhyo established the basis for a
Korean form of Buddhism: one that drew upon the Chinese models but,
in accordance with the needs of the Koreans, was essentially syncretic.

Second, that all experience is a creation of mind. He further developed this insight in his famous commentary on *The Awakening of Faith in the Mahayana*, a text attributed to the Indian scholar Ashvaghosa which propounds the philosophy of the 'One Mind'. Upon returning to Korea Wonhyo developed his own school, called the Popsong or Dharma Nature school, which was based upon his spiritual experience while seeking to resolve the tensions between the Buddhist traditions of his time.

The Bondage of Desire

273.

Sublime and majestic is the nirvanic delight of the Buddhas, for they have renounced the desires that bind one to the bottomless ocean of misery and instead have practised austerities. Yet sentient beings continue to come and go through the door of birth and death, precisely because they have been unable to renounce such desires. Although no one is preventing them, very few beings manage to reach the Buddhas' realms. Why? Because they insist on keeping desire, anger and ignorance in their possession. Although no one else encourages them, there are numerous beings who have stumbled into evil ways. And why is this? Because they cherish the four serpents and the five temptations as the innermost treasures of their minds.

Wonhyo, *On Cultivating Determination to Practise*

This passage is taken from a short text written by Wonhyo as an introduction and exhortation to practise Buddhism. Here he rephrases the fundamental Buddhist doctrine of the four noble truths: the suffering of birth and death is caused by desire and ignorance, while nirvana, the liberation from birth and death, is found through the practice of the path to enlightenment. The 'four serpents' refers to the four elements of materiality: earth, water, fire and air. The 'five temptations' are those of fame, wealth, sex, food and sleep. This text is still widely used today in Korea as a training manual for novice monks.

The Necessity of Moral Discipline and Wisdom

274.

*However well you practise meditation, without moral discipline you will
be just like someone who is shown the way to a treasure house but never
goes there. However well you endure austerities, without wisdom you
will be like a person who intends to go east but heads for the west.*

Wonhyo, *On Cultivating Determination to Practise*

This advice of Wonhyo is taken from the same text as the previous
passage. Although the message seems simple, it is one that is hard to
practise. The attainment of enlightenment is not simply a question of
developing concentration and undergoing austerities. Rather, the heart of
the practice lies in sound ethical behaviour and the cultivation of a
discerning mind. The greatest hindrances are not the inability to
concentrate well in meditation or the reluctance to subject one's body to
pain and hardship; far greater are the temptations to act against one's true
conscience or to succumb to fanciful views and opinions about the
spiritual life.

The Mutual Interpenetration of All Phenomena

275.

*Since Dharma-nature is round and interpenetrating, it is without any
sign of duality.*
All dharmas [phenomena] are unmoving and originally calm.
No name, no form; all [distinctions] are abolished.
*It is known through the wisdom of enlightenment, not by any other
level.*
*The true-nature is extremely profound, exceedingly subtle and
sublime.*
*It does not attach to self-nature, but manifests following [causal]
conditions.*
In one is all, in many is one.
One is identical to all, many is identical to one.
In one particle of dust are contained the ten directions.
And so it is with all particles of dust.
Incalculably long aeons are identical to a single thought-instant.
And a single thought-instant is identical to incalculably long aeons.

The nine times and the ten times are mutually identical,

Yet are not confused or mixed, but function separately.
The moment you begin to aspire with your heart, instantly perfect
enlightenment [is attained].

Uisang, 'Ocean Seal of Huayen Buddhism'

This piece is written by Uisang (625–702 CE), the monk who set out to China with Wonhyo. Although Wonhyo turned back to Korea, Uisang continued to China where he met the two great masters Chih-yen and Fa-tsang, respectively the Second and Third Patriarchs of the Huayen school of Chinese Buddhism. After receiving instruction from them, Uisang returned home to become the First Patriarch of the school in Korea. The text is the first half of his 'Ocean Seal of Huayen Buddhism', a diagrammatic presentation of the essential doctrines of the school. The Chinese characters are set out in a square 'map', which is designed in such a way that the reader both begins and ends in the centre.

The Huayen doctrine is based on the mystical and poetic vision enshrined in the massive *Avatamsaka Sutra*. The central idea is that of the mutual interpenetration of all phenomena. This can be understood as an extension of the Indian Buddhist doctrine of interdependent origination. But whereas the Indians interpreted this doctrine to show how all effects are invariably preceded by their causes and all causes invariably followed by their effects, the Chinese took it to mean that, in a sense, every single thing in the universe creates and contains everything else. Uisang's text inevitably reminds us of William Blake's celebrated verse:

To see a world in a grain of sand,
And Heaven in a wild flower,
Hold Infinity in the palm of your hand,
And Eternity in an hour!

Philosophy with Meditation

276.

Listening to the Dharma is like treading on thin ice: you must direct your eyes and ears and listen to the profound words. Clear your thoughts of emotions and sense-objects and appreciate the recondite meaning. After the master has left the hall, sit silently and reflect upon his lecture. If you have any doubts, consult those who have understood. Ponder it in the evening; inquire about it in the morning. Try not to fall short in your understanding by so much as a strand of silk or hair. If you practise in this way, you will be able to develop right faith and be one who has embraced the path.

Chinul, *Admonitions to Beginning Students*

These are the words of Chinul (1158–1210 CE), also known by his posthumous title of Bojo. Chinul is often regarded as the founder of the mature form of Korean Buddhism. He was born at a time when Buddhism had polarised into two main factions: the scholarly schools known as Kyo and the more recent meditation school of Son, i.e. Zen. Chinul sought to integrate these two approaches and throughout his life both taught Buddhist philosophy, especially that of the Huayen school, and instructed people in Zen meditation.

His three main enlightenments came to him when reading passages from Buddhist scriptures. The passage quoted here from the short text, *Admonitions to Beginning Students*, reads like the transcript of a lecture, perhaps given to the monks of the monastery he founded, Songgwang Sa in Cholla Namdo Province. The understanding he requires of his students is both reflective as well as contemplative, thus unifying the philosophical and meditative traditions.

Pointing to Your Original Mind

277.

Question: In our case, what is this mind of void and calm, numinous awareness?

Chinul: What has just asked me this question is precisely your mind of void and calm, numinous awareness. Why not trace back its radiance rather than search for it outside? For your benefit I will now point straight to your original mind so that you can awaken to it. Clear your mind and listen to my words.

From morning to evening, throughout the twelve periods of the day, during all your actions and activities . . . ultimately who is it that is able to perform all these actions? Speak! . . . You should know that what is capable of seeing, hearing, moving and acting has to be your original mind: it is not your physical body. Furthermore, the four elements which make up the physical body are by nature void; they are like images in a mirror or the moon's reflection in water. How can they be clear and constantly aware, always bright and never obscured – and, upon activation, be able to put into operation sublime functions as numerous as the sands of the Ganges? For this reason it is said, 'Drawing water and carrying firewood are spiritual powers and sublime functions.'

There are many points at which to enter the noumenon. I will indicate one approach which will allow you to return to the source . . . Do you hear the sounds of that crow cawing and that magpie calling?

Student: Yes.

Chinul: Trace them back and listen to your hearing-nature. Do you hear any sounds?

Student: At that place, sounds and discriminations do not obtain.
Chinul: Marvellous! Marvellous! This is Avalokiteshvara's method for entering the noumenon. Let me ask you again. You said that sound and discriminations do not obtain at that place. But since they do not obtain, isn't the hearing-nature just empty space at such a time?
Student: Originally it is not empty. It is always bright and never obscured.
Chinul: What is this essence which is not empty?
Student: As it has no form or shape, words cannot describe it.
                                         The Collected Works of Chinul

This dialogue presents Chinul as a true Zen master, pushing his students back onto their original nature. He is not concerned here with elaborating any doctrinal points, but merely with the realisation of sudden enlightenment. He employs a traditional method of meditation, often used by Zen teachers, which originates from the *Surangama Sutra*. In this discourse the Buddha asks his assembled disciples to tell him what they have found to be the most effective means of realising enlightenment. Avalokiteshvara explains that through 'regulating the organ of hearing' the mind can best be quietened for meditation and opened to the possibility of enlightenment.

The Same or Different

278.

Chinul then ordered the monastery drum beaten to summon the monks of the community and, carrying his staff with six rings, he walked towards the Dharma hall. There he lit incense, ascended the platform, and proceeded to perform all the usual formalities. He then struck his staff and, after mentioning the circumstances surrounding the question and answers exchanged in his room the previous evening, said, 'The miraculous efficaciousness of the Zen Dharma is inconceivable. Today I have come here because I want to explain it fully to all of you in this assembly. If you ask me clear, unattached questions, this old man will give you clear, unattached answers.' He looked to the right and left and, rubbing his chest with his hands, said, 'The life of this mountain monk is now entirely in all of your hands. You are free to drag me aside or pull me down. Let anyone who has bones and tendons come forward.'
He then stretched his legs and, sitting on the seat, gave answers to the different questions put to him. His words were precise and the meaning detailed; his elocution was unimpaired. The events are recorded in the Death Record. Finally a monk asked, 'I am not clear whether the past manifestation of illness by Vimalakirti of Vaisali and today's sickness of

Chogye's Chinul are the same or different.' The master replied, 'You've only learned similarity and difference!' Then, picking up his staff, he struck it several times and said, 'A thousand things and ten thousand objects are all right here.' Finally, supported by his staff, he remained sitting immobile and quietly passed away.

The Collected Works of Chinul

This passage forms part of the inscription on Chinul's stele and would have been composed by his disciples shortly after his death. It depicts a man who has lived his life to the full, but is aware of and prepared for his impending death. The 'Death Record' was no doubt a more detailed account of the exchanges between Chinul and his disciples. Unfortunately, this work has been lost. The final question refers to the *Vimalakirtinirdesa Sutra*, a discourse in which a layman called Vimalakirti, a native of the town of Vaisali in India, uses sickness as a valuable occasion for teaching the Dharma. Chinul's last words express the immediacy of his experimental insight in the language of Huayen philosophy, reminding us of Uisang's phrase: 'In one particle of dust are contained the ten directions.'

The Cuckoo's Cry

279.

One day Sosan asked his teacher:
  'What is it like when one seeks for Buddha?'
  'It's like looking for an ox while riding on an ox.'
  'What is it like after you know Buddha?'
  'It is like coming home riding on an ox.'
  'How can I keep on practising Zen if I attain realisation?'
  'You should keep on practising Zen as a herdsman with a whip keeps his cow from trespassing on another's field.'

Soon after this exchange with his teacher, Sosan heard a cuckoo crying in the garden and attained partial realisation. He composed two verses to commemorate the occasion:

'Suddenly I hear a cuckoo singing outside the window.
The spring mountains which fill my eyes are all my old home.

Returning from drawing water, I turn my head.
Blue mountains in white clouds without number.'

Mu Seong Sunim, *Thousand Peaks: Korean Zen – Tradition and Teachers*

In 1392 CE the Koryo dynasty, in which Buddhism had thrived under the patronage of the state and the guidance of such able figures as Chinul, was replaced by the unsympathetic Yi dynasty. During this period, which lasted until 1912, Buddhism was suppressed by a neo-Confucianist regime that sought to eradicate the influence of the religion. The most notable monk of the Yi period was Sosan (1520–1604). He came to prominence during a brief period of Buddhist revival under Queen Munjong. Sosan is remembered not only for his Zen but also for his poetry and calligraphy as well as his nationalism. Towards the end of his life he organised the Buddhist monks into militia units to help defeat the Japanese invasion of 1592.

In this passage we see Sosan as a young man struggling to grasp the meaning of Zen from his teacher Puyong Yonggwan. As is traditional in all schools of Zen, he recorded the insight he gained after this exchange in poetic form. Shortly afterwards, his teacher confirmed his realisation and granted his transmission.

The Sudden and Gradual Paths

280.

But since in Dharma there are many aspects and people have many different capacities, it does no harm to set forth [expedient teachings].
    Comment: 'Dharma' means the one thing. 'People' means sentient beings. In Dharma there are the two aspects of immutability and changing-with-conditions. Among people, there are two kinds of capacities, some for sudden enlightenment, others for gradual cultivation. Thus there is no harm in setting forth written and spoken words. This is like the saying, 'In an official position, even a needle is not admitted; privately, a horse and cart are allowed in.'
    Although I have called all beings 'completely perfect', they are born without the eye of wisdom, and they submit themselves to samsara. Therefore, if not for the golden blades of [the Buddhas' and patriarchs'] appearance in the world, who would cut away the thick blinding membrane of ignorance? As for crossing the ocean of suffering and ascending the shore of happiness, this is all due to the great compassion of the Buddhas and patriarchs. Therefore, even with lifetimes numberless as the Ganges's sands, it is difficult to repay them even one part in ten thousand.
    This means that since beneficial new influences have been widely shown [by them], one feels gratitude to the Buddhas and patriarchs for their deep kindness.
    Summation: The king ascends the treasure palace; the common people break into song.

Mu Seong Sunim, *Thousand Peaks: Korean Zen –
Tradition and Teachers*

From his mid-forties until his early sixties, Sosan compiled a handbook for Zen students. This is his longest work and consists of his own explanations and comments upon a selection of sayings and previous Zen masters. These include both major Chinese teachers such as Huineng as well as his Korean predecessor, Chinul. Here, commenting on an unidentified text that states a common Buddhist notion, Sosan discusses the 'sudden' and 'gradual' paths to enlightenment. Following Tsungmi and Chinul, he sees no inherent contradiction between these views: for some the sudden approach is appropriate and for others the gradual; at times there are moments of sudden realisation, at other times periods of gradual cultivation. Although one may present oneself in public as an uncompromising advocate of the sudden path, in practice one uses the expedient means of gradual development. Yet, in a passage that reflects a strong devotional attitude more characteristic of Pure Land Buddhism than Zen, Sosan qualifies what he has said by pointing out that whatever path one follows, any realisation that follows is the result of the kindness of the Buddhas and patriarchs.

The Loneliness of Truth

281.

I look around in all directions,
But cannot find anyone to whom I may transmit my kasa and bowl.
O, I can find no one!
In spring, flowers are in full bloom on the mountain.
In autumn, the moon is bright and the wind is cool.
I sing a song of no birth, but who will ever listen to my song?
My life and fate, what shall I do?
The colour of the mountain is the eye
Of Avalokiteshvara Bodhisattva.
The sound of the river is the ear of Manjushri Bodhisattva.
Mr Chang and Mrs Lee are Vairochana Buddha
Sentient beings call on Buddha or Patriarch, Zen or Kyo,
But in origin all of them are one.

Mu Seong Sunim, *Thousand Peaks: Korean Zen –*
Tradition and Teachers

After more than five hundred years of suppression during the Yi dynasty, at the turn of the century Buddhists were at last granted more freedom and respect. But the tradition was inevitably weakened. In 1910 the already precarious situation of Korean Buddhism was further threatened by the Japanese occupation of the country. However, through the efforts of the monk Kyongho (1849–1912) and his disciples, the tradition was revived and saved.

The lines cited above were composed by Kyongho around 1880, shortly after his major enlightenment. His insight was confirmed by Master Yongam, an eleventh generation successor of Sosan. The poem, of which about a quarter is quoted here, expresses the loneliness of one who has glimpsed the profound truth of Zen, but can find no one to whom he can pass it on. The kasa, the monk's robe, and the bowl are traditionally regarded as the symbols of transmission that are conferred by a Zen teacher upon the disciple who will continue his lineage. Again the Huayen doctrine of the interpenetration of all things is suggested in the images of the colour of the mountain being the eye of Avalokiteshvara, the river the ear of Manjushri, and Mr Chang and Mrs Lee (i.e. ordinary people) Vairochana Buddha (the Buddha whose body, according to Huayen, is co-extensive with the universe). Following the syncretic tradition of Korean Buddhism, Kyongho then reaffirms, from the standpoint of mystical experience, the non-contradictoriness of the Zen and Kyo (doctrinal) schools.

What is the Head and What the Tail?

282.

Master Mangong was sitting alone in his room. I bowed to him and then told him that I wished to learn about a hwadu and could he please teach me one. Although he had seen me enter the room, he remained silent and did not even look at me. For about thirty minutes he just sat there with his eyes closed. This made me feel extremely nervous. I wondered whether he was acting in this way because I was so small and ugly. Since I could not practise well he would probably not teach me a hwadu anyway. Reflecting on all my shortcomings I began to feel depressed. Finally, I thought that I had better leave. But at that very moment he opened his eyes wide and shouted: 'Since you are incapable of knowing what is the head and what the tail, what kind of a hwadu (lit: "head of speech") are you talking about?' This gave me such a shock that I felt as though I had been struck by a ball. My chest felt heavy and my heart was beating rapidly. I was so distressed that he had just scolded me and taught me nothing. I felt so ashamed that I could not stand the thought of facing anyone. So I left quietly by the back door without asking him anything further.

During the first twenty-one days of the retreat this sense of self-reproach grew stronger and would not abate. It reached a point where I could no longer sleep. I stopped talking and did not ask the others about anything. After the other nuns had gone to sleep in the meditation hall at eleven-thirty, I would go to the small recreation room and spend the rest of the night sitting there by myself. Gradually, a very vivid and tranquil state of mind began to develop.

All my distracted thoughts and feelings of distress disappeared. My mind was left in a vivid, pure and quiescent state. Sometimes the thought 'What is this?' would arise by itself. As the thinking ceased the sense of self-reproach became weaker. Then it felt as though a single thought arose up and pierced the top of my head. This then took the form of a voice which said: 'Since there is originally no head or tail, where can either of them be?'

Seonkyong Sunim, *The Life of a Korean Zen Nun*

One of Kyongho's most brilliant disciples was Mangong (1872–1946). During his lifetime Mangong was renowned both as a gifted and highly respected teacher, as well as an important figure in the Korean resistance to Japanese colonialist policy. The speaker in the passage quoted above is a nun called Seonkyong Sunim (b. 1903). Seonkyong became a nun when she was eighteen but it was not until she was thirty-two that she received instruction in Zen practice. This episode describes her first and only meeting with Mangong, who died a year later. She asks Mangong to give her a hwadu, a technical term that refers both to the place from where thought originates (hence its literal meaning 'head of speech'), as well as the vital point of a koan* that is used to turn the mind back to this place. In Korea, self-reproach is sometimes considered, along with doubt and faith, as one of the three basic attitudes required in Zen practice. Without knowing what she was doing, Seonkyong intensified her self-reproach to the point where it actually triggered an awakening into the true meaning of Mangong's seemingly dismissive remark. 'What is this?' is a classic hwadu or koan which has its origin in the encounter between the Sixth Patriarch Huineng and his disciple Huaijang.

Investigating a Hwadu

283.

The purpose of practising Zen meditation is to awaken the mind. Such practise does not involve just sitting quietly and trying to calm and pacify the mind. Nor does it entail contemplating the breath. Instead it involves direct inquiry into a hwadu. An example of a hwadu would be a question such as 'What is this?' or 'What is this mind?' What you are searching for can be called by many different names: mind, spirit, soul,

---

*Literally 'public case'. In the Zen Buddhist tradition a koan is the record of a person's enlightenment and it is used in meditation as a focus and trigger for deep spiritual inquiry.

true nature, and so forth. But such designations are merely labels. You should put aside all these names and reflect on the fact that the true master of the body is more than just the label 'mind'. The master of the body is not the Buddha, for it is not yet awakened. Nor is it anything material, because it cannot be physically given away or received. Nor is it simply empty space, for empty space cannot pose questions or have knowledge of good and evil.

Hence there is a master who rules this body who is neither the label 'mind', the Buddha, a material thing nor empty space. Having negated these four possibilities, a question will arise as to what this master really is. If you continue inquiring in this way, the questioning will become more intense. Finally, when the mass of questioning enlarges to a critical point, it will suddenly burst. The entire universe will be shattered and only your original nature will appear before you. In this way you will awaken.

Kusan Sunim, *The Way of Korean Zen*

Kusan Sunim (1909–83), the author of this passage, brings us into the modern world. Ordained in 1938, Kusan spent many years in intensive meditation and finally received transmission from his teacher Hyobong (1888–1966). Kusan also spent many years restoring the Korean monastic order after the departure of the Japanese. During the last ten years of his life, he allowed foreign monks to study at his monastery – Songgwang Sa, founded by Chinul – and on three occasions travelled and lectured in Europe and America. Here he explains how to meditate on a hwadu. He would give this kind of instruction to whoever came to see him: monks, university professors, foreign tourists, peasants from nearby villages. His message was clear and straightforward but totally demanding. He emphasised focusing one's deepest questioning or doubt upon the true nature of mind. Eventually, this doubt would congeal into a solid mass and then burst. At that moment enlightenment is attained.

Casting a Fishing Line of One Thousand Feet

284.

Today is the last day of the lunar month. The new moon is so bright that its light pervades the entire Dharmadhatu. Long ago Master Nanchuan once took his assembly of monks to look at the moon. So is this moon I am talking of the same as or different from the moon that Master Nanchuan gazed at? Those of you monks who are endowed with the Dharma eye, say something!

Even though you may claim to have awakened, I would still give you thirty blows. How many more would those who have not awakened receive?

Casting a fishing line of a thousand feet into the ocean of space,
The clouds disperse, the waves settle, and the coral grows.
The fish and the dragon sleep deeply and do not move.
Load the ship full with the moon, pull the oar and depart.

Kusan Sunim, *The Way of Korean Zen*

Traditionally, Zen training monasteries in Korea conduct two three-month meditation retreats a year, one in summer and one in winter. For the full ninety days, the monks or the nuns sit in meditation for ten to twelve hours daily, concentrating on their hwadu. To encourage them in their practice, the Zen master gives a Dharma lecture on the day before each new and full moon. The above text is the 'formal' part of such a lecture given by Kusan Sunim during the winter retreat at Songgwang Sa in 1981–82. In the true Zen fashion this lecture is enigmatic, paradoxical and confrontational. Kusan strives to break his students' minds out of their habitual state of slumber and conventionality. He intersperses his delivery with abrupt shouts and the pounding of his Zen staff on the dais, and chants the poem in a high-pitched, quavering rhythm. After the 'formal' part of the lecture, Kusan would then explain what he meant in more intelligible language and offer advice on how to further one's meditation practice. Nanchuan (784–834 CE) was a famous Chinese Zen master of the Tang dynasty.

The Arrival

285.

All sentient beings are sailing in a boat that is crossing the ocean. Man is one with the boat. The ocean is one with the land. Everything you see is in constant activity and motion. But there is one thing alone that is majestic yet totally natural. All things rest within its embrace. You are frequently caught up in bustling crowds. But do you ever perceive this one unmoving thing? By understanding it, you reach the realm of freedom.

The four great elements break apart from one another. The eye and its objects of sight drift away from one another. Do you know where they go? Upon discovering their destination, you will arrive at the jewelled palace. Do you have any of those jewels in your own home?

When you can kick and overturn the earth, and touch the sun with your hands, only then will you have arrived.

Kusan Sunim, *The Way of Korean Zen*

Here Kusan gives a metaphorical and poetic description of enlightenment. Again the Huayen notion of the interpenetration of all things is suggested. But the main point is the grandeur of the true mind, the ultimate truth of all things, that stands radiant and unchanging in the midst of the world's bustle and change. Death too, if you are properly prepared, affords a chance to glimpse the original nature. But you do not have to wait until then: right here and now you have the opportunity to transform your vision of the world.

The Resonating Bell

286.

> *Originally this metal was ugly rocks. Then the rocks were heated for a long time over a very hot fire, until finally they became liquid. Now this liquid will be poured into a mould and will take the shape of a big, beautiful bell, and when it cools someone will strike the bell, and the beautiful sound will fill the whole universe.*
>
> *We are all like rocks. And when we practise hard, we heat up our hearts making a big, hot flame, which melts our condition, situation and opinion until we become like molten metal, ready to assume the shape of a great bodhisattva who, when struck with the cry for help, makes a big, deep sound, which resonates and fills the whole universe and makes everybody happy.*
>
> Mu Seong Sunim, *Thousand Peaks: Korean Zen –
> Tradition and Teachers*

This passage was composed in English by a living Korean Zen master, currently based in the United States, called Seung Sahn (b. 1927). He received transmission at the young age of twenty-three from Kobong (1890–1961). After spending ten years in Japan and Hong Kong, he arrived penniless in the United States in 1971. He now has centres and monasteries throughout the country as well as in such unlikely places as Poland. In addressing a Western audience, he seeks to make the wisdom of the Korean Zen tradition relevant and intelligible for modern times. This simple yet beautiful metaphor of spiritual transformation describes the process in which the ordinary unenlightened individual becomes an enlightened bodhisattva, whose sole function is to achieve the happiness and well-being of the whole universe.

The Water of Life

287.

Many people like honey better than water. I think water is better than honey. Honey tastes good, but if you only eat honey, it is not good for you. It is possible to take much water, but only a little honey. Zen is very clear, simple and necessary, like water. Every day you need water, and every day you need Zen, but most people prefer honey. Zen is clear, but not interesting to them. Most people have desires, and Zen is cutting off desires, so people don't like this. Their whole life is only desire. If you practise Zen, then your life is only clear like water, with no taste, like water.

Mu Seong Sunim, *Thousand Peaks: Korean Zen –*
Tradition and Teachers

The meaning of this text is as clear as water. Any commentary would only make it murky.

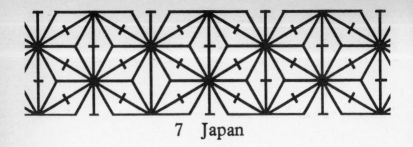

7 Japan

Shingon

Compiled with commentary by Stephen Hodge

Shingon Buddhism is the Japanese form of the mantra way or tantra (see
p. 10) introduced by Kobo Daishi (774–835 CE) following his return from
his sojourn in China in 806 CE. Unlike other forms of Buddhism taught in
Japan, Shingon retains many purely Indian elements, to the extent that it
is often regarded by the Japanese themselves as the most 'foreign' of all
their schools. This is probably because the transmission of the basic
teachings to China by the Indian masters Subhakara-simha (637–735
CE), Vajra-bodhi (671–741 CE) and Amogha-vajra (705–774 CE) had been
completed less than thirty years before Kobo Daishi in his turn
transmitted them to Japan. However, having said this, we must also
remember that Kobo Daishi himself was a spiritual master of great
creativity and a prolific writer, so it is not surprising that we find many
fresh insights in Shingon Buddhism that originated with him. In this
section, I shall try to deal with the most important elements of Shingon
teachings, both those found in the basic scriptural authorities such as the
Maha-vairochana Tantra and those found in the writings of Kobo Daishi
himself.

There is a basic problem which all religions, Buddhism included, have
had to deal with, and that is how to express that which is inherently
inexpressible. While the *via negativa* of the early Mahayana Buddhism
and the Madhyamikas is well known, alternative and contrasting
solutions were also developed and taught. This may be illustrated by the
famous line from the *Heart Sutra* which states that 'colour-form is
nothingness (shunyata) and nothingness is colour-form'. Generally
speaking, the emphasis has always been to show that all phenomena
(dharmas) such as colour-form are nothingness rather than to
demonstrate how nothingness is the phenomenal. However, it is in tantric
Buddhism that we encounter the most dramatic attempts both
theoretically and practically to 'express the inexpressible' in positive
terms. It is perhaps due to this that we find very affirmative language used
in the tantras about matters that many religions reject or view with
suspicion. In part this viewpoint is grounded on the belief that
enlightenment or the potential for it is the primordial essence of all beings,

and indeed of the entire universe. It is said that the only difference between us and Buddhas is that they truly know this, while we do not.

The Source of Dharma

288.

I am the primordial being of the universe, called the Support of the World. Supreme and primordially at peace, I teach the unequalled Dharma.

Maha-vairochana Tantra

Enlightenment, the basic all-pervading ground of reality, is personified as the primordial Buddha Maha-vairochana who speaks here. This ground is also known as the Dharmakaya, the embodiment of reality or truth. Though primordially and perpetually unmoving, the Dharmakaya (or Maha-vairochana) is identified as the source of the Dharma. Normally the Dharma is understood to mean just the Buddhist teachings, but here it encompasses all spiritual teachings that lead beings to the direct realisation and attainment of truth.

The Essence of Dharmakaya

289.

In ordinary Buddhist teachings, the elements are considered to be non-sentient, but in tantric teaching they are regarded as the symbolic embodiment of the Tathagata [enlightenment, eternal Buddha]. The great elements are not independent of the mind. Though differences do exist between matter and mind, in their essential nature they are the same. Matter is no other than mind, and mind is no other than matter. Without any obstruction they interpenetrate each other.

Kobo Daishi

To explain how Maha-vairochana (primordial Buddha) pervades all things and all beings, Kobo Daishi taught that the Dharmakaya (embodiment of reality) has three aspects – its essence, attributes and functions. Here he speaks of the essence of the Dharmakaya. Basing himself upon the *Maha-vairochana Tantra*, he explains that the five elemental forces – earth, water, fire, wind and space – traditionally thought to form the material universe, are in fact manifestations of the qualities of the Dharmakaya. To these he adds a sixth element, that of consciousness. Together these are the body and mind of Maha-vairochana integrated in a state of eternal harmony. These six interact to create all Buddhas, beings and the universe. They are simultaneously the creating and the created. Therefore, all phenomena are essentially the same in their constituents, and no difference exists between mind and body, whether of Buddhas or of ordinary beings. They are non-dual.

The Attributes of Dharmakaya

290.

All existence is interrelated horizontally and vertically without end, like images in mirrors or like the rays of lamps. This existence is in that one, and that is in this. The being of Maha-vairochana is the being of creatures, and vice versa. They are not identical but are nevertheless identical; they are not different but are nevertheless different.

Kobo Daishi

The second part of the Dharmakaya (all-pervading reality) is its attributes. These attributes appear or radiate out from the Dharmakaya like rays of light or reflections, and they are the manifested forms of the six elements through which we perceive Maha-vairochana (the primordial Buddha). Kobo Daishi divides these attributes into four modes, that is, the four mandalas. Properly speaking, a mandala is the multi-dimensional configuration of the manifested qualities of the Dharmakaya. The first of the four is the Great Mandala, which is the universe itself, the physical extension of Maha-vairochana. The second is the Samaya Mandala, the individualisation of Maha-vairochana's omnipresent compassion. The third is the Dharma Mandala, which is the dimension wherein the self-revelation and communication of reality-truth (Dharma) continually take place. Finally, there is the Action Mandala, which is the configuration of all movement in the universe. All four of these are inseparably related. When one is present, so are the other three.

The Functioning of Dharmakaya

291.

All the activities of [Maha-vairochana's] body, all the activities of his speech, and all the activities of his mind were seen by all of them to reveal the Dharma continually throughout all societies of beings.

Maha-vairochana Tantra

The third aspect of the Dharmakaya (embodiment of reality) is its functioning. Kobo Daishi identifies this with the activities of Maha-vairochana's (the primordial Buddha's) body, speech and mind, which, he says, are the expression of his compassion towards beings. These activities are seen or experienced in diverse forms suited to the needs and aspirations of all beings, for they appear as the various Buddhas, bodhisattvas or other teachers. With the growth of one's insight, one will ultimately come to view all forms, sounds and thoughts in the world as concrete expressions of the Dharmakaya which are perpetually engaged in revealing truth.

The Compassion of the Dharmakaya

292.

These masters of great compassion become perfectly awakened to enlightenment in order to save completely unlimited societies of beings. They teach the Dharma according to the inclinations of the many different societies of beings.

Maha-vairochana Tantra

Through the inherent compassion of the Dharmakaya (embodiment of reality), we encounter beings throughout the universe who embody both that compassion and the process of becoming enlightened as teachers and models for us. These teachers are not necessarily 'Buddhists' in a narrow sense, but include all those who act for the welfare and benefit of living beings. So, due to the cultural or historical situation in which one finds oneself, one may not be able to become a 'Buddhist' but must follow some other faith. This does not matter, as whatever religion you follow will eventually lead you to enlightenment, for whatever is good is linked to truth.

The Inherent Buddha Teachings

293.

The Buddha Dharma is not all remote. It is in our minds, it is close to us. Suchness is nowhere external. Where can we find it if not within our bodies?

Kobo Daishi

So the Dharmakaya is constantly making itself known – it is truth revealing truth. We always have access to the Dharma, which leads us to the realisation of truth for it inheres within us as a part of our very being. Buddhism has always stressed the immediacy and urgency of liberation and enlightenment. It is not something which needs a special time or place to be experienced. It is present right here and now.

The Inherent Source of Truth

294.

Where is the Dharmakaya? It is not far away; it is in our bodies. The source of wisdom? In our minds; indeed, it is close to us!

                                                                Kobo Daishi

Not only is the Dharma which leads us to enlightenment constantly available but, indeed, the source of truth, the Dharmakaya itself, is ever present – both in our bodies and our minds. There is nowhere we can go where it is not present, for, as we have seen, it is the very ground of being which is inherent in all things.

Perfect Buddhahood

295.

Foolish people blinded by ignorance who do not know this seek Buddhahood elsewhere, but do not realise it exists here. Buddhahood will not be attained even in any other world system. The mind itself is perfect Buddhahood – no other Buddhahood than that is taught.

                                                                Maha-vairochana Tantra

In fact, we may only 'attain' enlightenment because we are already enlightened. We are not aware of this due to a basic misunderstanding (*avidya*) of the nature of reality. Just as water which is inherently clear and pure, becomes opaque when disturbed by the wind, so do our minds lose their clarity when disturbed by ignorance. Because of the profound misunderstanding concerning the way things truly are, we come to experience ourselves as separate from the world around us. Then we become subject to the emotional afflictions of greed, hatred, pride and so forth that serve to isolate us even further from truth.

What Is Enlightenment?

296.

What is enlightenment? It is to know your mind as it really is. That is the supreme, full and prefect enlightenment. Therein neither exists nor can be perceived the slightest bit of Dharma. Why is that? Because enlightenment has the same attribute as space. Therein there is neither that which becomes enlightened nor that to which one is enlightened.
Maha-vairochana Tantra

Now we come to the heart of the matter. Not only is your mind the focal point of cognition and experience but also, as we have seen, it is inherently or potentially enlightened. If you cut through the obscuring veil of misunderstanding and emotional afflictions, you will know your mind as it really is. But enlightenment is without duality or separateness, and it is free from any of the Dharma's forms or concepts by which we normally experience ourselves and the world. It is a totality without parts, for it is not a thing but rather a process which involves the entire universe.

Where Is Enlightenment?

297.

Enlightenment should be sought in one's mind. Why is that? Because the mind is utterly pure by nature. It is neither internal nor is it external. Nor is to be found between the two. The mind has not been seen, is not seen, nor will be seen by any of the Tathagata Arhat Samyak-sambuddhas. It is not blue, not yellow, not red, not white, not purple, not transparent, not short, not long, not round, not square, not bright, not dark, not male, not female and not neuter.
Maha-vairochana Tantra

Due to our basic misunderstanding of the true nature of things, we come to believe that we who perceive the world and the objects we perceive are completely distinct and separate. Yet the true nature of mind is neither the inner perceiving subject nor the external perceived objects. It is not even a combination of the two. In the course of separating ourselves from what we perceive, we break the essential unity of reality and project or superimpose upon it our own mentally constructed images of what we think reality is, just as a film is projected upon a blank white screen. These images and concepts are useful to a degree if we see them for what they are, but we seldom do and instead we mistake them for reality itself. This shows the depth of our misunderstanding – the fact that we cannot even perceive reality unless it is through the veil of such images and concepts.

Knowing the Mind

298.

Therefore if a son or daughter of good family wishes fully to know enlightenment, they should know their own minds. And how is the mind to be fully known? Even though you search, you will not find it in any precepts, colours, shapes, sense objects, form, feeling, ideation, motivation, or consciousness, nor in any I and mind, nor in any perceiving subject, nor in perceived objects, nor in the pure or the impure . . . nor in any other perceptual data.

Maha-vairochana Tantra

The method of realising enlightenment is by knowing the mind as it really is. To do this you must first search for it everywhere, but eventually you will understand that it cannot be found, because it cannot be made an object as its true nature lies outside the realm of dualistic perception. Yet although the importance of the mind has been repeatedly stressed, this is not a form of idealism which is actually alien to Buddhism. It should be clear that what is referred to here as the 'mind' unites both the external world and what we normally call the mind.

The Essential Openness of the Mind

299.

There arises the mind whose essential nature is openness, without substance, which is without attributes, without perceptual forms, which transcends all conceptual proliferations, which is limitless like space, which is the ground of all dharmas [phenomena], which is separate from the conditioned and the unconditioned realms, which is free from actions and activities, separate from eye, ear, nose, tongue and body, and is without any self-existent nature whatsoever.

Maha-vairochana Tantra

When we have searched for the mind, exhausted all possibilities and discarded all concepts and beliefs about it, then the mind as it truly is in reality arises of its own accord. This mind is identical to enlightenment or the Dharmakaya. Just as space is not anything in itself and so can accommodate all objects, likewise this mind acts as the ground of all. In fact, it is said in some texts that the mind, enlightenment and space are identical.

Suchness

300.

You can realise suchness here and now. Walk on and on until you reach perfect peace, go on and on until you attain the primordial source.
Kobo Daishi

Once again Kobo Daishi urges us with insistence – suchness, another term for the true nature of reality or enlightenment, is present here and now. All you have to do is to make the effort to see this. The responsibility is yours alone.

This Very World is the Pure Land

301.

I am sure that I would not offend Buddha or God by telling you a secret: if you could take peaceful and anxiety-free steps while walking on earth, there would be no need for you to go to the Pure Land or to the Kingdom of God. There is a simple reason for this: samsara [the cycle of birth and death] and the Pure Land [the highest realm] both come from the mind. When you are peaceful, joyful and free, samsara is transformed into the Pure Land, and you don't need to go anywhere. Then, even if I had supernatural power, I would not have to use it.
Thich Nhat Hanh, *Guide to Walking Meditation*

These words were, in fact, written by a great modern Vietnamese Zen master, but he also speaks of the same truth taught by the tantras. The possibility for either samsara or nirvana lies within your mind – it all depends on your point of view.

No Arising, No Perishing

302.

Bodhisattvas who engage in the bodhisattva practice by way of mantras will become fully awakened to the supreme and perfect enlightenment in this very lifetime. What is the reason for that? Because that which is called 'life' is only applied as an idea arising by the Buddha, and that idea also perishes for bodhisattvas prior to their attaining the holistic state [samadhi] wherein they directly experience the nature of dharmas [phenomena].

Maha-vairochana Tantra

Those who have directly experienced reality realise that in truth there is no arising and no perishing. One of the basic teachings of Buddhism is that all things (phenomena) are impermanent. But these do not really exist, since they are actually no more than mental constructs which we project upon reality, and what does not really exist cannot be said to be born or to die. Conversely, the Dharmakaya, enlightenment or reality, is unchanging and so is ever present.

The Pure Phenomena of Bliss

303.

The pure phenomenon of bliss is the bodhisattva state,
The pure phenomenon of the arrow of desire is the bodhisattva state,
The pure phenomenon of sexual contact is the bodhisattva state,
The pure phenomenon of binding love is the bodhisattva state,
The pure phenomenon of freedom in all things is the bodhisattva state,
The pure phenomenon of beholding is the bodhisattva state,
The pure phenomenon of joy is the bodhisattva state,
The pure phenomenon of love [for others] is the bodhisattva state,
The pure phenomenon of pride is the bodhisattva state,
The pure phenomenon of adornment is the bodhisattva state,
The pure phenomenon of satisfaction is the bodhisattva state,
The pure phenomenon of radiance is the bodhisattva state,
The pure phenomenon of physical ease is the bodhisattva state,
The pure phenomenon of colour-form is the bodhisattva state,
The pure phenomenon of sound is the bodhisattva state,
The pure phenomenon of fragrance is the bodhisattva state,
And the pure phenomenon of taste is the bodhisattva state.
Why is that?

Because all dharmas are open in nature and so are inherently pure.
Prajna-paramita Naya Sutra

All things are pure for one who directly experiences reality. Moreover, to
be enlightened, to know things as they truly are, is characterised by bliss.
According to the tantras, ordinary beings can experience something of
this in the bliss of orgasm. Indeed, there are tantric techniques which
utilise sexual yoga as a means to perceive reality, for at the moment of
orgasm one transcends the usual narrow confines of oneself and one's
projections. This passage deals with the various elements involved in
sexual love.

The Perfection of Insight

304.

If someone hears just once this method of the perfection of insight by
which one engages in the pure nature of all dharmas [phenomena], then
all obscurations will be extinguished until they reach the source of
enlightenment. Even though they have accumulated the obscurations
linked with emotional afflictions, dharmas and karmic actions, they
will never be born in such miserable states of existence as the hell realms.
Even after having done evil, they will be purified immediately without
difficulty. Whoever also upholds it, recites it daily and thinks correctly
of it, will become master of all dharmas in this very world by the
attainment of the indestructible holistic state [vajra-samadhi] of the
sameness of all dharmas. They will experience delight, gladness and
bliss in all dharmas.

Prajna-paramita Naya Sutra

This describes the great benefits of engaging in the tantric methods
implied by the previous passage. If correctly used, they bestow total
freedom and liberation because they are a means of transcending the
ordinary self.

The Five Faults

305.

Bodhisattvas who desire to enter this union [samaya] with the mandala
and the mudras of the secret matrix should separate themselves by a long

*distance from five factors. What are those five? Avarice, harming
beings, doubt, laziness, and disbelief in the mantras and so forth.*
Maha-vairochana Tantra

It would be wrong to suppose that a person who practises the tantric
methods to attain total freedom is free from all self-discipline and
responsibility. In addition to cultivating the compassion required from all
Buddhists, the five faults mentioned here are to be completely overcome
because they impede one's practice and reinforce the mistaken belief in
separateness, bringing harm both to oneself and to others.

Ritual

306.

*Moreover in future ages there will appear beings who have weak minds,
who are confused by mere actions, and who are attached to material
things. Since they do not understand this method, these confused beings
expect results with good or bad qualities from physical objects, time and
activities. It is for their sakes I expound this ritual.*
Maha-vairochana Tantra

The passages we have already looked at teach the most direct path to the
understanding and experience of truth. Unfortunately not everybody has
a sufficient degree of ability to benefit from these teachings, and so
alternative approaches must be provided for those who need them. The
tantras are especially noteworthy for the wide range of methods and
practices they offer to accommodate people of all levels of ability and
interest. While some people find internal meditative practices most
suitable, others need external props in the form of rituals. When properly
understood, a tantric ritual acts as a model for us to grasp the significance
of the teachings. Hence the paintings of mandalas or statues of the
Buddhas used in these rituals are attempts to represent the intrinsically
existent mandalas and Buddhas, as models for those who cannot see the
real thing.

The Master

307.

The master should have his mind fixed upon enlightenment, be endowed with insight, be firm, be compassionate, be skilled in the arts, be ever wise in the methods of the perfection of insight, know the differences between the three ways, be skilled in the true nature of mantras, know the inclinations of beings, have trust in the Buddhas and bodhisattvas, have the initiation and permission to perform the task of drawing the mandala, be strenuous and decisive in the practice of the mantras, be well born, be skilled in practice, have attained the union of opposites and be established in mind directed towards enlightenment.

Maha-vairochana Tantra

Regardless of the tantric approach one follows, the importance of a spiritual teacher to act as your guide is always emphasised. Tantric teachings are often said to be secret, but this is not in the sense that they are only for a small elite. It is because they are so powerful and so easily misunderstood that care is needed in their use. It is said that the tantric devotee uses the poison which kills ordinary people to gain liberation. It is for this reason that you need a teacher. But when looking for a teacher, it is vital that he or she is genuine and trustworthy, for there are many charlatans who are more interested in gaining control of you than leading you to liberation. Therefore, most tantric texts include a section like this passage, describing the qualities one should look for in a teacher.

Jodo Shu and Jodo Shinshu

Commentary for Jodo Shu by Honen
Commentary for Jodo Shinshu by Takashi Tsuji and Philip Karl Eidmann

In Pure Land Buddhist teachings, Amida Buddha is the embodiment of great wisdom and compassion. He has attained Buddhahood by fulfilling the vow to bring all sentient beings who say his name to birth in the sphere of enlightenment, his Pure Land.

In the Jodo tradition birth in the Pure Land focuses on the absolute value of calling upon Amida Buddha's name – Namu Amida Buddha – without a doubt of his mercy. This invocation is called Nembutsu. The simple formula of exclusive recitation of the sacred name was first practised in Japan by Honen (1133–1212 CE) who abandoned all other Buddhist meditative practices in favour of absolute faith in the saving power of Amida Buddha and the essential accompaniment of the recitation of Nembutsu.

Honen's faith was inspired by the writings by Zendo (613–681 CE), the Chinese teacher of Pure Land doctrine. It was while reading Zendo's *Commentary on the Sutra of Meditation on Amida Buddha* that Honen resolved to embark upon a life of simple faith. Honen believed that the Nembutsu's special virtue lay in the fact that the Buddha himself had chosen it as the only way to salvation and its efficacy was explicitly asserted in Amida's Original Vow (the Eighteenth Vow, *The Larger Sutra on Amida Buddha*) and in *The Sutra of Meditation on Amida Buddha (The Sutra of Contemplation on the Buddha of Immeasurable Life)*. The aim of Jodo is birth into the Pure Land, which is attained by absolute faith in the 'Other Power' of Amida Buddha. Honen said that our self-generated efforts are ineffectual for enlightenment since it is the power and compassion of Amida Buddha working within us that lead us at death to the ultimate and absolute reality of the Pure Land.

In contrast to the Jodo view of Amida's coming and final salvation, Honen's pupil, Shinran (1173–1262 CE), expressed the idea of having fulfilled the cause of our birth in ordinary life. While stressing the importance of saying the Nembutsu, Shinran advocated the centrality of shinjin in the act of Nembutsu. Shinjin, which is often translated as 'faith', points to the true and real human mind given by Amida and equal to Amida's mind. He said that this mind is attained when we entrust ourselves to the Other Power or the power of Amida's Original Vow so that the defiled mind becomes equal to the pure mind of Amida. When shinjin is realised the Nembutsu flows spontaneously and the Original Vow, which has been accomplished prior to any and all life, is a reality which is encountered in the present moment. In the Shin tradition, from the time that we attain shinjin, the Nembutsu repetitions are prompted by joyous gratitude towards Amida Buddha for his saving mercy and are not directed towards salvation in the Pure Land.

The readings in the Jodo Shinshu section are drawn from the *Shinshu Shogyo Zensho*, Volume II, a collection of Shinran's teachings, and from the *Tannisho*, compiled within a generation of the death of Shinran. The first half of the *Tannisho* is a collection of sayings from Shinran and the second half is a critique by the *Tannisho*'s compiler of misinterpretations of Shinran's teachings. His testimony not only clarifies Shinran's intent but also reflects his determination to preserve the teachings that changed his life.

With acknowledgement to Kenjo S. Urakami and Professor Denis Hirota.

Jodo Shu

308.

If those beings who in immeasurable and innumerable Buddha-lands, after they have heard my name, when I shall have obtained bodhi, should direct their thought to be born in that Buddha-land of mine, and should for that purpose bring their stock of merit to maturity, if these should not be born in that Buddha-land, even those who have ten times repeated the thought [of that Buddha-land through the Nembutsu] . . . then may I not obtain the highest perfect knowledge.

The Eighteenth Vow (the Original Vow),
The Larger Sutra on Amida Buddha

Amida Buddha, as a Buddha-to-be called Hozo-Bosatsu, determined to build a perfect Buddha-land for the people and took the forty-eight vows for that purpose in the presence of the Buddha Sejizaio-Nyorai. One of the forty-eight vows is the Original Vow, which is designed to guide and receive all human beings into his Pure Land.

Amida Buddha fulfilled his forty-eight vows and is now in his Pure Land. Therefore, without doubt, you will be received into the Pure Land by reciting Amida Buddha's name (the recitation is referred to as Nembutsu).

The practice of Nembutsu produces merits which equal the merits of all other practices, though each has its own merit.

Nembutsu can be likened to a building and other practices to parts of the building such as the ridge, beam, pillar and so on. The practice of Nembutsu is therefore a manifestation of all the practices. Therefore Amida Buddha selected the original practice of Nembutsu from among many practices and designed it for the Original Vow.

Nembutsu can be practised at any time and anywhere by anyone. Therefore Amida Buddha selected the easy practice of Nembutsu for his Original Vow since his vows are to receive all human beings into his Pure Land unconditionally.

If the building of Buddha's statues or pagodas were the conditions for acceptance into his Pure Land, there would be no possibility for the poor people, and indeed there are more of the poor than the rich.

If wisdom or ability were the conditions, there would be no possibility for the unintelligent or talentless, and actually wise or capable men are few.

If knowledge and scholarship were asked for, there would be no opportunity for the uneducated, and as a matter of fact learned men are few in number.

If abidance by the Buddhist precepts were the conditions, there would be no chance for those unable to abide by them. Practically, all people are offenders while very few observe precepts.

All other practices are difficult and are not practicable for ordinary people. The purpose of Amida Buddha's Original Vow is to guide all human beings, and nine out of ten are ordinary people.

There is no hope for ordinary people to be received into the Pure Land if the Original Vow requires unattainable practices.

This is the reason why Amida Buddha compassionately designed the original yet easy practice of Nembutsu as the condition of the Original Vow for all to be received into his Pure Land.

309.

The Buddha said to Ananda and Vaidehi, 'The sentient beings in the lowest rank of the lowest grade of birth are those who commit such evil acts as the five grave offences and the ten transgressions and are burdened with various kinds of evil. These foolish beings, because of their evil acts, shall fall into the evil realms of existence, and for the passage of many kalpas receive endless sufferings.

'When the life of such a foolish person is about to end, he meets a virtuous and learned teacher who comforts him in various ways, expounds for him the exquisite teachings, and urges him to be mindful of the Buddha. But this person is too tormented by pain to be mindful of the Buddha. Then the virtuous friend says, "If you cannot be mindful of the Buddha, you should say that you take refuge in the Buddha of Immeasurable Life". And so, with a sincere mind and an uninterrupted voice, this person says "Namu Amida Butsu" manifesting ten moments of thought; and, because he says the Buddha's name with every thought-

moment, *the evil karma binding him to birth and death for eighty kotis of kalpas is eliminated.*

'*When his life comes to an end, this person sees a sun-like golden lotus appearing in front of him. And in the interval of a single thought-moment, he immediately attains birth in a lotus flower in the World of Utmost Bliss.*'

The Sutra of Contemplation on the Buddha of Immeasurable Life,
Meditations 33–5

Do not have any doubt about being received into the Pure Land, though it is impossible for us to eradicate the illusion of worldly desire within ourselves. It is stated that we are full of worldly passions derived from our ceaseless greed, anger and ignorance.

We aspire to go to Amida Buddha's Pure Land although there are many Buddha-lands in this universe. It is because even someone who repeats acts of wickedness, called the ten vices and the five rebellious acts, such as killing, can be received into his Pure Land.

We admire Amida Buddha among many Buddhas in the universe as he will appear and guide a person who recites Nembutsu even three to five times.

We select the practice of Nembutsu from many religious practices as Amida Buddha designed the Original Vow to receive all human beings who practice Nembutsu.

We are convinced that we will be received into the Pure Land according to the Original Vow. To be received into the Pure Land, we should have firm belief in the Original Vow (see no. 308).

It is the utmost joy for us to be born a human being, to learn of the Original Vow, to be inspired to practise Nembutsu, to be freed from the agonies of the repetition of life and death, so we can be received into the Pure Land which is so difficult to attain.

310.

Spring

In the dawning spring sky,
*   the mist of worldly passions covers good nature*
Though the unrestricted light of Amida Buddha
*   dissipates the mist in a short time.*

Summer

There is not a single day in my mind
*   that I do not long to commune with Amida Buddha*
Even the geraniums remind me of a meeting with him
*   as its name 'aoi' is associated with 'au' – to meet.*

Autumn

When Amida Buddha tinges one's heart with his compassion
  his face is brightened with joy and hope
Just as leaves are beautifully tinted with red
  when the autumn comes.

Winter

If O-Nembutsu is recited
  amidst the falling snow of worldly desire,
Deeply laid wickedness melts away before long
  by the warm light of Amida Buddha.

                                    Poems of Honen

Jodo Shinshu

311.

If those beings in immeasurable and innumerable Buddha-lands, after
they have heard my name, when I shall have obtained bodhi, should
direct their thought to be born in that Buddha-land of mine, and should
for that purpose bring their stock of merit to maturity, if these should not
be born in that Buddha-land, even those who have only ten times
repeated the thought [of that Buddha-land through the Nembutsu]...
then may I not obtain the highest perfect knowledge.
                          The Eighteenth Vow (the Original Vow),
                              The Larger Sutra on Amida Buddha

Faith has three aspects: sincerity, faith and the wish to be born in Amida
Buddha's land. It is not blind faith in something one does not understand,
but a religious experience that involves our whole person. When we fully
realise the significance of Namu Amida Butsu (the invocation of Amida
Buddha's name referred to as Nembutsu), faith is awakened, and when
faith is awakened, we realise that so profound a spiritual experience can
only happen through the grace of Amida Buddha. Faith, therefore, is a
gift from Amida Buddha.

312.

When we believe that we are to be born in the Pure Land, being saved by
Amida's Inconceivable Vow, there rises up within us the desire to utter

the Nembutsu. At that moment we share in the benefit of being embraced and not forsaken.

Tannisho, ch. 1, page 15

Amida, who accumulated goodness and virtue, for the benefit of all beings transfers them to human beings through the medium of the name, Namu Amida Butsu. He gives them to us, human beings of the ten quarters of the universe, when we hear this name and realise the significance of Namu Amida Butsu. It is the working of Amida's great compassion throughout timeless time, not starting yesterday or the day before, but something that has been going on through eternity. Sentient beings come to that realisation, and when that awakening occurs the name becomes faith. We are no longer isolated beings living alone in a vast universe but are one with Amida Buddha and will never be the same again.

313.

What is called external power is as much to say that there is no difference between this or that.

Shinshu Shogyo Zensho, Vol. II, page 671

The external power is the power of the main vow of the Tathagata.

Shinshu Shogyo Zensho, Vol. II, page 35

The external power by which the ordinary person attains enlightenment is the activity of the Buddha. This activity is not clearly understood by us but it has existed since time immemorial. Any attempt to consider its aspects cannot possibly succeed. Yet we must understand that it is not some metaphysical force which we cannot see or describe. The external power is itself the force of non-discrimination.

When a Buddha attains enlightenment, at that instant he sends forth his boundless compassion and wisdom. That compassion and wisdom, as well as his preaching and living in the world, all affect those human beings who come after him in time. We are, after all, endlessly related to all and everything in the universe. The example of the Buddha and his compassion is always ready to influence us. When our unconscious good deeds manifest their fruit as a receptive state of mind, the compassion of Buddha makes itself felt.

314.

The reason is that, as those who practise good by their self-power lack the mind to rely wholly on the Other Power, they are not in accordance

with the Original Vow of Amida. However, if they convert their minds
of self-power and trust the Other Power, their birth in the True Land of
Recompense is assured.

   Amida made his vow out of compassion for us who are full of evil
passions, and who are unable to set ourselves free from samsara by any
practice.

Tannisho, Ch. 111, pages 22–3

If we are willing to follow the law of self-power, it is certainly easier for a
good man to succeed. Jodo Shinshu, however, is a religion beyond good
and evil. Amida Buddha is not concerned with those who can actually
achieve enlightenment through their own power, since they possess the
capabilities, but those individuals who haven't any capability of achieving
enlightenment. They are the object of Amida's compassion.

315.

The Nembutsu is the unimpeded single path. The reason is that the gods
of heaven and earth bow in reverence to the followers of faith, and maras
[those belonging to the devil's realm] and non-Buddhists cannot harm
them. Nor can various good deeds surpass the Nembutsu.

Tannisho, ch. 7, page 30

If we have firm conviction and deep faith in the path of enlightenment,
nothing will trouble us. Sin and its karmic effects cannot harm us. It
doesn't mean that we will become pure; it doesn't mean that we will
become completely free from sin and all its karmic effects, but it does
mean that despite our limitations, finiteness, and despite all our greed,
anger and folly, we will be able to overcome anger and frustration. If there
was ever a man who led a tumultuous life, who lived a life of loneliness and
separation, and who met obstacles at every turn of the road, it was
Shinran. But despite that, Shinran was able to find peace by reciting the
Nembutsu.

316.

Some people say that a person who is not afraid of evil because Amida's
Original Vow is inconceivable is putting too much reliance on the
Original Vow and their ignorance about the past karma of good and
evil.

   A good mind arises due to the influence of the past good acts, and evil
things are thought and done due to the words of past evils. 'We should
know that the committing of a trifling sin,' said the late master, 'as
minute as a particle of dust on the tip of a rabbit's or a sheep's hair, is
without exception due to our past evil karma.'

Tannisho, ch. 13, pages 48–9

In timeless time Amida Buddha understood human nature. If all beings were good and pure, there would be no use for Amida Buddha. Amida's existence becomes significant because of the evil of human beings. Shin is a religion which brings salvation and enlightenment to all sentient beings whose intelligence is limited and who are full of greed, anger and hatred.

Good and evil deeds are a result of karmic conditions and arise spontaneously. If we sow seeds of evil all our life, we cannot suddenly change our evil ways and we become so accustomed to evil that the desire to do good may not even arise. This is why the moral life has to be cultivated like a gardener cultivates the seeds and plants with painstaking care in order to produce perfect flowers.

317.

At the moment when one thought of faith arises in us, due to Amida's light shining upon us, we are endowed with the diamond faith and received into the Rightly Established State, and when life ends, all passions and all evil hindrances are turned [into bodhi] and we are enlightened into the truth of birthlessness. Without the Compassionate Vow, how can we, paltry sinners, ever be freed from birth and death? Thus thinking, we should bear in mind that the Nembutsu we utter throughout life is entirely for acknowledging our indebtedness to the Tathagata's great compassion and expressing our gratitude to his benevolence. To believe that each utterance of the Nembutsu can extinguish our sins amounts to endeavouring to erase the sins for ourselves and, thereby, attain birth [in the Pure Land].

Tannisho, ch. 14, pages 58–9

The Nembutsu is not a means to an end. In other Pure Land schools the Nembutsu is used for acquiring merit; for example, two recitations are more meritorious than one and twenty better than ten. But in Shin the quantity of the recitations is not important; what really matters is the sincere recitation of the Nembutsu with a singleness of faith in Amida Buddha. Therefore Shinran did not recite the Nembutsu for the purpose of filial piety, for extinguishing sins or for any other purpose. He recited the Nembutsu in order to be brought into direct communion with Amida Buddha and be one with the Other Power.

318.

The awakening of faith ... is faith serene, deep and broad ... It is a true awakening of faith, diamond hard and unshakable. It is pure faith ... it is single-pointedness of mind.

Shinshu Shogyo Zensho, Vol. II, page 48

Shinran believed the awakening of faith to be the most vital and important religious experience for the ordinary human for by this awakening the believer becomes equal to the highest rank of bodhisattva.

The awakening of faith in Shin is an instant of perfect egolessness, and is a religious experience which changes our whole destiny. The effects of this awakening are of two kinds. One kind of effect is immediate. The other kind of effect manifests itself at death and directs our rebirth into nirvana (see no. 319).

319.

Nirvana is called extinction, non-action, peaceful happiness, eternal happiness...

Shinshu Shogyo Zensho, Vol. II, page 630

Nirvana is boundless, infinite, endless, eternal, unoriginated. To know it requires a realisation more real than the five senses and the mind can produce. It is this realisation that the goal of Buddhist meditation is said to be. Outside of realising this state no word can define nirvana. To name it Shinran adopted the traditional term, the Pure Land. For Shinran this Pure Land was itself the state of nirvana, not the Pure Land which traditionally precedes nirvana in other Buddhist schools. Shinran called the idea of the other heavenly pure realm 'an apparitional realm'. The true Pure Land, the realm of nirvana, is beyond description. To know it directly, this is the whole goal and purpose of Shin, as it is of all Buddhism.

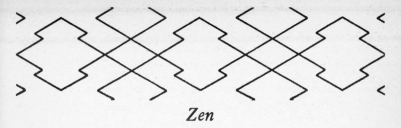

Zen

Compiled with commentary by a Zen scholar and author

The Buddha began his teaching in India with a logical analysis of experience, together with experiments in living and in meditation. India had always had a strong intellectual tradition, including the development of logic, and marvellous Sanskrit grammar (compiled by Panini long before the Buddha lived), a feat of analysis unsurpassed even today. Not surprisingly, within a few centuries of the Buddha's death, his followers had developed extremely powerful dialectical systems. Perhaps Buddhism would not have been widely accepted in India without such justification in terms of logical analysis.

But it meant that words began to be coined, or adapted, to express what the Buddha had refused to try to express. All religions have this problem on their mystical side: how can people be attracted to practise unless words are used? But if words are used, self-contradictions arise.

While Indian thinkers thought it better to attempt some sort of answer on logical lines, when Buddhism spread to China, this logical approach was overshadowed. The Chinese, a practical people, do not trust logic absolutely; they know that logic needs hard precise edges for its application, whereas in the world edges are fuzzy. Precision is attained only by ignoring irregularities in the hope that they will not be significant.

Because the Chinese did not trust logic, they did not study it much, and so often could not understand the highly developed arguments of Indian Buddhism. But they revered the sutras and translated them into beautiful prose. Many more were composed in China on the basis of their own experience, again often in beautiful language. One result was a tendency in Chinese Buddhism to quote sutras without fully understanding them. The Indians had quoted too, but had understood what the words said (though not necessarily what was beyond the words). The Chinese were often quoting for beauty of language, feeling that was enough without going further into it.

Zen was a purifying reaction against veneration of mere words. As will be seen (see no. 320), in its Indian form it was mainly a question of purification from outer attachments and inner 'gaspings' of desire. Then the essence of the heart is realised. It is not a question of Buddha-making – the Buddha is already there in fullness – it is only Buddha-realisation.

As time went on, Zen assisted the inner purification by the method of setting riddle-like questions which could not be answered by quotation. 'What was your original face before you were born?' The method became a system in one of the branches of Zen, called Rinzai by the Japanese. The other main extant branch, Soto, uses them but not as an essential element. If the riddles (koan) become like a fixed syllabus, with sometimes a Chinese historical background which has to be learnt, the point may become lost. Some masters in Japan therefore gave riddles to lay pupils arising from an immediate situation, for example:

A famous painter, Kano Tanyu, was commissioned to paint a great dragon on the huge ceiling of Myoshinji temple. He was asked to do it 'from life'. He protested that though he had painted many dragons he had never actually seen one. The Abbot of Myoshinji insisted, however, and Tanyu spent the next two years practising Zen assiduously in the expectation of seeing a dragon. One day something happened, and he rushed excitedly to the teacher saying: 'By your grace I have today seen the form of a live dragon!' 'Oh, have you? Good. But tell me, what did his roar sound like?' At this query the painter was again at a loss, and for one further year he laboured on at his spiritual practices. What he painted at the end of the year was the dragon of Myoshinji, a supreme masterpiece in the history of art, remarkable for the technique but far more for the life which the artist has infused into it. It seems as if it contains the great life which embraces heaven and earth, the universe and man also. It was to pierce through to this reality that the master painter Tanyu poured out his heart's blood for three years. But when the one experience of reality was attained, there was no need to seek any further.

                          Zen Master Amukuku Sessan (see also no. 326)

Note: Zen is the Japanese pronunciation of the Sanskrit word *dhyana* and the Chinese word *chan*; following this precedent, names are usually given as the Japanese pronounce them.

The Heart Essence beyond Thinking

320.

Bodhidharma [sixth century CE] stayed in the Shorinji monastery, where he meditated facing a wall for nine years. He refused to see inquirers; finally one man proved his sincerity by standing waiting in the snow. Then the teacher said only: 'Outwardly cease from associations; inwardly have no hankerings in the heart. When your mind is like an upright wall, you can enter the way.'

The disciple tried in various ways to say what was the heart-nature, but could not grasp the way. The teacher said only: 'No, no!' He did not explain the heart-nature beyond thinking. One day the disciple told him: 'I know how to cease from associations.' 'By annihilating them, is it not so?' asked the teacher. 'Not by annihilating', said the disciple. 'What is this experience of not annihilating?' demanded the teacher. 'I know it completely and for ever, but words cannot reach to it,' replied the pupil. 'That is the very heart-essence transmitted by all the Buddhas,' said the teacher, 'have no doubt about it.'

'The Transmission of the Light'

This short passage, dated around 1000 CE, contains the main points of the Zen training. There is a heart-essence beyond thinking which is sought by ceasing from outer attachments and from inner longings. By meditation and living on these lines, the mind becomes motionless like an upright wall; the way opens up. The disciple increases his concentration by wrestling with mental formulations. These are rejected, but the effort brings him to a state beyond thoughts which is not, however, an annihilation like sleep.

Thinking cannot be transcended until it has been brought to stillness, 'like an upright wall'. The mind seems to face a blank wall. This direct method requires tremendous fortitude. In another account, the great teacher tells this disciple: 'It can be done only by enduring the unendurable and practising what is most difficult.'

Bodhidharma met opposition from highly placed scholars of Buddhism. One tradition says that they tried to poison him six times, and six times he became aware of it and stopped eating. Tradition also says that he lived to 150 years. His would-be murderers all died – of old age. This is a great teaching: the truth outlives its attackers.

Neither For Nor Against

321.

The perfect way is not difficult:
It is just not picking and choosing

Only when freed from hate and love,
It reveals itself fully and without disguise.
A tenth of an inch's difference,
And heaven and earth are set apart:
If you want to see it manifest,
Take no thought either for or against it.

To set up what you like against what you dislike –
This is the disease of the mind:
When the deep meaning [of the Way] is not understood
Peace of mind is disturbed and nothing is gained.
[The Way is] perfect like unto vast space,

With nothing wanting, nothing superfluous:
It is indeed due to making choice
That its suchness is lost sight of.
Pursue not the outer entanglements,
Dwell not in the inner void;
When the mind rests serene in the oneness of things,
The dualism vanishes by itself.

Inscribed on the Heart of Faith

What! Aren't we to choose between stale bread and a fresh loaf? If I'm to learn French, don't I have to choose a French teacher?

That is not the meaning of 'not picking and choosing'. Certainly I take the fresh bread when both are there. But when there is only stale bread, I am to eat it thankfully, knowing that there are many who have no bread to eat or anything else.

As for learning French, how many likes and dislikes can get in the way: 'No, I never did well at that. The teacher didn't like me because I'm from the South. I used to cut his classes.'

'But he was a good teacher?'

'Yes, they said he was very good. But I just couldn't stand him.'

That is picking and choosing. 'Not picking and choosing' does not prohibit taking appropriate action to meet circumstances. But when the time comes to look a fool, to be despised for sticking to an important point, then accept it without inner grinding of teeth.

There is a Zen poem:

Every day we sweep up the leaves that fall in the garden;
But we don't hate the trees for dropping them.

Vastness, No Holiness! (Rinzai)

322.

THE INTRODUCTION

To see smoke beyond the mountain is to know there is fire; to see a horn over the wall is to know there is an ox. From one corner displayed to know clearly the other three is only skill in inference, and to a monk an everyday affair. But when he can cut off all the streams of thought, he is free to spring up in the east or sink down in the west, to go against or with, along or across, to give or take. At that time say, of whom is this the action? Let us look at Setcho's riddle.

THE CASE

The Ryo Emperor Bu asked the teacher Bodhidharma:
  'What is the first principle of the holy truth?'
  Bodhidharma said: 'Vastness, no holiness!'
  Quoth the emperor: 'Who is it that confronts us?'
  Bodhidharma said: 'Know not.'
  The emperor did not understand, and Bodhidharma crossed the river and went to Gi. Later the emperor asked Abbot Shiko, who said:
  'Does Your Majesty yet know who is this man, or not?'
  The emperor said '[I] know not.'
  Shiko said: 'It is the bodhisattva Kannon, who is transmitting the seal of the Buddha heart.'
  The emperor in regret would have sent an envoy to ask him to return, but Shiko said: 'Though an emperor send an envoy for him, nay, though the whole people go after him, never never will he turn back.'

THE HYMN

The holy truth is vastness –
How to speak and hit the mark?
'Who is it that confronts us?'
And he replied: 'Know not.'
So in the night he crossed the river.
How could he prevent the thorn-bushes growing after him?
Though all the people pursue, he will not come again;
For a thousand, ten thousand ages we are thinking after him.
Cease from thinking. The pure breeze,
Circling the earth, has no bounds.

Setcho looks to the left and right, and says: 'Is the Patriarch here?'
  He replies: 'He is.'
  'Then call him, that he may wash my feet.'
            Bodhidharma's 'Vastness!', *Hekiganroku*

Hekiganroku and *Shoyoroku* (see no. 323) are two Chinese koan (riddle) anthologies read and translated by Japanese Zen masters on the basis of their own oral Zen teachings and experience.
  Hekiganroku, favoured by the Rinzai sect, is a set of 100 cases compiled by Setcho (979–1052 CE) of the Ummon Zen sect. Setcho added his own poems and comments to these cases and these were later expanded by the Rinzai master Engo (1063–1135 CE).
  The case of Bodhidharma and the emperor occurs in both *Hekiganroku* and *Shoyoroku* but is flavoured by the particular emphasis of Rinzai and Soto Zen respectively. In this reading we see the central role of the koan discipline in Rinzai.
  Emperor Bu was renowned for his spiritual devotion and generous financing of monasteries. When Bodhidharma visited the capital in 527

CE, the emperor asked what merit he had gained from his pious actions. To his astonishment, he was told: 'None.' This prompted the question in this case study: 'What is the first principle of the holy truth?', and the famous reply, 'Vastness, no holiness!'

Vastness, No Holiness! (Soto)

323.

THE INTRODUCTION

In olden days Benka offered an unpolished jewel to kings, but they thought it a pebble and punished him cruelly. At night a rare gem is thrown to a man, but in alarm he clutches for his sword. An unexpected guest, but none to play the host; the borrowed virtue is not the real virtue. A priceless treasure, but he knows not what to do with it; the head of a dead cat – try him with that!

THE CASE

The Ryo emperor asked the great teacher:
 'What is the first principle of the holy truth?'
 Bodhidharma said: 'Vastness, no holiness!'
 Quoth the emperor: 'Who is it that confronts us?'
 Bodhidharma said: 'Know not.'
When the emperor did not understand, the teacher crossed the river and went to Shorinji temple: nine years facing the wall.

THE HYMN

Vastness, no holiness!
The moment came, but there was a gap between.
Like a master axeman, he would have cut the mud from the face but
 never harmed the flesh – Oh, profit!
Instead – Oh loss! The pot smashed to the ground, but he never turned
 his head.
Alone, alone, he sits at Shorinji in the cold;
Silent, silent, he upholds the great tradition.
In the clear autumn sky the moon's frosty disc is wheeling;
The Milky Way pales, the stars of the Dipper hang low.
When the heir comes, he in turn will receive robe and bowl;
From this arises medicine but also illness for men and gods.
 'Vastness, No Holiness', *Shoyoroku*

'Vastness' has its original meaning of 'emptiness'. The hymns can alert the mind, stimulate it, and concentrate it. But ultimately there has to be a jump beyond the mind – into Bodhidharma's vastness.

When the emperor did not understand, Bodhidharma went to the Shorinji temple at Gi where he meditated sitting in front of a wall for nine years.

This version of Bodhidharma and the Emperor is from *Shoyoroku*, the anthology of Chinese koans preferred by the Japanese Soto Zen tradition. Like *Hekiganroku* (see no. 322), it contains 100 cases, in this instance compiled by Wanshi (1090–1157 CE) of the Soto sect and then expanded by another Soto master, Bansho (1165–1246 CE).

Meditation Practice

324.

> *Zen practice means meditation practice . . . Keep body and mind at rest – cut off all mental activity. Do not think about time or circumstances, nor cling to good or bad thoughts. Zazen is not self-consciousness or self-contemplation. Do not try to make a Buddha . . .*
>
> *Use a small round cushion. Do not sit on the middle of the cushion but place the front part under your hips. Cross your legs, in either full lotus or half lotus, and put them on the mat . . .*
>
> *Keep your back straight, ears above shoulders, and nose above navel. Sit like a mountain. Think the unthinkable. How to think the unthinkable? Think nothing . . . This meditation sitting is not a means to enlightenment; it is Buddha in fullness. Meditation is pure, natural enlightenment.*
>
> Dogen, *Shobogenzo*

'Don't try to make a Buddha.' A Buddha can never be made, even by perfect meditation, out of what is not a Buddha already, any more than a mirror can be made, even by perfect polishing, out of a brick. But a Buddha, already there but not recognised, can be realised most easily in meditation. In fact, meditation is simply realisation.

Dogen, the thirteenth-century founder of Soto Zen (see p. 278), says this realisation of Zazen meditation must pervade the whole of life. When one picks up a toothbrush, one thinks: 'The toothbrush is taken in our hand, for the benefit of all beings. May the Dharma [Buddha teachings] be given to their mind so that they are naturally purified. With this action, may the delusion-teeth of all be purified.'

This understanding is encapsulated in Dogen's advice: 'To learn the Way is to learn self. To learn self is to forget self. To forget self is to perceive self as all things. To realise this is to cast off body and mind of self-and-others.'

The Song of Meditation

325.

All beings are from the very beginning Buddhas.
It is like water and ice:
Apart from water, no ice.
Outside living beings, no Buddhas.
Not knowing it is near, they seek it afar. What a pity!
It is like someone in the water who cries out for thirst;
It is like the child of a rich house who has strayed among the poor.
The cause of our circling through the six worlds
Is that we are on the dark paths of ignorance.
Dark path upon dark path treading,
When shall we escape from birth-and-death?
The Zen meditation of the Mahayana
Is beyond all our praise.
Giving and morality and the other perfections,
Taking of the name, repentance, discipline,
And the many other right actions,
All come back to the practice of meditation.
By the merit of a single sitting
He destroys innumerable accumulated sins.
How should there be wrong paths for him?
The Pure Land paradise is not far.
When in reverence this truth is heard even once,
He who praises it and gladly embraces it has merit without end.
How much more he who turns within
And confirms directly his own nature,
That his own nature is no-nature –
Such has transcended vain words.
The gate opens, and cause and effect are one;
Straight runs the way – not two, not three.
Taking as form the form of no-form,
Going or returning, he is ever at home.
Taking as thought the thought of no-thought,
Singing and dancing, all is the voice of truth.
Wide is the heaven of boundless samadhi,
Radiant the full moon of the fourfold wisdom.
What remains to be sought? Nirvana is clear before him,
This very place the lotus paradise, this very body the Buddha.

Hakuin, 'Song of Meditation'

With Hakuin, the eighteenth-century reformer of Rinzai Zen in Japan, Zen came particularly close to lay people. He wrote many works in the vernacular instead of classical Chinese, and among them this 'Song of

Meditation' is one of the best known.

When members of the audience of a modern Zen priest complained that it was impossible to practise Zen in the polluted air of Tokyo, he shouted cheerfully at them: '"This very place the lotus paradise, this very body the Buddha." You are in Tokyo, so Tokyo is your lotus paradise: now be Buddha.'

The Very First Jizo

326.

Sakawa Koresada, a direct retainer of the Uesugi family, entered the main hall at Kenchoji and prayed to the Jizo-of-a-Thousand-Forms there. Then he asked the attendant monk in charge of the hall: 'Of these thousand forms of Jizo, which is the very first Jizo?'

The attendant said, 'In the breast of the retainer before me are a thousand thoughts and ten thousand imaginings; which of these is the very first one?'

The samurai was silent.

The attendant said again, 'Of the thousand forms of Jizo, the very first Jizo is the Buddha-lord who is always using those thousand forms.'

The warrior said, 'Who is this Buddha-lord?'

The attendant suddenly caught him and twisted his nose.

The samurai immediately had a realisation.

TESTS

(1) *Which is the very first Jizo out of the thousand-formed Jizo?*
(2) *Which is the very first out of the thousand thoughts and ten thousand imaginings?*
(3) *What did Koresada realise when his nose was twisted?*

Shonan Kottoroku, Warrior Koan

Rinzai Zen

Compiled with commentary by Myokyo-ni

As a Buddhist school, the Zen school is firmly based on the Buddhist principles common to all schools. It also shows itself to be an offspring of the developed Mahayana teachings. So what then distinguishes the Zen school? Mahayana developed perhaps the deepest philosophical and psychological systems ever known. However, this brings with it the inherent danger of getting stuck at the intellectual or words level. Perhaps the Zen school is a reaction against just that – an unspoken return to basic principles. Being aware of the glibness of words, it insists on personal experience and insight, and stresses the actual expression of this insight. But expression may also lend itself to empty imitation, so the Zen school traditionally insists on trained and proved teachers who can help their students to walk the way they have gone themselves and who can confirm their clear seeing, their insight-understanding. In that sense, the Zen masters are guides rather than teachers.

The Zen school claims its origin from the Buddha himself. Once when he was to preach to a large assembly, he simply and silently raised up a flower. None in the audience understood except Kasyapa, one of his oldest disciples, who smiled. This is said to have started the 'transmission from heart to heart', the transmission of the heart seal.

The Indian monk Bodhidharma is credited with bringing this school to China. After long perseverance, his future successor Eka finally gained an interview with him. Zen masters have never been propagators. Eka's plea was that since his heart was not at peace, could the great Indian monk set it at rest. When Bodhidharma replied: 'Show your heart and I shall set it at rest for you', Eka had to concede that he could not find or produce it. 'There then, I have set your heart at rest for you', commented Bodhidharma. At that, Eka awakened.

As a special transmission which does not stand on the scriptures, the Zen school has no particular canon of sutras nor indeed any specific sutra on which to build its corpus of teachings. It might equally be said that it has no such teachings. However, far from being averse to the scriptures, Zen masters have always been extremely well versed in them, quoting from them freely as befitted audience and occasion.

This is illustrated in these selections in which the diverse teachings are again and again referred to and often explained in a direct and immediate way that is specific to the Zen school. However, without a deep knowledge of the Buddhist teachings and the points that are being elucidated, there is a danger of misunderstanding Zen sayings as meaningless paradoxes. If these quotations prompt the interested reader to a deeper study of the Buddhist scriptures and the Buddha's Way, and to the practice thereof, then they have indeed fulfilled their purpose. As a selection they are humbly offered in gratitude for years of training undergone in Japan under two masters, both now dead, to whom any merit of this contribution is due – the faults being mine.

The Transmission of the Heart Seal

327.

A special transmission outside the teachings;
Not standing on written words or letters.
Directly pointing to the human heart,
Seeing into its nature and becoming Buddha.

Bodhidharma

With these words Bodhidharma summed up the Zen school and its aim. The 'special transmission' refers to the handing on of the heart seal – insight matching insight. Mere words, intellectual or academic knowledge is not sufficient; a whole dimension is missing. Words alone often lead to misunderstanding and arguments. A smile of appreciation as understanding touches the heart – from heart to heart, both seeing, knowing 'as one'.

Paradox

328.

Jinshu: The body is the Tree of Awakening,
*   The heart is a bright mirror [supported] on a stand.*
*   Carefully keep always wiping it*
*   So that no dust can settle.*

Eno: There is no Tree of Awakening,
*   The bright mirror has no stand.*
*   When all is void and empty,*
*   Where could dust settle?*

Platform Sutra of the Sixth Patriarch

When the succession to the Fifth Chinese Patriarch was under consideration, his main disciple, Jinshu, was generally expected to become his heir. To present his insight, he composed the above verse. Eno (Hui Neng), who in fact became the Sixth Patriarch, countered with another verse.

The teaching analogies of the Zen school are themselves pointers and, like these two verses, make up matched pairs which, though apparently paradoxical, point to a coherent whole. When contemplated, the above verses reflect each other like two mirrors making a point as important now as it was then: one is not possible without the other; the chicken comes out of the egg, but without the chicken, no egg.

The Knight and the Monk

329.

> *The mountain is the mountain*
> *And the Way is the same as of old.*
> *Verily what has changed*
> *Is my own heart.*

Traditional training story

A knight in medieval Japan deserted his liege lord after a long inner struggle because he felt an overwhelming vocation for the Zen life. He had to leave secretly as, according to the knightly code, such action was inconceivable. He entered a remote mountain monastery where he trained for some twelve years without leaving the mountain. Then he set out on pilgrimage. Before long he encountered a knight on horseback who recognised him and made to strike him down but then, loathe to sully his sword, decided against it. Instead the knight just spat into the monk's face as he rode by. As the monk wiped away the spittle, it flashed across his mind how different his reaction to such an insult would have been in days gone by. Deeply moved, he turned towards the mountain area where he had done his training, bowed, and composed the above poem.

The Passing of All Things

330.

> *Give rise to a heart that does not settle down anywhere.*

Diamond Sutra

All conditioned things are in constant flux, and so we should avoid clinging fast to or over-reacting against what is in the process of passing anyway.

This is not new or specially Eastern. The mystic poet Blake also found that 'Whoever ties to his heart a joy, does the winged life destroy'. But between knowing something and actually living not only according to that, but 'in-formed' by that, is anything but easy. Training, too, makes for change.

Absence of Fear

331.

In the absence of thought coverings, there can be no fear.

Heart Sutra

Both this and the last reading sound key themes of the vast Mahaprajnaparamita teachings. Every 'I' must experience itself as insecure for, being but a temporary bundle, fears of all kinds of losses beset us. Illness, old age and death await everyone. But would such commotion and unease prevail if we did not think about 'my' gain and loss? In Buddhism we have the wonderful analogy of the wave and the ocean. Waves are stirred up by the winds of the afflicting passions. But if a wave were aware of being nothing but ocean, would not its fear of plunging down cease?

Master Hakuin said that the great death was the condition for genuine insight. Only then both 'I' and fear have gone. 'I' and fear are not two. They are like the back and palm of one hand. With fear gone, including fear of death, most problems also fall away. What remains in the light of genuine insight is compassion and the strength to put this into action. Together these three comprise the empty heart, devoid of ego and therefore devoid of afflicting passions. There is a natural rededication in joy and service.

The Four Great Vows

332.

Sentient beings are numberless,
I vow to assist them.
The afflicting passions are countless,

I vow to outgrow them.
The Dharma teachings are manifold,
I vow to study them.
The Buddha Way is peerless,
I vow to walk it to the end.

The Four Great Vows

This aspiration sets our feet on the path, and is reaffirmed daily. As it becomes the companion of our daily life, it also releases strength to keep going. This is the helping power of the vow. As the veils of delusion thin and the sight clears, it is the little things that light up and warm the heart.

The Patriarchal Teachings

333.

Now that you have devoutly taken refuge in the three treasures [Buddha, Dharma, Sangha], I shall expound to you the teachings of the Mahaprajnaparamita. Good friends, although you recite it, you do not understand its meaning, so I shall explain. Listen all! Mahaprajnaparamita is a Sanskrit term; it means the Great Wisdom Gone Beyond, which has reached the 'other shore'. This Dharma [Buddha teachings] must be practised; it has nothing to do with recitations. If you recite it and do not practise it, it will be like an illusion or a phantom or speck of dew. The Dharmabody of the practitioner is the same as that of the Buddha.

What does 'maha' mean? It means 'great'. The capacity of the heart is as that of empty space. Do not sit with a mind fixed on emptiness, for then you will fall into the empty emptiness. [True] emptiness includes the sun, moon, stars and planets, the great earth, mountains and rivers, all trees and grasses, bad men and good men, bad things and good things, heavens and hells. They are all within this emptiness. The emptiness of man's nature is also the same.

Platform Sutra of the Sixth Patriarch

The inner light is beyond both praise and abuse,
Like unto space it knows no boundaries;
Yet it is right here with us ever retaining its serenity and fullness;
It is only when you seek it that you lose it.
You cannot take hold of it, nor can you get rid of it;
While you can do neither, it goes on its own way.
You remain silent and it speaks; you speak and it is silent;
The great gate of compassion is wide open with no obstructions before it. . . .

Should someone ask me what teaching I understand,
I tell him that it is the power of the Mahaprajnaparamita.
Yoka Daishi, 'Song of Enlightenment'

Yoka Daishi (d. 713 CE) is one of the heirs of the Sixth Patriarch, Hui Neng. His 'Song of Enlightenment' and the Third Patriarch's 'On Faith in the Heart' have guided the footsteps of all students of Zen. These excerpts may perhaps give the flavour of the 'patriarchal teachings'.

Attachment to Form

334.

Committing evils or practising goodness – both are the outcome of attachment to form. When evils are committed on account of attachment to form one has to suffer transmigration; when goodness is practised on account of attachment to form, one has to go through a life of hardships. It is better therefore to see all at once into the essence of the Dharma as you listen to this discourse.
Huang-po, *On the Transmission of the Heart Seal*

Basic to all Buddhism are the three signs or marks of being, namely: impermanence, non-'I' (devoid of 'I' or self-nature) and suffering. We carry an unnecessary load of suffering because we cannot accept impermanence and non-'I'. We cannot do so because the three fires (also three poisons) of wanting, ill-will and delusion burn within us. In their diverse combinations, these are the source of our problems. Driven by the three fires, 'I' whirls on the wheel of life and change – this world we know full of suffering. Or rather, 'I' imagines itself to do so, to be bound upon that wheel. By means of diligently walking the Buddha's Way, the sight is cleared and genuine insight arises. If in that clear seeing no 'I' is to be found, the fires die down and there is deliverance from the wheel, from the ocean of birth and death.

The Empty Heart

335.

By the Dharma is meant the heart, for there is no Dharma apart from heart. Heart is no other than the Dharma, for there is no heart apart from the Dharma. This heart in itself is empty [mushin], and there is no such empty heart either. When the empty heart is sought after by the heart, this is making it a particular object of thought. There is only testimony of silence, it goes beyond thinking. Therefore it is said that the Dharma cuts off the passage to words and puts an end to all forms of mental activities.

This heart is the source, the pure Buddha-nature that is inherent in all of us. All sentient beings, however mean and degraded, are not in this particular respect different from Buddhas and bodhisattvas – they are all of one substance. Only because of their imagination and false discriminations, sentient beings work out their karma and reap its result, while in their Buddha-nature itself there is nothing correspond-ing to it. The essence is empty and allows everything to pass through; it is quiet and at rest, it is illuminating, it is peaceful and productive of bliss. When you have within yourself a deep insight into this, you immediately realise that all that you need is there in perfection and in abundance, and nothing is at all wanting or lacking in you.

Huang-po, *On the Transmission of the Heart Seal*

We cannot conceive an 'I'-less state, and even a state of a somewhat diminished 'I' is hard to grasp unless we have undergone training to that end. Nor is it helpful to try to deny 'I' while strongly feeling 'I'. 'I', when it comes into contact with the three signs of being (impermanence, non-'I' and suffering), is usually incapable of accepting what is contrary to its deluded wants or notions. Then the three fires (wanting, ill-will and delusion) flare up. In other words, we emotionally react either for or against, with varying degrees of intensity. We all know to our cost what tremendous energy is locked up in these passions of 'ours'.

Deliverance from the passions which afflict us is possible. However, this is not achieved by cutting off the emotions as 'I' would like so as to free 'myself' from them, for 'I' is another of the deluded notions. What is possible is a valid transformation of the emotional energy which then reveals itself as the inherent ever-present Buddha-nature. When not obstructed by 'I' or 'my' desires and notions, be they good or bad, the Buddha-nature then acts of itself, through us, in 'right' response to the situation. This functioning is the opposite of 'as I want it, everything goes'. The very 'I' that likes and dislikes, that wants 'my way', is the cloud that has been dispelled.

Self-reliance

336.

But students nowadays do not succeed because they suffer from lack of self-reliance. Because of this lack, you run busily hither and thither, are

*driven around by circumstances and kept whirling by the ten thousand
things. You cannot find deliverance thus. But if you can stop your heart
from its ceaseless running after wisps of the will, you are not different
from the Buddha and patriarchs. Do you want to know the Buddha?
None other than he who here in your presence is now listening to the
Dharma. Just because you lack self-reliance, you turn to the outside and
run about seeking. Even if you find something there, it is only words and
letters, and never the living spirit of the patriarchs. Do not be deceived.*

　　　　　　　　　　　　　　　　The Zen Teaching of Rinzai

Needless to say, this 'self-reliance' has nothing to do with 'I', 'me', 'mine'
but is the free and unobstructed functioning of the Buddha-nature itself,
which is our own being since time out of mind. It entails a sloughing off or
wearing away of the obstacles in 'us' which prevent the clear awareness of
the Buddha-nature or heart. Paraphrasing Master Rinzai, this is the one
who here in your presence is reading these words. Do you know him? For
he has always been there since the beginning of time. This one, the true
face, the Buddha-nature inherent in all of us, is what the Sixth Patriarch
Hui Neng pointed to by his question (see below).

The True Face

337.

*Two monks were arguing about a flag that was fluttering in the wind.
One monk said it was the wind that caused the flag to flutter. The other
firmly held that it was the flag itself that moved. Their argument
became heated, when the Sixth Patriarch happened to come by. Hearing
the clamour the two raised, he pithily commented, 'It is neither the wind
nor the flag, it is the heart of the two venerables that moves.'*

　　　　　　　　　　　　　Platform Sutra of the Sixth Patriarch

*Before thinking good and bad, what is the true face before father and
mother were born?*

　　　　　　　　　　　　　Platform Sutra of the Sixth Patriarch

Before we can with confidence hand ourselves over to that 'great
functioning' which arises from the insight into the Buddha-nature which
is our true face, there is the long way of training to wean us from our
habitual split into this and that, the need or no need to wipe the mirror.

The Three Stages

338.

> There is a reality even prior to heaven and earth;
> Indeed, it has no form, much less a name;
> Eyes fail to see it;
> It has no voice for ears to detect.
> To call it heart or Buddha violates its nature,
> For it then becomes like an imaginary flower in the sky;
> It is not heart, nor Buddha;
> Absolutely quiet, and yet illuminating in a mysterious way,
> It allows itself to be perceived only by the clear-eyed.
> It is Dharma truly beyond form and sound;
> It is Tao having nothing to do with words.
> Wishing to entice the blind,
> The Buddha has playfully let words escape his golden mouth;
> Heaven and earth are ever since filled with entangling briars.
> O my good worthy friends gathered here,
> If you desire to listen to the thunderous voice of the Dharma,
> Exhaust your words, empty your thoughts out,
> For then you may come to recognise this one essence.
> Says Hui the brother, 'The Buddhadharma
> Is not to be given up to mere human sentiments.'
>
> The National Teacher, Daio

The established teachings express a way of looking at words that helps us to wean ourselves from our ingrained, short-sighted, one-sided notions. Training with the body then helps to establish this new, fuller attitude. What is known in the head alone is easily forgotten, but what is learned with the body is learned for good. What I think I know tends to desert me at just the critical moment, but once I have learnt to ride a bicycle, once the skill has been acquired, even after twenty years of not having been on one, it has not been forgotten, cannot be unlearnt. Hence the three stages of hearing with the ear (or reading with the eye), pondering in the heart, and practising with the body.

The Middle Way

339.

> *Just as a man who has started out on a long journey sees before him a great stretch of water, on this side full of doubts and fears, on the other*

shore safe and free from fears. But there is no boat to cross over, no causeway to pass from this to the other shore. Then he thinks of fashioning a raft from branches and leaves and paddling across. Having thus done and arrived at the other shore, he would have finished with that raft that served him well for the crossing. I liken my teaching to a raft – having reached the other shore by means of it, it is to be left behind, not be taken along. Understanding the parable of the raft, you must leave righteous ways behind, not to speak of not righteous ways.

Majjhima Nikaya, i, 134 (abridged)

We human beings are always prone to cling to one or the other side, not seeing the wood for the trees or the trees for the wood. Therefore, the Buddha preached the Middle Way – not only between indulgence and austerity, but in a deeper and more existential sense as 'suffering and the Way out of suffering'. At its profoundest level, the Middle Way does not imply rejection of suffering, but rather its transcendence by leading through suffering to the end of it. For the pilgrim walking the Way of the Buddha, this Way is itself the discipline which produces clear seeing and the strength to act in accordance with it. Then the Way ends; the walker is free of all 'I'-biased and deluded seeing. He himself has become the Way, acting out of his true nature which is the Buddha-nature, and thus acting as bodhisattva to benefit all sentient beings.

This reading is from the southern (Theravada) canon, and yet shows the seeds of all the features that later give rise to the developed Mahayana, particularly the Mahaprajnaparamita teachings of emptiness and transcendence.

Soto Zen

Compiled with commentary by the Reverend Daishin Morgan

All schools of Buddhism have developed out of a desire to live and express the true teaching of the Buddha within the changing circumstances of different times and cultures. The Zen school developed in sixth-century China, out of an earnest desire to keep to the essential spirit of Shakyamuni, the historical Buddha, which was in danger of becoming buried beneath a mountain of erudite analysis and formalistic practice. The Early Zen tradition of China evolved out of the intensely practical nature of the Chinese mind and it is because of its insistence upon practical application and direct experience that Zen is particularly suited to the needs of Western society.

The object of the Zen tradition is to point directly to the Buddha-nature, the true essence of man, without relying upon words or scriptures. Direct experience of this true nature is what enlightenment in Zen is all about. This does not mean words and scriptures are not used, but that they should be recognised as fingers pointing to the moon and not worshipped as something fixed as though they could define the nature of truth. Zen, in practice, has a deep respect for forms and traditions but is always willing to adapt and change them to fit the circumstances of the individual. Just as the artist must adapt his or her work to the medium, so the Zen master must adapt his or her teaching to the needs of the disciple.

The main focus is always upon meditation; in fact the word 'Zen' literally means 'meditation'. This meditation is, however, not something done in isolation from the rest of life; it is the means through which one comes to know the source of right action and personal responsibility. Our way of viewing the world is coloured by a myriad of ideas, impressions and opinions, to such an extent that we do not see the real world at all – only our own idea of the real world. To remedy this situation we must gradually learn how to let go of all ideas and opinions, including the most cherished, and see directly that which is before us. It is out of clarity that ignorance is dispelled and it is only through ignorance that we act destructively or cause suffering. Once any being truly understands what they are doing to themselves and others when they act out of greed, hate or delusion, then they will immediately cease from perpetrating those evils. Human beings are not evil at root; they have no fallen nature but the same nature as the Buddha. Like the sun that is obscured by clouds, they cannot see that true nature or act upon it until they learn how to dispel the clouds of ignorance.

Meditation is the art of being still and aware of whatever arises without judgement. If hate arises then be still within the heart of the hate and know it fully. This is not to indulge it and it is certainly not to suppress it. When you hate, acknowledge to yourself that that is what is happening and feel the hate fully. When you do so with an open heart you will know what hate is and there will arise such a revulsion that you will never willingly hate another being. This is to find the true meaning of the precept 'Do not be angry'. Without this insight we do not really know why we should not hate and so we continue to hate.

Zen is the very essence of Buddhism, and as such it was transmitted to Japan where it still flourishes today in a form that harmonises with the best of Japanese culture. The process of assimilation is now underway in the West. Monasteries, temples and lay meditation groups are springing up all over Europe and the United States as Western people rediscover for themselves, and in their own cultural setting, the direct way of enlightenment.

Throssel Hole Priory in England is such a Buddhist monastery and follows the Serene Reflection Meditation tradition (Soto Zen). It was founded in 1972 by the Rev. Roshi P. T. N. H. Jiyu-Kennett, the Abbess and Spiritual Director of Shastra Abbey, headquarters of the Order of Buddhist Contemplatives of the Soto Zen Church and Zen Mission Society, USA. She is the author of several books including *Zen Is Eternal Life* (Shastra Abbey Press, 1987) and *The Liturgy of the Order of Buddhist Contemplatives for the Laity* (Shastra Abbey Press, 1987) from which many of the translations that I have included are taken.

I have selected the quotations with the view of showing something of the mind of meditation and how it finds expression in daily life. As well as quotations from the Buddha, many of the quotations below are from the writings of Zen Master Dogen (1200–1253), the founder of Soto Zen, the largest of the Zen schools in Japan. Although the recorded sayings of Shakyamuni Buddha are deeply revered in Zen, whenever an individual penetrates to the same understanding that the Buddha possessed, their contributions to the development of the teaching are similarly highly regarded. In this way the canonical literature of Buddhism is continually growing and developing.

The Illusion of Birth and Death

340.

The most important question for all Buddhists is how to understand birth and death completely, for then, should you be able to find the

Buddha within birth and death, they both vanish. All you have to do is realise that birth and death, as such, should not be avoided and they will cease to exist, for then, if you can understand that birth and death are nirvana itself, there is not only no necessity to avoid them but also nothing to search for that is called nirvana.

Dogen, 'Shushogi'

The truth is not to be found outside this life; if we do not know it here and now, there is nowhere else to find it. It is through complete acceptance of life that liberation is found. Both birth and death are illusions, for in reality there is no begining and no end. It is because we cling to the notion of being separate from the eternal Buddha-nature that we think we have something to lose or something to gain. It is enough to be still within our own heart, which is none other than the heart of Buddha, and then the action of saving all sentient beings arises freely and naturally. This is beyond passivity and activity for it is the awakening to the heart of wisdom.

Studying Oneself

341.

When one studies Buddhism, one studies oneself; when one studies oneself, one forgets oneself; when one forgets oneself, one is enlightened by everything, and this very enlightenment breaks the bonds of clinging to both body and mind not only for oneself but for all beings as well. If the enlightenment is true, it even wipes out clinging to enlightenment. Therefore, it is imperative that we return to, and live in, the world of ordinary men.

Dogen, 'Genjo-Koan'

To study oneself is not to apply all sorts of theories or to analyse or make comparisons; it is simply to be still within the silence of the heart and see directly that which is. When one can embrace the fearful and the compassionate, the horrors and beauties that appear and disappear, then one forgets oneself for there is only infinite compassion. This infinite compassion can then move freely and manifest itself for the benefit of all beings.

Enlightened action arises from the Buddha heart that all beings possess. My task is to follow that Buddha absolutely. There is then no praise or blame, no good or evil, there is just the work of a Buddha. If others are helped that is nothing to do with me for I am not to be found. As soon as I think I am helping others I fall into delusion.

Casting off Mind and Body

342.

*There is no reason why we people of the present day cannot understand.
All you have to do is cease from erudition, withdraw within and reflect
upon yourself. Should you be able to cast off body and mind naturally,
the Buddha-mind will immediately manifest itself; if you want to find it
quickly you must start at once. You should meditate in a quiet room, eat
and drink moderately, cut all ties, give up everything, think of neither
good nor evil, consider neither right nor wrong ... neither trying to
think nor trying not to think; just sitting with no deliberate thought is
the important aspect of Zazen [meditation].*

Dogen, 'Rules for Meditation'

To cast off body and mind is to find enlightenment. There is a way of
being and doing that is not based upon selfishness, that arises from the
true source of compassion, love and wisdom. This true way is beyond that
of the plaster-cast saint (the image of religion rather than its true heart).
To follow such a way we have to become spiritual adults willing to go into
the darkness where everything is surrendered, even the sense of who we
are and the things that give our lives meaning or safety. When we are
willing to be really still then the truth appears and the self falls away. This
is done by sitting up straight and looking within. Pay no heed to thoughts
as they arise, no matter how wonderful or terrible they may seem; just
keep letting them go, returning always to the stillness that underlies
everything.

Training

343.

*Understand clearly that the truth appears naturally and then your
mind will be free from doubts and vacillation ... Do not discuss the wise
and the ignorant, there is only one thing – to train hard for this is true
enlightenment; training and enlightenment are naturally undefiled. To
live by Zen is the same as to live an ordinary daily life ... All activity is
permeated with pure Zazen [meditation]. The means of training are a
thousandfold but pure Zazen must be done.*

Dogen, 'Rules for Meditation'

The truth appears naturally because it is the foundation of our being; by
trusting it absolutely, there is no need to divide the world into the good

and evil, the wise and the foolish, or any other pair of opposites. When we look with the heart, we are able to see the heart of others and appropriate action arises from this wisdom. It is through judgement of ourselves and others that we believe we and they are inadequate, are lacking something, or do not measure up to some arbitrary standard. This is how we condemn ourselves. The point is not that there are no standards, but that true standards are not to be found in any formula but by living in the presence of the eternal Buddha. Every activity can become meditation, yet without the commitment to set aside some time each day for formal practice, we will not develop the insight necessary to see how each action is indeed one with the truth.

The Essence of the Buddhist Life

344.

The three pure precepts of the Buddha.
Cease from evil.
Do only good.
Do good for others.

Keizan, 'Kyojukaimon'

This is the essence of the Buddhist life. 'Cease from evil' is the foundation, for unless we cleanse our own delusion we shall continue to create suffering for ourselves and others. There is a way in which a being can know that which is truly good to do in every situation, but such vision only comes from taking refuge in the Buddha. Such refuge is taken by always seeking the guidance of the Buddha within our own hearts. This going for refuge is embodied within meditation which is at the heart of practice. One cannot see the Buddha-nature without cleansing the heart. Our true heart is fundamentally one with the universe and therefore is deeply in tune with others. This true heart 'knows' what is good to do even though 'we' may not know with our heads. The key to right action is having the humility to ask guidance of that which is greater than the self-centred ego and then to follow that guidance absolutely. Without helping others there can be no ceasing from evil. Buddhism recognises no absolutely separate individual; all are intimately connected and all have a common essence, so every action, even those done in secret, conditions the world in which we live.

Confession

345.

Here is the way in which to make an act of perfect contrition. 'May all the Buddhas and ancestors who have become enlightened have compassion upon us, free us from the obstacle of suffering which we have inherited from our past existence, and lead us in such a way that we may share the merit that fills the universe, for they, in the past, were as we are now, and we will be as they in the future. All the evil committed by me is caused by beginningless greed, hate and delusion; all the evil is committed by my body, in my speech and in my thoughts; I now confess everything wholeheartedly.' By this act of recognition of our past behaviour, and therefore our contrition, we open the way for the Buddhas and ancestors to help us naturally. Bearing this in mind, we should sit up straight in the presence of the Buddha and repeat the above act of contrition, thereby cutting the roots of our evil-doing.

Dogen, 'Shushogi'

Buddhism has no judgement or punishment. Each action has its result and so we will reap the consequences of all that we do. Unless we understand the full extent of a mistake, there will be a tendency to repeat it. When we fully acknowledge what we have done by sitting up straight in the presence of the Buddha, then there is no grovelling attempt to avoid the inevitable consequences but a courageous and straightforward look at the real nature of the mistake without indulging in condemnation or excuses. This is true acceptance and through this we come to experience the living reality of the infinite compassion of the Buddha. When the consequences of past mistakes are experienced there is no complaining or confusion because of the 'unfairness' of the world since, having confronted ourselves in the stillness of meditation, we find that, even though we have made mistakes, there is that which is for ever unstained within us. It is not unusual for people to weep with gratitude when they experience such compassion.

The Body of Dharma

346.

The Dharmakaya [cosmic Buddha], though manifesting itself in the triple world [past, present and future], is free from impurities and desires. It unfolds here, there and everywhere, responding to the call of karma. It is not an individual reality, it is not a false existence, but is universal and pure. It comes from nowhere; it does not assert itself, nor is it subject to annihilation. It is for ever serene and eternal. It is the One, devoid of all determinations. This body of Dharma has no boundary, no quarters, but is embodied in all bodies. Its freedom or spontaneity is incomprehensible, its spiritual presence in things corporeal is incomprehensible. All forms of corporeality are involved therein; it is able to create all things. Assuming any concrete material body as required by the nature and condition of karma, it illuminates all creation. Though it is the treasure of the intelligence it is void of particularity. There is no place within the universe where this body does not prevail. The universe becomes, but this body for ever remains. It is free from all opposites and contraries, yet it is working in all things to bring them to nirvana.

It benefits us by destroying evils, all good things thus being quickened to growth; it benefits us with its universal illumination which vanquishes the darkness of ignorance harboured in all beings; it benefits us through its great loving heart which delivers all beings from the misery of birth and death.

Avatamsaka Sutra

When the self is left behind the great discovery is made. There is an unborn, an undying and uncreated which embraces all existence. It is not a dry principle but a warm, living reality that cannot ever be expressed in words. Buddhism looks at the ultimate in a way that is radically different from other traditions. It does not see the universe as having a beginning or an end, although any individual part will certainly come to an end. There is therefore no creator, no divine director whose plan we are living out. Our being is the result of multiple causes like waves on an ocean. Each wave conditions the next, as do the winds and tides. We are the result of an infinite number of causes, not the creation of a divine being. Nevertheless, there is that which is the true nature of existence beyond the changing appearances. This true nature has no substance and yet it exists. There is no God in Buddhism, nor is there a vacuum, but a truth that must be experienced directly.

Impermanence

347.

Thus shall ye think of all this fleeting world;
A star at dawn, a bubble in a stream;
A flash of lightning in a summer cloud,
A flickering lamp, a phantom and a dream.

Diamond Sutra

All things are subject to change and are no lasting refuge. Fundamentally they are but illusions with no permanent substance. By recognising this truth we can stop clinging to this world and so set ourselves free to act in accordance with our true nature which is limitless compassion, love and wisdom.

The Mind That Abides Nowhere

348.

Bodhisattvas should forsake all conceptions of form and resolve to develop the mind of supreme enlightenment. Their minds should not abide in form, sound, smell, taste, touch and Dharma. Their minds should abide nowhere. If their minds abide somewhere it will be in falsehood.

Diamond Sutra

The mind that abides nowhere is not in a state of vacuity but, on the contrary, is truly alive. If I let my mind abide in the thought, 'I am adequate', I fall into pride; if I abide in the thought, 'I am inadequate', I fall into despair. Either alternative is false, for the truth lies in confronting directly, beyond words, the reality of what I am.

The Practical and Diligent Cook

349.

The Zen temple regulations state that the desire for Buddhahood must for ever be kept active within the mind of the tenzo priest [cook], and he must, at various times, devise such dishes as will create great pleasure for the monks who partake thereof.

When rice and vegetables are being examined and washed it is imperative that the cook be both single-minded and practical, ensuring that the work is done to the very best of his ability and without allowing contempt for any foodstuff to arise in his mind. He must be diligent in all his work without discriminating against one thing as opposed to another. Although he dwells within the ocean of merit he must never waste so much as one drop of that ocean's water – not even if he has his hut upon the very summit of the mountain of good works. However minute may be the merit of anything he does, he must never forget to accumulate that merit even if it seems to him to be infinitesimally small and therefore not worth bothering about.

Dogen, 'Tenzo-Kyokan'

Zen always places great emphasis upon practicality. All jobs when performed with a sincere heart can reveal the true way. There is nothing holy and nothing unholy. Pleasure is a source of suffering when it is clung to, but a severe regime of asceticism can be a source of delusion too, leading to a hardness and lack of warmth and sympathy. Apple pie and custard is not the answer to the problem of life, but every now and then it certainly helps!

The cook must be single minded yet practical; never waste anything but not serve up food that will be inedible. There are vegetables that can be cooked and eaten; there are vegetbles that can be placed upon the compost heap; both compost and food have the Buddha-nature. The key element is that the cook must not be seeking the approval of others, but must seek to cook with a sincere and pure heart as an offering to the three treasures (Buddha, Dharma, Sangha).

The Five Thoughts Recited before Eating

350.

> *We must think deeply of the ways and means by which this food has come.*
> *We must consider our merit when accepting it.*
> *We must protect ourselves from error by excluding greed from our minds.*
> *We will eat lest we become lean and die.*
> *We accept this food so that we may become enlightened.*
>
>   Shobo genzo, 'Mealtime Regulations'

Before eating, all trainees recite the above verse for it reminds us how intimately we are connected to the universe and how we must be aware of the effect our actions have on beings of all kinds. Most Buddhists are vegetarians because of the knowledge that all beings know suffering and when the heart is open the suffering of others can never be ignored. We are responsible for our actions, for the fact that we must take life in order to live, even if the life that we take is that of a vegetable. So that it shall not be wasted, the Zen trainee strives to make the best possible use of that life by realising enlightenment and simultaneously working for the good of all things. Every action of life can serve as a reminder of the true purpose of existence and a means of realising that purpose.

The Seeds of Enlightenment

351.

Therefore we should know that all sorts of defilements, trouble, anxiety and distress are the seeds of the Tathagata [enlightenment, the eternal Buddha]. This is like one who does not plunge into the ocean and will never find the priceless pearl. Likewise, a man who does not enter the ocean of defilement and trouble will never win the gem of all knowledge.

Vimalakirti Nirdesa Sutra

The difficulties, pleasures and pains of life are the very things that will lead us to enlightenment. They reveal where we still cling to delusion and present the opportunity to let go. Nobody realises enlightenment in abstraction but within the very heart and turmoil that make up this world. To seek to avoid pain is only to condemn ourselves to further pain, but to have the courage to face the pain without judgement of ourselves or others and without making excuses is to see the cause of the pain directly. The discipline of the religious life is to be for ever willing to enter hell if that is what is necessary, for when there is no holding back there is no hell.

The Essence of Compassion

352.

Just listen to the life of Kanzeon.
To calls from every quarter he responds;
Of oceanic depth his holy vows . . .
When people hear his name, and see his form,
And think of him not vainly in their hearts,
All forms of ill in all the worlds shall cease.
If, wishing harm, an enemy should try
To push another in a fiery pit,
The victim should, on Kanzeon's great power
Think, and straightaway that fiery pit shall be
Transformed into a cool and silver lake . . .
If bound in chains, in prison, let a man
Just think of Kanzeon's great holy power,
At once the shackles will then set him free . . .
He is a light pure, spotless like the sun,
With wisdom does he darkness all dispel,
Subverting all effects of wind and fire;
His all-illuminating light fills all the world.

'The Scripture of Kanzeon Bosatsu', *Lotus Sutra*, ch. 25

This is part of a scripture recited every morning in Zen monasteries. Kanzeon is the personification of compassion, the cure of all pain and suffering. By calling upon great compassion one knows no disaster – even though a bomb may go off or one is confronted with grief and pain. There is a true refuge that nothing can destroy, which is found by calling with a pure heart upon the compassion that is the essence of the universe. When we offer ourselves up in faith to the essence of compassion, then the veils of separation fall away and we discover the indestructible Buddhahood that is our true nature. When this happens there is no clinging to life or death, for in order to call upon great compassion we have to abandon the idea that our imaginary self is the centre of the universe and the idea that our self is in control.

The Illusion of Male and Female

353.

> *Sariputra, one of the Buddha's disciples, is one day confronted by a goddess who points out to him that although he has made progress in his training he still clings to forms. He is greatly impressed by her wisdom and asks her: 'Why do you not change your female bodily form?'*
>
> *The goddess replied, 'For the last twelve years I have been looking in vain for a female bodily form; so what do you want me to change? This is like an illusionist who creates an illusory woman. All phenomena are unreal, so why have you asked me to change my unreal body?' Thereat, she used her supernatural powers to change Sariputra into a heavenly goddess and herself into a man similar to Sariputra, and asked him: 'Why do you not change your female form?'*
>
> *[Disconcerted] Sariputra replied: 'I do not know why I have turned into a goddess.' The goddess said; 'Sariputra, if you can change your female body, all women should also be able to change into men. You are not a woman but appear in female bodily form. Similarly, all women, though they appear in female form, are fundamentally not women. Hence the Buddha said, "All things are neither male nor female."'*
>
> *Vimalakirti Nirdesa Sutra*

In the heart of the true religion there is no distinction between male and female. The Buddha's teaching on this must not be confused with the expediences that, rightly or wrongly, have been adopted down the centuries to cope with cultural prejudice. The Buddha-nature makes no distinction between male and female; those who are caught up in forms do not know the truth. Always we must look to the heart of a being otherwise we only meet our own fears and prejudices.

The Teachings of All Things

354.

When we wish to teach and enlighten all things by ourselves, we are deluded; when all things teach and enlighten us, we are enlightened.

Dogen, 'Genjo-Koan'

It is presumptuous to try to convert the world, but when we realise the true emptiness of self, the whole world becomes the realm of enlightenment. Enlightenment, or nirvana, is here and now, but without sincere training we will never realise it.

The Teachings of the Master

355.

A master archer hits a target at a hundred yards because he skill possesses.
But to make two arrows meet in mid-air – head-on – goes far beyond the skill of ordinary man.
In this superior activity of no-mind
See! the wooden figure sings and the stone maiden dances.
This is far beyond all common consciousness
Beyond all thinking.
The retainer serves his lord the emperor;
His father does the child obey.
Without obedience there is no filial piety
And, if there is no service, no advice.
Such action and most unpretentious work
All foolish seem and dull.
But those who practice thus this law continually shall in all worlds
Be called Lord of Lords unto eternity.

Tozan Ryokai, 'Most Excellent Mirror – Samadhi'

This passage speaks of the manner in which Zen is taught. To speak about the truth is easy enough, but to make two arrows meet the words must come straight from the heart. When we live from the Buddha-nature even the wooden figure sings and the hardest of stone hearts is shown how to dance. The Zen master is the retainer who serves his lord the eternal Buddha and the child is the disciple who serves his master. The master's job is to point to the truth and get himself out of the way so that the disciple comes to know the eternal Buddha directly for himself. This is achieved through following the master's teaching. The master points the way by always following the eternal Buddha's teaching which, because of his greater experience, he hears constantly within his heart. Such service may seem unspectacular, but it leads to the deepest enlightenment.

Zen

Gentling the bull

Translation* and Commentary by D. T. Suzuki

Searching for the Bull

356.

*Alone in the wilderness, lost in the jungle, the boy is searching,
    searching!
The swelling waters, the far-away mountains, and the unending path;
Exhausted and in despair, he knows not where to go,
He only hears the evening cicadas singing in the maple-woods.*

The beast has never gone astray, and what is the use of searching for him?
The reason why the cowherd is not on intimate terms with him is because
the cowherd himself has violated his own innermost nature. The beast is
lost, for the cowherd has himself been led out of the way through his
deluding senses. His home is receding farther away from him, and byways
and crossways are ever confused. Desire for gain and fear of loss burn like
fire; ideas of right and wrong shoot up like a phalanx.

Seeing the Traces

357.

*By the stream and under the trees, scattered are the traces of the lost:
The sweet-scented grasses are growing thick – did he find the way?*

---

*The Suzuki translation refers to the 'ox' but this has been changed to 'bull' in
accord with recent Japanese scholarship which emphasises the unruly nature of
the buffalo species referred to in the original Japanese.

However remote over the hills and far away the beast may wander,
His nose reaches the heavens and none can conceal it.

By the aid of the sutras and by inquiring into the doctrines, he has come to
understand something, he has found the traces. He now knows that
vessels, however varied, are all of gold, and that the objective world is a
reflection of the self. Yet he is unable to distinguish what is good from
what is not, his mind is still confused as to truth and falsehood. As he has
not yet entered the gate, he is provisionally said to have noticed the traces.

Seeing the Bull

358.

On yonder branch perches a nightingale cheerfully singing;
The sun is warm, and a soothing breeze blows, on the bank the willows
are green;
The bull is there all by himself, nowhere is he to hide himself;
The splendid head decorated with stately horns – what painter can
reproduce him?

The boy finds the way by the sound he hears; he sees thereby into the
origin of things, and all his senses are in harmonious order. In all his
activities, it is manifestly present. It is like the salt in water and the glue in
colour (see no. 233). (It is there though not distinguishable as an
individual entity.) When the eye is properly directed, he will find that it is
no other than himself.

Catching the Bull

359.

With the energy of his whole being, the boy has at last taken hold of the
bull:
But how wild his will, how ungovernable his power!
At times he struts up a plateau,
When lo! he is lost again in a misty impenetrable mountain pass.

Lost long in the wilderness, the boy has at last found the bull and his
hands are on him. But, owing to the overwhelming pressure of the outside
world, the bull is hard to keep under control. He constantly longs for the

old sweet-scented field. The wild nature is still unruly and altogether refuses to be broken. If the cowherd wishes to see the bull completely in harmony with himself, he will surely use the whip freely.

Herding the Bull

360.

> *The boy is not to separate himself with his whip and tether,*
> *Lest the animal should wander away into a world of defilements;*
> *When he is properly tended to, he will grow pure and docile;*
> *Without a chain, nothing binding, he will by himself follow the cowherd.*

When a thought moves, another follows, and then another – an endless train of thoughts is thus awakened. Through enlightenment all this turns into truth; but falsehood asserts itself when confusion prevails. Things oppress us not because of an objective world, but because of a self-deceiving mind. Do not let the nose-string loose, hold it tight, and allow no vacillation.

Coming Home on the Bull's Back

361.

> *Riding on the animal, he leisurely wends his way home;*
> *Enveloped in the evening mist, how tunefully the flute vanishes away!*
> *Singing a ditty, beating time, his heart is filled with a joy indescribable!*
> *That he is now one of those who know, need it be told?*

The struggle is over; gain and loss, the man is no more concerned with. He hums a rustic tune of the woodsman, he sings simple songs of the village-boy. Saddling himself on the bull's back, his eyes are fixed at things not of the earth, earthy. Even if he is called, he will not turn his head; however enticed, he will no more be kept back.

The Bull Forgotten, Leaving the Man Alone

362.

> *Riding on the animal, he is at last back in his home,*
> *Where lo! the bull is no more; the man alone sits serenely.*
> *Though the red sun is high up in the sky, he is still quietly dreaming,*
> *Under a straw-thatched roof are his whip and rope idly lying.*

The dharmas are one and the bull is symbolic. When you know that what you need is not the snare or net but the hare or fish; it is like gold separated from the dross, it is like the moon rising out of the clouds. The one ray of light serene and penetrating even before the days of creation.

The Bull and the Man Both Gone out of Sight

363.

> *All is empty – the whip, the rope, the man, and the bull:*
> *Who can ever survey the vastness of heaven?*
> *Over the furnace burning ablaze, not a flake of snow can fall:*
> *When this state of things obtains, manifest is the spirit of the ancient*
> *   master.*

All confusion is set aside and serenity alone prevails: even the idea of holiness does not obtain. He does not linger about where the Buddha is, and as to where there is no Buddha he speedily passes by. When there exists no form of dualism, even a thousand-eyed one fails to detect a loop-hole. A holiness before which birds offer flowers is but a farce.

It will be interesting to note what Eckhart, a mystic philosopher has said about this: 'A man shall become truly poor and as free from his creature will as he was when he was born. And I say to you, by the eternal truth, that as long as ye desire to fulfil the will of God, and have any desire after eternity and God, so long are ye not truly poor. He alone hath spiritual poverty who wills nothing, knows nothing, desires nothing.'

Returning to the Origin, back to the Source

364.

> *To return to the origin, to be back at the source – already a false step*
> *this!*
> *Far better it is to stay home, blind and deaf, and without much ado;*
> *Sitting in the hut, he takes no cognisance of things outside,*
> *Behold the streams flowing – whither nobody knows; and the flowers*
> *vividly red – for whom are they?*

From the very beginning, pure and immaculate, the man has never been affected by defilement. He watches the growth of things, while himself abiding in the immovable serenity of non-assertion. He does not identify himself with the maya-like transformations [that are going on about him], nor has he any use of himself [which is artificiality]. The waters are blue, the mountains are green; sitting alone, he observes things undergoing changes.

Entering the City with Bliss-bestowing Hands

365.

> *Bare-chested and bare-footed, he comes out into the marketplace;*
> *Daubed with mud and ashes, how broadly he smiles!*
> *There is no need for the miraculous power of the gods.*
> *For he touches, and lo! the dead trees are in full bloom.*

His thatched cottage gate is closed, and even the wisest know him not. No glimpses of his inner life are to be caught; for he goes on his own way without following the steps of the ancient sages. Carrying a gourd [symbol of emptiness] he goes out into the market, leaning against a staff he comes home. No extra property he has, for he knows that the desire to possess is the curse of human life. He is found in company with wine-bibbers and butchers, he and they are all converted into Buddhas.

Acknowledgements and References

THAILAND AND SRI LANKA

Acknowledgements

Arnold, Edwin, *The Light of Asia*, London, 1938
Reading: 116

Norman, K. R. (trans.), *The Elder's Verses: Theragatha and Therigatha*, Vol. I (1969), Vol. II (1971), Luzac, London
Readings: 20, 22, 24 (first reading), 31, 40, 53, 54, 66

Nyanaponika Thera, *The Heart of Buddhist Meditation*, Rider, London, 1975
Reading: 86

Saddhatissa, H. (trans.), *The Sutta Nipata*, Curzon Press, London, 1985
Readings: 3, 5, 51, 61 (first reading), 80, 82

Walshe, Maurice (trans.), *Thus Have I Heard*, Wisdom Publications, London, 1987
Readings: 11, 14, 15, 32, 88, 90

Chanting Book, Amaravati Publications, Great Gaddesden, Hemel Hempstead, Hertfordshire, 1987
Reading: 50

The Pali texts and English translations listed below are published by the Pali Text Society, PO Box 64, Henley-on-Thames, RG9 1ER

In Pali:

Vinayapitaka, H. Oldenberg (ed.), 5 vols., 1879–83

Digha Nikaya, T. W. Rhys Davids and J. E. Carpenter (eds.), 3 vols., 1889–1910

Majjhima Nikaya, V. Trenckner and R. Chalmers (eds.), 3 vols., 1888–1902

Anguttura Nikaya, R. Morris and E. Hardy (eds.), 5 vols., 1885–1900

Samyutta Nikaya, L. Freer (ed.), 5 vols., 1884–89

Udana, P. Steinthal (ed.),1 vol., 1885

Itivuttaka, E. Windisch (ed.), 1 vol., 1890

Sutta Nipata, Dines Andersen and Helmer Smith (eds.), 1 vol., 1913

Theragatha, H. Oldenberg (ed.), 1883, 2nd edn, 1966

Therigatha, R. Pischel (ed.), 1883, 2nd edn, 1966

In English translation:

Vinaya: The Book of the Discipline, I. B. Horner (trans.), 5 vols., 1938–52

Majjhima Nikaya: Middle Length Sayings, I. B. Horner (trans.), 3 vols., 1954–59

Anguttara Nikaya: The Book of the Gradual Sayings, F. L. Woodward and E. M. Hare (trans.), 5 vols., 1932–36

Samyutta Nikaya: The Book of the Kindred Sayings, C. A. F. Rhys Davids and F. L. Woodward (trans.), 5 vols., 1917–30

Udana: Verses of Uplift, and Itivuttaka: As It Was Said, F. L. Woodward (trans.), 1935

Sutta Nipata: The Group of Discourses, K. R. Norman (trans.), with alternative translation by I. B. Horner and the Ven. Walpola Rahula, 1984

References

Nanamoli Thera, *The Life of the Buddha*, Buddhist Publication Society, Kandy, Sri Lanka, 1972

Nanamoli Thera, *A Treasury of the Buddha's Words* (translation of the *Majjhima Nikaya*), Mahamakut Rajavidyalaya Press, Bangkok

Narada Thera, *The Dhammapada, Pali text and English translation*, BMS Publications, Kuala Lampur, 1978

Nyanaponika Thera, *The Heart of Buddhist Meditation*, Rider, London, 1975

Rhys Davids, T. W., and Stede, W., *Pali–English Dictionary*, Luzac, London, 1966

Radhakrishnan, S., *The Dhammapada, Pali text and English translation*, Oxford University Press, 1950

Saddhatissa, H. S. (trans.), *The Sutta Nipata* (see Acknowledgements)

Walshe, Maurice (trans.), *Thus Have I Heard* (see Acknowledgements)

INDIA

Acknowledgements

Conze, E. (ed.), *Vajracchedika Prajna Paramita Sutra*, ISMEO, Rome, 1959
Reading: 126

Dutt (ed.), *Samadhi-raja Sutra*, Mithila Institute, Darbhanga, 1961
Reading: 127

Klong-chen-pa, *Shin-rta-chen-po*
Reading: 119

Lamotte (ed.), *Samadhi-nirmocana Sutra*, Louvain University, Brussels, 1935
Reading: 134

Mitra (ed.), *Prajna Paramita Sutra in 8000 Verses*, Biblioteca Indica, Calcutta, 1888
Readings: 123, 125

Stael-Holstein, A. von (ed.), *Kashyapa-parivarta*, Shanghai, 1926
Readings: 116–18

Taisho Shinshu Daizokyo Kyokai, Vol. 13, Tokyo, 1924–35
Readings: 120–22

Tibetan Tripitaka, Peking Edition 1763–95; reprinted Otani
    University, Kyoto, 1957
Readings: 128–33, 135

Yuyama (ed.), *Ratna-guna-samcaya*, Cambridge University Press,
    1976
Reading: 124

TIBET

Acknowledgements

Amipa, S. G. (ed.), *A Waterdrop from the Glorious Sea*, Tibetan Institute,
    Rikon, 1976
Reading: 180

Batchelor, S. (ed.), *The Jewel in the Lotus*, Wisdom, London,
    1987
Readings: 138, 146, 181

Campbell, June (trans.), 'The Hundred Verses of Advice of the Padampa
    Sangyes to the People of Tingri', in *The Middle Way*, Vol. 49,
    No. 2, August 1974, London
Reading: 15

Chang, G. C. C. (trans.), *The Hundred Thousand Songs of Milarepa*,
    Shambhala, Berkeley, 1962
Reading: 148

Confession to the Thirty-five Buddhas and Vajrasattva Purification,
    Manjushri Institute (trans.), Ulverston, 1984
Reading: 152

Dalai Lama (Seventh), *Songs of Spiritual Change*, G. H. Mullin (trans.),
    Snow Lion, Ithaca, 1982
Readings: 203, 225

Dharmarakshita, *The Wheel of Sharp Weapons*, Library of Tibetan
    Works and Archives, Dharamsala, 1973
Reading: 174

Gyatso, Geshe Kelsang, quoted in oral teachings, Manjushri Institute,
    Ulverston
Reading: 147

Gyatso, Geshe Kelsang, *Joyful Path of Good Fortune*, Tharpa, London,
    1988
Readings: 164–72, 175, 186, 188

Gyatso, Geshe Kelsang, *Ocean of Nectar*, Tharpa, London (forthcoming)
Reading: 196

Gyaltsan, Jetsun Dragpa, *The Manjushri Tradition and the Zenpa Zidel*,
    Sakya Centre (trans.), Dehra Dun, 1968
Reading: 178

Gyaltsan, Panchen Lama Losang Chokyi, *Offering to the Spiritual Guide*, Manjushri Institute, Ulverston, 1987
Readings: 193–4, 198–202

Kuna Lama Rinpoche, *Teachings at Tushita*, Mahayana Publications, New Delhi, 1981
Reading: 206

Lingpa, Jigme, *The Dzogchen Preliminary Practice of the Innermost Essence*, Thondup/Beresford (trans.), Library of Tibetan Works and Archives, Dharamsala, 1982
Reading: 141

Lhalungpa, Lobsang P. (trans.), *The Life of Milarepa*, Paladin/Granada, St Albans, 1979
Reading: 140

The Migtsema Prayer, Manjushri Institute, Ulverston, 1987
Reading: 142

Mullin, G. H. (trans.), *Death and Dying: The Tibetan Tradition*, RKP/Arcana, London, 1986
Reading: 159

Nagarjuna/Sakya Pandit, *Elegant Sayings*, Dharma Publishing, Emeryville, 1977
Readings: 144, 192

Nyima, Tukan Chokyi, *A Fasting Retreat Practice*, Manjushri Institute, Ulverston, 1987
Reading: 150

Prayer for Developing Bodhichitta (Essence of Good Fortune), Manjushri Institute, Ulverston, 1986
Reading: 207

Rim, Geshe Lam, *A Necklace of Good Fortune*, Library of Tibetan Works and Archives, Dharamsala, 1982
Reading: 161

Shantideva, *A Guide to the Bodhisattva's Way of Life*, S. Batchelor (trans.), Library of Tibetan Works and Archives, Dharamsala, 1979
Readings: 151, 153–6, 158, 162, 177, 190–91, 214, 221, 225

Tangpa, Geshe Langri, *Eight Verses of Training the Mind*, Manjushri Institute, Ulverston, 1986
Readings: 149, 204

Tayang, Losang, and Losel, *One Hundred and Eight Verses in Praise of Great Compassion*, Thubten Losel (trans.), Mysore Printing and Publishing House, Mysore, 1984
Reading: 197

Thurman, R. (trans.), quoted in *Tsongkhapa's 'Speech of Gold'*, Princeton University Press
Reading: 136

Tsewang, Geshe Konchog, quoted in oral teachings, Manjushri Institute, Ulverston, 1987
Reading: 139

Tsondru, Geshe, *The Essence of Nectar*, Geshe L. Tharchin (trans.),

Library of Tibetan Works and Archives, Dharamsala, 1979
Readings: 195, 205, 219–20

Tsongkhapa, Je, *The Foundation of All Excellence*, Manjushri Institute, Ulverston, 1987
Readings: 137, 176, 179, 189, 222–4

Tsongkhapa, Je, *Song of the Stages of the Path*, J. Samuels (trans.), Manjushri Institute, Ulverston, 1988
Readings: 208, 210, 212, 215–6

Wangyal, Geshe, quoted in *The Jewelled Staircase*, Snow Lion, Ithaca, 1986
Reading: 145

Wheel of Life Prayer, Manjushri Institute (trans.), Ulverton, 1988
Reading: 187

Zangpo, Togme, *Thirty-Seven Practices*, Manjushri Institute, Ulverston, 1987
Readings: 143, 160, 182–4, 209, 211, 213, 217–8

Zangpo, Togme, and Tsongkhapa, Je, *The Thirty-Seven Practices of All Buddha's Sons and the Prayer of the Virtuous Beginning, Middle and End*, Library of Tibetan Works and Archives, Dharamsala, 1973
Reading: 173

CHINA

Acknowledgements

Chang, C. C., *The Buddhist Teaching of Totality*, Pennsylvania State University Press, 1971
Reading: 248

Luk, C., *Ch'an and Zen Teaching*, Series 1, Rider, London 1960
Readings: 234–9, 244, 266–7

Luk, C., *Ch'an and Zen Teaching*, Series 2, Rider, London, 1960
Readings: 259–63

Luk, C., *Ch'an and Zen Teachings*, Series 3, Rider, London 1962
Readings: 252–5

Luk, C., *The Vimalakirti Nirdesa Sutra*, Shambhala/Routledge & Kegan Paul, Berkeley, 1972
Readings: 240–41

Luk, C., *The Surangama Sutra*, Rider, London, 1959
Readings: 244–47

Luk, C., *The Secrets of Chinese Meditation*, Rider, London, 1964
Readings: 263–5, 267–9

Suzuki, D. T., *The Lankavatara Sutra*, Routledge & Kegan Paul, 1973
Readings: 242–3

Chinese Texts

Ching Te Ch'uan Teng Lu, Tao Yuan, (ed.), 1004 CE, reprinted Chen Shan Mei Co., Taipei, 1967

Readings: 231-2, 249, 250-51

Fa Hua Ching, Fa Kuang Scriptural Press, Taipei, 1975
Readings: 270, 271

Fu Tsu Hsin Yao, Tao An (ed.), Tai Yin Ching Chun, Taipei, 1974
Readings: 233, 256-8

Han Tang Fu Hsueh Si Hsiang Lun Chih, Bejing, 1974
Readings: 229-30

Hsu Yun Ho Shang Fa Hui, Chinese Buddhist Scriptural Press, Hong Kong, 1962
Readings: 266-7

Ssu Shih Erh Chang Ching, Buddhist Publishing House, Shanghai, 1933
Readings: 226-8

KOREA

Acknowledgements

Buswell, Robert E., Jr (trans.), *The Korean Approach to Zen: The Collected Works of Chinul*, University of Hawaii Press, Honolulu, 1983
Readings: 276-8

Sunim, Kusan, *The Way of Korean Zen*, Martine Fages (trans.), Stephen Batchelor (ed.), Weatherhill, Tokyo/New York, 1985
Readings: 283-5

Sunim, Mu Seong, *Thousand Peaks: Korean Zen - Tradition and Teachers*, Parallax, Berkeley, 1987
Readings: 272, 279, 280 (trans. R. Bernen), 281, 286, 287

Sunim, Seonkyong, *The Life of a Korean Zen Nun*, Martine Fages (trans.), Stephen Batchelor (ed.), unpublished manuscript
Reading: 282

Uisang, 'Ocean Seal of Huayen Buddhism', in Steve Odin, *Process Metaphysics and Hua Yen Buddhism*, State University of New York Press, Albany, 1982
Reading: 275

Wonhyo, *On Cultivating Determination to Practise*, Martine Fages (trans.), Stephen Batchelor (ed.), unpublished manuscript
Readings: 273-4

JAPAN

Shingon

Acknowledgements
Hanh, Thich Nhat, *Guide to Walking Meditation*, Kobo Daishi Zenshu, Vol. I
Readings: 289, 290, 293

ibid., Vol. III
Readings: 294, 300

Taisho Shinshu Daizokyo Kyokai, Tokyo, 1924–35, Vol. XVIII
Readings: 288, 291, 292, 296–8, 299, 306, 307
ibid., Vol. VIII
Readings: 303, 304
Tibetan Tripitaka, Peking Edition 1763–95; reprinted Otani University,
    Kyoto, 1957
Readings: 295, 302, 305

Jodo Shu

Acknowledgements

Kenjo S., Urakami (trans. and ed.), *Selected Sayings of St Honen*,
    Jodo-Shu Press, Hawaii, 1977
Reading: 310
Ryukoko University Translation Centre *The Sutra of Contemplation on
    the Buddha of Immeasurable Life as Expounded by Shakyamuni Buddha*,
    Kyoto, 1984
Reading: 309
Takakushu, Junjiro, *Amitayur-Dhyana Sutra, The Larger Sukhavati
    Vyuha*, in *Sacred Books of the East – Buddhist Mahayana Texts*,
    Vol. XLIX, Oxford University Press, 1894
Reading: 308

Jodo Shinshu

Acknowledgements

Tsuji, Takashi, *Shinshu Shogyo Zensho* in *Three Lectures on the Tannisho*,
    Vol. II, Bureau of Buddhist Education, San Francisco, 1967
Readings: 313, 318, 319
Takakushu, Junjiro, *Amitayur-Dhyana Sutra, The Larger Sukhavati
    Vyuha*, in *Sacred Books of the East – Buddhist Mahayana Texts*,
    Vol. XLIX, Oxford University Press, 1894
Reading: 311
Tsuji, Takashi, *The Tannisho, Notes Lamenting Differences*, Kyoto, 1962
Readings: 312, 314–7

References

Tsuji, Takashi, *Three Lectures on the Tannisho* (see Acknowledgements)
Eidmann, Philip Karl, *The Unimpeded Single Way*, Bureau of Buddhist
    Education, San Francisco, 1963

Zen

Acknowledgements

Dogen, *Shobogenzo*, Nishiyama (trans.), Daihokkaikaku, Tokyo, 1975
Reading: 324
Leggett, T., *A First Zen Reader*, Tuttle, 1960
Readings: introduction, 322–3, 325

Leggett, T., *The Warrior Koans*, Arkana, 1985
Reading: 326
Suzuki, D. T., *Essays in Zen Buddhism*, first series, Luzac, 1927
Readings: 320-1

Rinzai Zen

Acknowledgements

Blofeld, John, *Zen Teachings of Huang-Po*, Buddhist Society, London
Readings: 334-5
Conze, Edward (ed.), *Prajnaparamita: Selected Sayings from the Perfections of Wisdom*, Buddhist Society, London, 1976
Reading: 331
Leggett, T., *A First Zen Reader*, Tuttle, 1960
Reading: 329
Myokyo-ni, own translations
Readings: 327-8, 330, 332, 336-7
Suzuki, D. T., *Manual of Zen Buddhism*, Rider, London, 1950
Readings: 333 (second reading), 338
Woodward, F. L. (trans.), *Some Sayings of the Buddha*, Buddhist Society, London, 1973
Reading: 339
Wong, Mau-lam (trans.), *Sutra of Hui Neng*, Buddhist Society, London, 1953
Reading: 333 (first reading)

Soto Zen

The Liturgy of the Order of Buddhist Contemplatives for the Laity, Rev. Roshi Jiyu-Kennett (trans.), Shastra Abbey Press, 1987
Readings: 342-3, 352
Zen is Eternal Life, Rev. Roshi Jiyu-Kennett (trans.), 3rd edn, Shastra Abbey Press, 1987
Readings: 340-41, 344-5, 349-50, 354-5
Lu Kuan Yu (trans.), *Diamond Sutra*, Ci Hang Trust, Malaysia, 1987
Reading: 348
Luk, Charles, *Vimalakirti Nirdesa Sutra*, Shambhala/Routledge Kegan & Paul, Berkeley, 1972
Readings: 351, 353
Saunders, Kenneth (trans.), *Diamond Sutra*, Shambhala, Berkeley, 1969
Reading: 347
Suzuki, D. T. (trans.), *Avatamsaka Sutra* in Suzuki, B. L., *Outlines of Mahayana Buddhism*, 4th edn, George Allen & Unwin, London,1981
Reading: 346

Zen: Gentling The Bull

Suzuki, D. T., *Manual of Zen Buddhism*, Rider Books, London, 1950